W9-CLG-684

PROSE STYLE: A HANDBOOK FOR WRITERS

STONE & BELL
PROSE STYLE:
A HANDBOOK
FOR WRITERS
SECOND EDITION

WILFRED STONE

Stanford University

J. G. BELL

Stanford University Press

McGRAW-HILL BOOK COMPANY

New York, St. Louis, San Francisco, Düsseldorf, Johannesburg, Kuala Lumpur, London, Mexico, Montreal, New Delhi, Panama, Rio de Janeiro, Singapore, Sydney, Toronto

This book was set in Caledonia by Monotype Composition Company, Inc., and printed and bound by The Murray Printing Company.
The designer was Joan O'Connor;
the drawings were done by F. W. Taylor Company.
The editors were Cheryl Kupper, Robert Weber, and Helen Greenberg.
Sally Ellyson supervised production.

Prose Style: A HANDBOOK FOR WRITERS

Library of Congress Catalog Card Number 75-168462

2 3 4 5 6 7 8 9 0   MUMU   7 9 8 7 6 5 4 3 2

ISBN 07-061731-7

ACKNOWLEDGMENTS

The American Heritage Dictionary of the English Language, reprinted with the permission of the publisher.

Harry Anslinger and Will Oursler, from The Murderers, copyright Farrar, Straus & Giroux, Inc., reprinted with the permission of the publisher.

James Baldwin, excerpt from "What It Means To Be An American," The New York Times Book Review, January 25, 1959. © 1959 by The New York Times Company. Reprinted by permission.

Roy Bongartz, from "Three Meanies," in Esquire 74:110 (August 1970), reprinted with the permission of the publisher.

J. Bronowski, excerpt from Science and Human Values, Julian Messner, Inc., 1956.

Jerome Bruner, from The Personal Voice, edited by Albert Guerard. Reprinted by permission of the publisher, J. B. Lippincott Company.

Kenneth Burke, "Thomas Mann and André Gide," from Counterstatement by Kenneth Burke (Harrison-Blaine, 1931), reprinted with the permission of the author.

Herb Caen, excerpt from his column in the San Francisco Chronicle, February 16, 1964.

Stokely Carmichael, "What We Want," from *Crisis*, Peter Collier, ed., Harcourt, Brace, World, 1969, used with the permission of the Student National Coordinating Committee.

Joyce Cary, from *The Horse's Mouth* by Joyce Cary, published by Harper & Row, Inc., and reprinted with the permission of the publisher.

Eldridge Cleaver, from *Soul on Ice* by Eldridge Cleaver. Copyright © 1968, McGraw-Hill Book Company. Used with permission of McGraw-Hill Book Company.

David Denby, "Dirty Movies—Hard-Core and Soft," copyright © 1970, by The Atlantic Monthly Company, Boston, Mass. Reprinted with the permission of the author.

Loren Eiseley, excerpt from *The Immense Journey*, Random House, Inc., 1946.

Henry Watson Fowler, excerpt from *Modern English Usage*, Oxford University Press, rev. ed. 1965. By permission of The Clarendon Press, Oxford.

Charles Frankel, from *High on Foggy Bottom* by Charles Frankel, published by Harper & Row, 1969, and reprinted with the permission of the author.

Erich Fromm, from *Escape from Freedom* by Erich Fromm, published by Holt, Rinehart and Winston, Inc., and reprinted with the permission of the publisher.

Sir Ernest Gowers, excerpt from *Plain Words*, Alfred A. Knopf, Inc., 1954.

Irving Howe, "The Idea of the Modern" in *Literary Modernism*, ed. Irving Howe and published by the Fawcett Company. Reprinted with the permission of the author.

Julian Huxley, excerpt from *Man Stands Alone*, Harper & Row, Publishers, Inc.

James Joyce, excerpt from *A Portrait of the Artist as a Young Man* by James Joyce. Copyright 1916 by B. W. Huebsch, 1944 by Nora Joyce; copyright © 1964 by the Estate of James Joyce. All Rights Reserved. Reprinted by permission of The Viking Press, Inc., the Executors of the James Joyce Estate, and Jonathan Cape Ltd., publishers.

John Kaplan, from *Marijuana—The New Prohibition*, copyright © 1970 by John Kaplan, reprinted by permission of The World Publishing Company.

Kenneth Keniston, "Students, Drugs, and Protest: Drugs on Campus," in *The American Scholar* and reprinted from *Current*, February, 1969, with the permission of the author.

Martin Luther King, Jr., "Letter from Birmingham Jail," from *Why We Can't Wait*, by Martin Luther King, Jr., published by Harper & Row, Publishers, Inc., and reprinted with the permission of the publisher.

Edward Loomis, excerpt from *Heroic Love*, Alfred A. Knopf, Inc.

Dwight Macdonald, from *Against the American Grain* by Dwight Macdonald, copyright Random House, Inc., and reprinted with the permission of the publisher; and from "Purging the University," in *Newsweek*, July 13, 1970, with the permission of the publisher.

Dwight Macdonald, excerpt from *Memoirs of a Revolutionist* by Dwight Macdonald. Copyright © 1957 by Dwight Macdonald. Reprinted with permission of Farrar, Straus & Giroux, Inc.

Norman Mailer, excerpt reprinted by permission of G. P. Putnam's Sons from *The Presidential Papers* by Norman Mailer. © 1960, 1961, 1962, 1963 by Norman Mailer.

Vladimir Nabokov, from *Lolita* by Vladimir Nabokov. Copyright © 1955 by Vladimir Nabokov, and reprinted by permission of G. P. Putnam's Sons.

Oregon Journal, newsbreak reprinted in *The New Yorker*, July 16, 1966.

George Orwell, excerpt from "Politics and the English Language," *Shooting an Elephant and Other Essays*, Harcourt, Brace & World, Inc., and Martin Secker & Warburg Ltd.

The Oxford English Dictionary, reprinted with the permission of the Clarendon Press, Oxford, England.

V. L. Parrington, excerpt from *Main Currents in American Thought*, Harcourt, Brace & World, Inc.

Thomas R. Powell, excerpt from "Constitutional Metaphors," *The New Republic*, February 11, 1925.

Ramparts Magazine, "The Redress of Their Grievances," copyright Ramparts Magazine, Inc., 1967. By permission of the editors.

Mark Schorer, "Technique as Discovery," *Hudson Review*, I (Spring, 1948), as reprinted in *The World We Imagine: Selected Essays* by Mark Schorer, copyright 1968, Farrar, Straus & Giroux, Inc., and reprinted with the permission of the author.

S. R. Slavson, excerpt from *Reclaiming the Delinquent*, The Macmillan Company (Free Press), 1965.

David E. Smith, from *The New Social Drug: Cultural, Medical, and Legal Perspectives on Marijuana*, copyright © 1970. By permission of Prentice-Hall, Inc., Englewood Cliffs, New Jersey.

Alvin Toffler, from *Future Shock*, by Alvin Toffler, by permission of Random House, Inc.

Kenneth Tynan, excerpt from *Curtains*, Atheneum Publishers.

Gore Vidal, "The Republican National Convention," from *For Our Time* by Gore Vidal, reprinted from *The New York Review of Books* with the permission of the publisher. Copyright © 1968, New York Review, Inc.

George Wald, "A Generation in Search of a Future." Reprinted with the permission of George Wald.

Yvor Winters, excerpt from *The Brink of Darkness*, published 1965 by Alan Swallow. By permission of The Swallow Press, Incorporated, Chicago.

Philip Wylie, excerpt from *Generation of Vipers*, Holt, Rinehart & Winston, Inc.

CONTENTS

PREFACE
TO THE SECOND EDITION

The reception of the first edition of this book, published in 1968, has borne out our belief in the virtues of a short, readable, and more or less informal approach to the problems of writing. At the same time, its use in the classroom has shown up certain defects that we have tried to remedy in this new edition.

First, following advice from several users, we have modified the unconventional organization of the first edition in the direction of conventionality: Part 1 is now on general aspects of writing, Part 2 on rhetorical aspects, Part 3 on mechanical aspects, and Part 4 on the research paper. Second, we have virtually rewritten the chapter on paragraphs, with which users of the first edition rightly found fault, and the two chapters on the research paper, which were well received but whose topic would be approached rather differently today. Finally, we have rewritten substantial parts of other chapters, notably Chapter 1, and made other changes and additions throughout.

The resulting book is some fifty pages longer, for which we are sorry. We had hoped to keep it roughly the same length, but found the additions urged on us—notably, that we include a *complete* sample research paper and greatly expand our coverage of diction in Chapter 6 and the Index to Current Usage— too compelling to ignore. We can only hope that our critics were in fact as right as it seemed to us they were, and that the book's increased length is justified by its increased usefulness.

We are grateful to Alfred Appel, Jr., David Britt, John Hue-benthal, Alan Lichter, Robert Miles, Art Simpson, Oliver Stally-brass, Phyllis Thompson, and Pauline Wickham for their valuable criticisms and suggestions, and to Autumn Stanley for preparing the index.

WILFRED STONE
J. G. BELL

PREFACE
TO THE FIRST EDITION

The freshman of today is a more sophisticated person than his counterpart of ten years ago. He has been exposed to more information, has met more academic competition, has watched more TV, has had more of what the Victorians called "experience," and—the point here—has had more training in the fundamentals of English composition. Freshman English in college is still a going concern, perhaps more so than ever, but it has increasingly left its remedial aspect behind and gone on to more sophisticated things. For the student in such a course, or in any of the various other courses involving writing that Freshman English has splintered into during the last few years, a new kind of handbook is needed. We think this book is the proper kind.

First of all, it is short. It makes no attempt to be encyclopedic, or to provide lists of all the pitfalls that the beginning writer might possibly encounter. We have assumed that in fundamental matters the student needs to be reminded, not taught from the ground up, and that so far as possible the old rules and caveats should be not merely repeated but related organically to the writer's purposes. We have written a shortwinded book, partly to keep it interesting, but mostly to focus students' attention on what we think is most important to their development as writers.

Second, it is designed to be read and not just referred to. Most teachers of Freshman English will remember that semester or quarter when they never did get around to using the old-fashioned handbook—except perhaps for occasional reference. It was too mechanical, too heavy, too removed from what a good Freshman English class is all about. Such a book is like a fire extinguisher on the wall: there in case it is needed, but often dusty from disuse. We have tried to write a different sort of book, one that a teacher can hand his students early in the course with the advice "Read this through, learn what you can from it, try to practice what it preaches, and keep it handy when you are writing."

Third, it ranges far beyond such basic matters as syntax, diction, and usage. It is also a guidebook to style, to research strategies, and even to the kind of person the writer ought to be. We present writing as a three-way relationship between writer, reader, and written work—as a liaison among all three elements, not a mechanical operation. We have made much of questions of tone, style, and imagery, for these are important parts of the "voice" that readers hear in a writer's work and to which they fundamentally respond.

Finally, the book is the combined effort of a college teacher and a professional editor: the first an authority of sorts on what students need and want in their early maturity as writers, the second an authority on writing as such. As we point out more than once in the text, the college writer must be both writer and editor. How very different the two talents are, and how they complement each other, we have discovered only in the course of writing this book.

WILFRED STONE
J. G. BELL

PART 1
THE WRITER AND
HIS MESSAGE

1

ABOUT WRITING

Often the beginning writer thinks of good writing as something to imitate rather than something to create. Surrounded as he is by handbooks, anthologies, sourcebooks, and other weighty repositories of precept and example, he feels frustrated, even despairing. Do people really think he is capable of learning overnight to write like Norman Mailer or George Orwell? If they do, he can see only one hope: rote learning and imitation. To be a writer, he must set aside the Joe Smith he is and write like some Joseph W. Smith he is not, never was, but vaguely supposes he ought to be. From this point of view, writing is not saying what one thinks or feels; it is acting in a play written by others.

We think this point of view is mistaken. In our opinion, learning to write well is a matter of finding your own voice and using it—*your* voice, not someone else's. If Joe Smith is who you are, Joe Smith is the one your reader wants to hear from. A writer should put himself into the act, write his own part. Nothing less, in the long run, makes writing worth reading. Not that the act of writing is ever entirely a private performance; far from it.

Writing takes place in an environment, in a context, and the writer who ignores this context is likely to end up speaking some sort of private language. Let us examine briefly the three elements of this context—the writer, his audience, and his writing.

THE WRITER

Writing starts with the writer. He must have something to say, must want to say it, and must learn how to say it clearly and well. The easiest of these three requirements is the last: the rules and conventions of good writing. They can be learned, and a good part of this book is given over to instruction in them. What cannot be learned (at least in the same way) is self-confidence, belief in yourself and the validity and importance of what you write. Many students contemplate that blank sheet of paper in despair. How can I have anything to say that the teacher or anybody else will want to hear? What do I know about history, psychology, politics, science—or even myself? I am young, yet I am supposed to speak from ripe experience. I am a beginner, yet I am supposed to write like a professional. How can I measure up?

The answer is: Don't try so hard. Don't try to be "professional"; try to be honest with yourself, with your own feelings and thoughts, and with the ideas you encounter in your reading. There is nearly always some point where you and your experience intersect with those ideas, some point where you can speak with authority. The point may be only a tiny corner of a large issue, and may take some pondering to find; but authority is none the less real for being asserted in a small matter. Writing about Shakespeare or the Second World War is inherently no more interesting than writing about your roommate. The interest depends not on the size of the subject, but on what you have to say.

Let us assume that for several weeks your class has been reading and discussing essays on what your teacher calls "the identity crisis of American life." The readings have included Thoreau's "Civil Disobedience," Jerome Bruner's "Myth and Identity," Erich Fromm's "The Illusion of Individuality," Martin Luther

King's "Letter from a Birmingham Jail," George Wald's "A Generation in Search of a Future," and excerpts from *The Autobiography of Malcolm X* and Eldridge Cleaver's *Soul on Ice*. These essays may have fascinated, bored, or upset you; they may have made you angry; or they may have left you feeling uninvolved, outside it all, uneasy and perhaps a little guilty at the spectacle of passions you do not share.

Then suddenly a political issue on your campus leads to a sit-in. Students are arrested, and a demonstration protesting their arrest leads to a riot, arson, and further arrests. The crisis you have been reading about comes home to you; some of its issues are being dramatized outside your dormitory window. You may be as confused about these issues as you were a week ago, but at least they are no longer academic. Your instructor asks for an essay relating your recent reading to the campus unrest, emphasizing so far as possible your personal reaction to the events of the past few days. Did your courage get tested in any way? Did anything change your attitude toward violence? Toward authority, law and order, freedom? These are questions you had encountered earlier in the course, but at that time the jails of Concord and Birmingham had seemed far away. Now things have changed. You are part of the scene and can write as something of an authority.

But what to say? The problem is still difficult, since you have been asked to be specific and to avoid sweeping generalities. Perhaps your best course is to pattern your paper on the lines of a scientific experiment. The experimenter's basic concern is with some widely accepted generalization or theory; he seeks to discover whether that theory is true, false, or true only with certain qualifications. In the same way you can start with some passage in your reading that caught your attention and put it to the test. Does the passage square with your recent experience, or does it miss something central? Does what you have seen or felt bear out the writer's views or contradict them?

A paper of this sort has three components: the passage you choose to examine, a statement of your experience, and your reflections on the first in the light of the second. There are other ways of constructing a paper, but this classic structure is a good one for the present assignment. Your first job, then, is to choose that core passage from your reading. Perhaps you remember Thoreau's ringing statement about corrupt government:

> Unjust laws exist; shall we be content to obey them, or shall we endeavor to amend them, and obey them until we have succeeded, or shall we transgress them at once? Men generally, under such a government as this, think that they ought to wait until they have persuaded the majority to alter them. They think that, if they should resist, the remedy would be worse than the evil. But it is the fault of the government itself that the remedy *is* worse than the evil. *It* makes it worse. Why is it not more apt to anticipate for reform? Why does it not cherish its wise minority? Why does it cry and resist before it is hurt? Why does it not encourage its citizens to be on the alert to point out its faults, and do better than it would have them? Why does it always crucify Christ, and ex-communicate Copernicus and Luther, and pronounce Washington and Franklin rebels?

Or this statement by Martin Luther King:

> You express a great deal of anxiety over our willingness to break laws. This is certainly a legitimate concern. Since we so diligently urge people to obey the Supreme Court's decision of 1954 outlawing segregation in the public schools, at first glance it may seem rather paradoxical for us consciously to break laws. One may well ask: "How can you advocate breaking some laws and obeying others?" The answer lies in the fact that there are two types of laws: just and unjust. I would be the first to advocate obeying just laws. Conversely, one has a moral responsibility to disobey unjust laws. I would agree with St. Augustine that "an unjust law is no law at all."
> Now, what is the difference between the two? How does one determine whether a law is just or unjust? . . . Any law that uplifts human personality is just. Any law that degrades human personality is unjust. All segregation

statutes are unjust because segregation distorts the soul and damages the personality. It gives the segregator a false sense of superiority and the segregatee a false sense of inferiority. Segregation, to use the terminology of the Jewish philosopher Martin Buber, substitutes an "I-it" relationship for an "I-thou" relationship and ends up relegating persons to the status of things.

Perhaps your experience has been more private, and can better be measured against this passage from Erich Fromm:

> . . . Modern man lives under the illusion that he knows what he wants, while he actually wants what he is *supposed* to want. . . . Modern man is ready to take great risks when he tries to achieve the aims which are supposed to be "his"; but he is deeply afraid of taking the risk and the responsibility of giving himself his own aims. . . .
>
> By conforming with the expectations of others, by not being different, these doubts about one's own identity are silenced and a certain security is gained. However, the price is high. Giving up spontaneity and individuality results in a thwarting of life. Psychologically the automaton, while being alive biologically, is dead emotionally and mentally. While he goes through the motions of living, his life runs through his hands like sand.

Why did I join that demonstration, you may ask yourself. Did I take part because I believed in its goals or because everybody I knew was taking part? Or alternatively: Is my disgust at the demonstrators' antics genuine, or am I an unwitting slave to conventions I do not consciously accept?

Possibly you have been struck by Bruner's contention that although we all live by "myths" and are constantly creating new myths to live by, our society is impoverished by having no one unifying myth that we can all believe in. As a fledgling activist, you are ready to give your all for the cause, but what *is* the cause? The dictatorship of the proletariat seems to have produced mainly tyranny. The welfare of the downtrodden seems no dearer to campus revolutionaries than to government reformers,

and most of the downtrodden themselves seemingly prefer re-
form to revolution. Peace is a good cause, but how can one
achieve it through violence and arson? The university's administration seems to you bullheaded on some points, but what
noble principle—what unifying myth—justifies the vandalism
committed during the sit-in? What is the vandals' vision of the
uncorrupt society, their prescription for human happiness? Perhaps this passage by Bruner focuses some of your thinking:

> In our own time, in the American culture, there is a deep
> problem generated by the confusion that has befallen the
> myth of the happy man. It reflects itself in the American
> personality. There still lingers the innocent Christian con-
> ception that happiness is the natural state of man—or at least
> of the child and of man as innocent—and that it is something
> that we have done or failed to do as individuals that creates
> a rather Protestantized and private unhappiness. The im-
> pact of Freud has begun to destroy this myth, to replace it.
> Our popular films now, with artistry, depict the child as
> murderer. A generation of playwrights has destroyed the
> remnants of the myth of Horatio Alger, replacing it with
> the image of Arthur Miller's salesman dying by entropy, an
> object of compassion. We are no longer a "mythologically
> instructed community." And so one finds a new generation
> struggling to find or to create a satisfactory and challenging
> mythic image.
>
> Two such images seem to be emerging in the new genera-
> tion. One is that of the hipsters and the squares; the other
> is the idealization of creative wholeness. The first is the
> myth of the uncommitted wandering hero, capable of the
> hour's subjectivity—its "kicks"—participating in a new in-
> wardness.

You may recognize something of yourself in this description,
and perhaps something of your activist friends. Yet by your
lights Bruner altogether misses the complexity of the new generation's world view, which you see as having more to do with
the older generation's attitude toward war, social injustice, and
destruction of the environment than with its residual myths of

happiness through faith or business success. How to define the new cause, the new myth, so that everyone can accept it is beyond you. But after your experience of the last few days, you may be convinced that it is equally beyond Bruner, in which case that could be the theme of your paper.

Or perhaps you have come to feel that political bickering can blind people to what they really want. A passage by George Wald makes this point in global terms:

> I think we've reached a point of great decision, not just for our nation, not only for all humanity, but for life upon the Earth. . . . The thought that we're in competition with Russians or with Chinese is all a mistake, and trivial. Only mutual destruction lies that way. We are one species, with a world to win. There's life all over this universe, but in the universe we are the only men.
>
> Our business is with life, not death. Our challenge is to give what account we can of what becomes of life in the solar system, this corner of the universe that is our home, and, most of all, what becomes of men—all men of all nations, colors, and creeds. It has become one world, a world for all men. It is only such a world that now can offer us life and the chance to go on.

The choice of a passage does not automatically provide you with a subject or a theme (for the distinction, see pp. 18–20). You must find your subject and theme by deciding where, in this broad context of social transition and revolution, you find yourself. If you are a conservative, you may want to attack Martin Luther King's self-serving distinction between just and unjust laws, or to criticize Wald's airy dismissal of our differences with the Russians and the Chinese. If you are a radical, you may want to deride King for his moderation or Bruner for his apparent insensitivity to the issues of a world on fire.

If, as is more likely, you are neither notably conservative nor notably radical, you may have to think a little harder. So much the better. Norman Mailer once wrote that "one must be with it, or doomed not to swing"; but the with-it swinger of the left or right will produce a more predictable and less interesting paper than the out-of-it groper in the center, provided only that the groper's experience is honestly reported. Here is part of a student theme that partly fails on this last point:

> I wasn't really in the sit-in but was riding around on my motorcycle between the Union Courtyard and the fountain, and saw most of what went on. There was a rock band inside; the demonstrators were clearly dug in for an all-night stand. Once as I drove by—watching for the police, since it is illegal to drive there—the wind must have been blowing our way, since a strong smell of marijuana filled the air. I remember thinking, "Man, if the pigs came now, they could have one helluva bust."
>
> Later that night, twenty-three (I believe) students were arrested, and the next day this cruel, oppressive University allowed the remaining demonstrators to have an open mike in front of the Union to complain about the "police brutality" and the violent tactics used to clear the courtyard of trespassers. If they had only been told when the police were coming, they said, they would have cleared out of the courtyard and the Union peacefully. But they were blitzkrieged and had no chance. This argument must have been dreamed up by simpletons.
>
> I am sympathetic with most of the aims of the sit-inners: I am against the Vietnam War and against racism and against pollution and against imperialism and against bumper stickers. But I couldn't believe how stupidly naive and idealistic those demonstrators were in their claims and complaints. Most of the people in the sit-in were newcomers and didn't realize they were playing in the big leagues. None of the leaders got caught; most of those in the police net were freshmen and sophomores who didn't know they were just being played for suckers. Even so, how could they be so boneheaded as to think they could break the law and get away with it? I can agree with Thoreau or Martin Luther King that there are times when unjust laws must be broken—and maybe this was one of those times—but I don't think much of people who break the law and then don't expect to take the consequences. I

was on their side on the issues, but I have no sympathy with people who want to have their cake and eat it too.

Is this a good theme? The writing is clear and vigorous, but what about the argument? It is more than a little confused. Does the writer sympathize with the radicals, as some of his language and his private lawbreaking suggest, or is his contempt for them genuine? On the evidence he seems to be torn both ways; like the sit-inners he describes, he wants to have his cake and eat it too. There is nothing wrong with ambivalence if the writer sees it himself and admits it. But this writer does not see his ambivalence, or does not see that it shows; he tries in vain to sell us an argument that he himself only half believes. There are other signs as well of the writer's confusion, notably his ineffectual efforts at humor. Those bumper stickers, for example, are a cheap gag made for its own sake; they don't belong in the same sentence with Vietnam.

Let us now consider part of another theme by a girl in the same class:

That dilemma-filled week drained me of emotions and tears and radical vigor. I was distressed by the entire chain of events. I had never before been exposed to people whose answer to problems is destruction, and my initial response to trashing and police on campus was: "What good will all of this do? Someone is going to get hurt." Some dorm friends replied that trashing was not in itself bad, it was just a bad tactic to use at the time. I could not agree.

So, I set about with some friends who shared my views to organize a demonstration against violence—and in those days we all thought many times of Thoreau and Gandhi and Martin Luther King. I had done enough organizing in high school to know two days was not enough time to organize a demonstration, but we went to work. I also worried about our motives. I feared being thought a reactionary; and I feared being inactive at a time when I thought something must be done. Was this the right thing?

Right or wrong, it took place and was a "success"—if such a word can apply to an affair like this. More than a thousand people came to our mass meeting, march, and con-vocation; and that Monday night restored my belief that bringing people together is a good thing and can accomplish something. A feeling of pride and love filled me as I sat on the floor in the Round Room afterwards and listened to radicals and revolutionaries, intellectuals and hospital work-ers, the violent and the passive, discuss non-violence as a way of life. I thought of Eldridge Cleaver's remark in *Soul on Ice* where he said, "There is in America today a genera-tion of white youth that is truly worthy of a black man's respect, and this is a rare event in the foul annals of Ameri-can history." I had the good feeling that the people in that room were members of that "white generation."

The theme concludes with this paragraph:

Throughout the entire semester I have been confronted by challenges to my ideals, my values, my politics, and my health. I cried when I became so involved that I felt only frustration over minor setbacks or unkind remarks. In retrospect, however, I know I thrived on involvement; I understand the need and consider it my duty to do some-thing to satisfy it. I cannot do it all myself, but I must do something.

How does this theme compare with the first? It is much better. The writer is clearly trying to come to grips with her own convictions and actions; she can be reasonably objective even about emotion-packed experiences, and can relate her feel-ings more or less naturally to the reading she has been doing. Her writing is sometimes clumsy, but her paper is one that few critics would want to pick at. Why? It is on the level. It is an intelligent response, deeply felt, to a serious issue. However much we may differ with the opinions of such a writer, we have to respect her.

Good writing, in short, begins in self-knowledge (or some degree of it) and helps provoke further self-knowledge. "How do I know what I mean till I see what I say?" said the old lady, and she has a point. We are not saying that all good writing consists of confessions of humility, cowardice, confusion, or faith. In writing, as in talking, you are under no obligation to reveal matters that you would rather keep to yourself. We are saying only that what you do write should be true to your experience, true to your vision of the way things are—not your mother's vision, not your teacher's vision, not your political party's vision, *your* vision. The reader usually knows when you are saying what you mean. He also usually knows when you are saying what you think you ought to say, or what you hope somebody will think is profound. When you say what you mean, he will keep on reading. When your mind turns off, so will his.

THE AUDIENCE

Without an audience or the hope of an audience, most writers would have no motive for writing. Writing is a medium of communication. It carries your thoughts not only out from you, but in to someone else. How you write will depend on who that someone else is: you write one way in a letter to a child, another way in a business letter, still another way in a love letter. The differences are not only in what you want to say, but in what will interest your reader, and in what ideas and words you think he can grasp.

What is true of a letter is equally true of a theme or a report. If you are a scientist writing for scientists, a clergyman for clergymen, a labor leader for union members, you will feel free to use terms that a lay audience would not understand without an explanation. The same assumptions about the educational and intellectual level of your readers will govern other decisions as well. For example, they may determine the length of your sentences and paragraphs (inexperienced readers like them short), the complexity of your syntax, the level of detail.

If you are addressing a general audience—as, let us say, a writer for *Life* or *Harper's*—you will adjust your writing to the presumed capacities of a much wider range of readers. If you use technical language, you will be sure to explain what it means; if you deal with complex issues, you will state them in clear and simple terms; if you take a position on a controversial topic, you will be concerned with how readers may react to what you say. If, by contrast, you ignore your readers' capacities, or even if you over-estimate or underestimate them, your words will be imperfectly understood at best, and probably will go unread.

To say that a writer must think constantly of his readers, must anticipate their confusions and choose his words accordingly, is not to contradict what we said earlier about the need for honesty and courage. The purpose of writing is to say something, not to get published. If you temporize or compromise your principles, if you oversimplify to the point of misrepresenting, if you pander to the prejudices of an editor or a teacher, you will not be the kind of writer that we are asking you to admire. Your integrity as a writer comes first. When we place attention to your reader's capacities as a very close second, it is only because a writer's integrity has no meaning if his writing is impossible for anyone to read.

We have spoken here in terms of publication, and of a wide range of readers. Though you are not literally writing for publication, you should imagine that you are—and that your teacher is not your audience so much as your editor, receiving and judging a manuscript you have sent him at his request. If the manuscript is something that he thinks would interest the readers of his magazine, he will accept it; if not, he will send it back. Your teacher, to be sure, is an audience, too, and since he may be your most attentive and critical reader, you can hardly be indifferent to his reactions. But his personal reactions are secondary to his views on how your imaginary audience will react, and on what revisions might make its reaction more favorable. In short, you should think of him as an editor helping you to ask wise and honest questions about the effect of your words.

From this point of view, consider the following excerpts from still another student theme:

> In *Soul on Ice* Eldridge Cleaver says that "The myth of the strong black woman is the other side of the coin of the myth of the beautiful dumb blonde." Now I don't know anything about strong black women (though I'd like to), but I have had some acquaintance with dumb blondes, and after reading Bruner on myths I have a pretty good idea of what a myth is. Cleaver goes on to say: "The white man turned

the white woman into a weak-minded, weak-bodied, delicate freak, a sex pot, and placed her on a pedestal: he turned the black woman into a strong self-reliant Amazon and deposited her in his kitchen—that's the secret of Aunt Jemima's bandanna."

Maybe that's Cleaver's myth, but the dumb blonde I know most about spent most of her time trying to get off that pedestal and get me into bed—after marriage, that is. She was so dumb she didn't even know that marriage as an institution is dead. She was an honest-to-God throwback to the Victorian era. Mae West and Marilyn Monroe might never have lived so far as she was concerned. Sex pot, hell! The only pot she cared about was the one at the end of the rainbow.

This writer is addressing that most narrow and parochial of audiences, his own classmates—and a narrow segment of them, at that. His motive is to make them laugh, or perhaps to get a rise out of his teacher. These aims, though not wrong in themselves, are here too low and limited. Cleaver is raising a serious issue; in making sport of it, our writer is misjudging his audience and prejudicing his case much the way our first writer (p. 10) prejudiced his. He has chosen to play the adolescent in a place where maturity is expected, and the reader is irritated, just as you might be irritated by your little brother's pranks when you are trying to study.

THE WRITING

We come finally to the third element in our three-way relationship, writing itself. Much of this book is given over to the rules or conventions that make for clear writing, but conventions are only part of the story. To approach the task of writing only through rules—through learning what is proper and improper, grammatical and ungrammatical, conventional and vulgar—is, we feel, a dead end. The rules are important, but there is a big difference between knowing the rules and knowing how to write, and an even bigger difference between writing "correctly" and writing well.

The best writers tend to be people with something on their minds that they want to get off, curious people who want to discover things, or think things through, and tell others what they have come up with. They may be well organized or not, they may or may not get good grades; there seems to be no correlation between the various standard forms of academic excellence and the instinct for expressing oneself in writing. The heart of writing is not rules but this instinct or motivation. If the writer is not motivated, what he writes will not be worth reading; if he is, he will find out where to put his commas and how to write good paragraphs almost as a by-product of his motivation.

There are many varieties of writing, ranging from formal through informal and colloquial to slangy, varieties that reflect both the writer's approach and his assumptions about his audience. There is nothing "wrong" or "right" about any of these varieties as such; each has its place, each its charm. Our concern in this book will be with so-called Standard English, the kind that most educated people write for publication, or public attention, on subjects they are serious about. This definition obviously covers a lot of ground, from the smooth professional journalism of *Time* and *Newsweek* to the academese of *Classical Philology*, from the bright, empty cadences of a television commercial to the earnest exhortations of a Sunday sermon.

Standard English is a variety of usage, not an indication of quality; Standard English is not necessarily good English. Indeed, a great deal of what passes for Standard English in American writing, even at the most exalted levels, is graceless and unclear. That is one reason why books like this one are necessary. These days the writing of business executives, government officials, engineers, social scientists, and educationists is particularly awful. Here, for example, is a communiqué written by an elementary school principal to inform parents of a proposed curriculum change:

> The highly structured nature of grade level standards is well recognized. While a majority of pupils may be operating on what is defined as average or standard, the very fact that material is so identified tends to lead to conformity. Pupils in this school tend, traditionally, to operate above

these standards. The teacher usually groups to handle the variation found in the verbal and performance operations of the class. To us, therefore, it was more logical to relate the child to his success and mastery of the subject area sequence rather than to the number on the textbook.

Here is a fair rendering of the same paragraph in Standard English, without the bewildering passives, the elusive abstractions, and the pseudoscientific jargon:

Most of you parents have had firsthand experience with the old-fashioned grading system, in which children stay with other children of the same age from first grade through sixth regardless of differences in ability. I feel (and the teachers agree) that this system has flaws and needs changing. At present, when a student shows special ability, he is put in a special group within his grade. Under the new system, a child would advance beyond his grade in subjects he is especially good at and stay with his grade in other subjects. If, for example, a third-grade child were good at mathematics and reading, he could do fourth-, fifth-, or even sixth-grade work in these subjects as his talents permitted, while remaining at the third-grade level for his other subjects.

In the rewritten piece we know who is doing the speaking (or writing), we know who is responsible for the ideas being proposed, and we can understand what is being said. The double-talk and the ambiguity of the original were entirely unnecessary. What seemed hard to understand was in fact extremely simple.

Not everything can be made simple, but most things—even the most complicated things—can be said clearly. In fact, the more complicated the message, the greater the writer's responsibility to make it clear. Good writing is a matter of communication, of getting something across. Our school principal's failure to communicate is only one of many possible kinds. Another is what teachers ironically call "fine writing," which comes from the notion that writing to be good must be flowery, or polysyllabic, or larded with quotations or foreign words. Fine writing is the kind of prose that says "Joseph traversed the path to his domicile" instead of "Joe went home." At best this style sets up a kind of static between the sender and the receiver; at worst it has to be translated to be understood.

In the pages that follow, we will have a lot to say about tone, imagery, grammar, sentence structure, and diction. We will invoke rules and conventions. But it should not be forgotten that these rules and conventions are means, not ends. The aim of writing may be defined as follows: to spare your reader the error of misunderstanding your message, and the pain of translating it, by making it as clear as possible from the outset. Rules and conventions are useful only to the extent that they serve this end.

SUBJECT AND THEME

As we have seen, your first practical step in doing a piece of writing is to choose your subject; your second is to decide what you are going to say about that subject, or what your "theme" will be. For example, the subject of George Orwell's well-known essay "Politics and the English Language" is stated in the title. The theme is established in the first few paragraphs, and can be paraphrased as follows: "When a civilization is decadent, as ours is, the language of that civilization becomes decadent, too. By cleaning up the language—ridding it of its bad habits—we can reverse the process of political decay." Behind all of Orwell's examples of stale language lies this theme; indeed, this theme is the point of his essay, its *raison d'être*. In a formal argument the theme is the proposition or contention to be proved. In an informal essay proof as such may not be called for, but the theme must be backed up by example and reasoning.

Choosing a Subject

In choosing a subject, look for something that you care about, that you respond to, that hits you where you live. If your teacher offers a choice of subjects none of which interests you, or one broad subject on which you feel you have nothing to say, the problem is a little harder. In this situation, two words of advice.

First, take your time deciding: a quick, what-the-hell decision may lead to hours of anguish or tedium, whereas another ten minutes' thought might turn up an angle or aspect of the subject that you would enjoy exploring. Second, use your imagination. The fact that A. E. Housman's poetry bores you is not necessarily a reason to avoid writing about it. Why not write about *why* Housman bores you, why you like some other poet better, or even why you don't like poetry at all (if you don't), giving examples from Housman? If your essay is up to standard in other respects, your teacher will not object to this slight departure from the assigned topic.

Just as there is probably no such thing as an inherently dull human being, so there is probably no such thing as an inherently dull subject—if, that is, we get far enough below the surface to reach that point of intimacy where affection and sympathy come into play. A girl may not be interested in politics. Then let her choose a politician whose looks she likes, listen to him, read about him, write about her reaction to what he says. Everybody is interested in people; and this girl might even end up interested in politics after all. A boy may have no taste for classical music. Then let him read a biography of Mozart, think about Mozart's amazing career and the universal acclaim for his works today, and write whatever comes to mind. Somewhere along the way he will certainly want to listen to a few records, if only to hear what it was that made such a stir in 1769 or 1787. He may end up liking classical music better; people often dislike things only because they know nothing about them. If one aspect of a subject bores you, look for another that doesn't. If all aspects bore you, try another subject. If all subjects bore you, you had better see a psychiatrist. The extremes of boredom are a condition in the writer, not in what there is to write about.

Choosing a Theme

Choosing a theme is a much more difficult task. Finding a theme in a subject means finding a point of view toward it. Some people bring to serious subjects a built-in point of view: that of a Christian, a Communist, a self-made man, or whatever.

But most college students are not so endowed. For them, finding a point of view is part of a hard, even harrowing, search for moral, spiritual, and intellectual values.

Where this search will take a student he does not know and we do not know; nor do we have any basis, in the circumstances, for recommending one point of view over another. Our Mozart man may end up writing that he does not see what the fuss over Mozart is all about, that for his part he prefers Dixieland or acid rock. Our politics girl may end up by coming out with flags flying for some fool with nothing more between his ears than a handsome head of hair. Well and good. Say what you think. If you don't know what you think, try arguing both ways—Mozart is terrible, Mozart is wonderful—and see which argument you feel more comfortable with, which one you feel readier to defend.

You will be "wrong" sometimes, maybe often; no matter, that is part of getting educated. In particular, your teacher's opinion of Mozart, or of politics, is irrelevant to what you write. You are writing not to please him, or spite him, or flatter him, but to make a reasoned presentation of your own views to a wider, if hypothetical, audience. He will grade you not on the degree to which you manage to say what he thinks, but on how well you have said what you yourself think.

Writing, as a transaction between writer, subject matter, and audience, begins and ends with the writer. His integrity, his perception, his tact—in short, his qualities of character—are what finally make the difference between worthwhile writing and junk. Intelligence, education, and maturity help. But what is needed most of all is that the writer seek to understand and elucidate that most vital of all subjects, himself.

2
LOGIC AND EVIDENCE

A sound argument is not the automatic result of being right or well-intentioned. If a child says he knows that the moon revolves around the earth because it is there at night and not in the daytime, he is right about what the moon does but his reasoning is unsound. When Mother says Johnny was bad to hit his sister, she is saying what she honestly thinks; but is her reasoning sound? If she knew the whole story, she might have congratulated him on his restraint.

An important part of Aristotle's pioneering study of logic in the fourth century B.C. was his naming of logical fallacies, those errors in reasoning that he found common enough to classify. Since then, logicians have refined and qualified this list, but all the fallacies Aristotle identified are still in evidence, and many of his names and definitions are still used. No matter how well an argument is researched, no matter how well it is written, a logical fallacy or error of reasoning will weaken it. The writer who has a fine style but cannot think straight is not a good writer. Style and logic are inseparable parts of the written fabric, and in the best prose become virtually one and the same thing.

Most of us have an instinctive sense for logical error, even when we cannot put our finger on what is wrong. After a disappointing lecture, we may say nothing more profound than "What a windbag!"—yet our reaction probably indicates that the speaker has been guilty of one or more of Aristotle's logical fallacies. You're arguing in a circle! Two wrongs don't make a right! But that doesn't follow! These familiar phrases point to the presence of the classical fallacies known respectively as *petitio principii, tu quoque,* and *non sequitur.* We shall pay only passing attention to these ancient terms, and very little attention to these three fallacies in particular. Indeed, our aim in this chapter is not to give an exhaustive treatment of the subject, but simply to identify some logical fallacies that are frequently encountered and to clarify a few logical principles.[1]

A fallacy is an erroneous or unjustified inference. An inference is a logical relationship expressible by the formula *if P, then Q*: if this statement (*P*) is true, it follows that this other statement (*Q*) must be true. This relationship can be expressed more completely as a syllogism, a three-term relationship consisting of a premise (major premise), a middle term (minor premise), and a conclusion:

Premise
    All men are mortal.   ⎫
Middle term   ⎬ P
    Socrates is a man.   ⎭
Conclusion
    Therefore Socrates is mortal.   Q

This classic syllogism contains no fallacy; the premises are sound and lead inexorably to the sound conclusion. In a fallacious argument, by contrast, either the premise or the path from the

[1] Those who are interested in fallacies not touched on in this chapter, or in the Latin names of those for which we use English terms, should consult a good elementary logic text, e.g. Monroe C. Beardsley, *Thinking Straight,* 3d ed. (New York, 1966). There is an excellent chapter on logic, geared to the use of words in writing, in Richard D. Altick, *Preface to Critical Reading,* 5th ed. (New York, 1968).

premise to the conclusion is erroneous; either P is wrong, or the statement *if P, then Q* is wrong, or both.

Most noninductive arguments, if labored over long enough, can be reduced to syllogistic form, but for writers this exercise is not very helpful. Modern logicians tend to substitute letter and number symbols for words and sentences, and with good reason: the written language is not as precise an instrument as they require. The statement "I intend to pay my bills on time after this" seems simple enough at first; yet when we ask just what "I" means in this context, or whether the speaker is making a moral commitment or expressing mere future purpose, we get into profound philosophical problems. This book is not concerned with such tangles, but the beginning writer should be aware that they exist. Words are symbols, imperfect symbols invented and used for the most part by nonlogicians. A large part of the writer's job is fashioning clear and logically sound statements out of these imperfect materials. It is not an easy job.

But neither—given some basic common sense and a little care and thought—is it an impossible job. These qualities, alas, are missing in the following essay, which is an only slightly modified version of a paper actually submitted in an English class. The superscript numbers, indicating various logical fallacies committed by the writer, are keyed to the numbered headings in the subsequent discussion.

An American Myth

One of the most persistent American myths[1] I know is that all the poor people in the world,[1] the people to whom we shell out millions in aid every year, are unhappy[1] just because they are poor. Sitting where we are on our mountain of luxury, we feel that if people do not have television sets, two cars in the garage, paid vacations, and a nice house in the suburbs, they are unhappy.[9] It just is not so. I can say with absolute assurance— from personal observation in Turkey, Syria, Egypt, Lebanon, Greece, and Mexico[3]—that the poor are not unhappy if we leave them alone.[9] They do not enjoy themselves in the same way we do, but their lives are nevertheless full of pleasure. They have their own holidays and dances and rituals—which are entirely different from ours—but this is their own culture and they like it.

Nor do the poor suffer or feel pain in the same way we would under similar conditions;[9] they have grown used to their lot and are happy in it if left alone.   We forget that often the loveliest flowers grow on manure[4] heaps.[8]

To prove my thesis, look at what happened in 1965 after we sent millions of tons of wheat to India during the famine.[3]   Instead of making the country contented, there were food riots all over North India and some fighting with Pakistan.[5]   The people were more ungrateful, not less.   And the same thing some years ago in Egypt; after all our help, Egypt let the Russians build the Aswan Dam and the country was overrun with "Yankee Go Home" signs.[5]   We stirred the people up with our aid, with a vision of luxury to which they were not accustomed, and then nothing would satisfy them.

The same thesis applies to the poor at home.   Our welfare rolls are filled on the one hand with deadbeats[2] too lazy to work and on the other with hopheads[2] who won't work on principle.[6]   Why do we go on subsidizing whores[2] who have a child a year—each one by a different father?   If we cut off the supplies, these people would straighten out and join the same civilized society that the rest of us live in and pay taxes in.[5]   Why do we do it?   Because we are infected[2] by the sentimental idea that these people cannot help themselves, and that if we do not help them we will be Bad Samaritans.   Actually we are Bad Samaritans doing what we do now, for these people—once they get used to living on handouts—lose all pride and self-respect, like zoo animals.[8]

How many of our policy makers have actually been in a slum? They think it is terrible because it is so unlike the place *they* live. But my father has worked in embassies all over the Middle East and I have had plenty of opportunity to see slums.   Actually slums are no worse than any other place once you get used to them; they are just different.[9]   "There's no place like home" applies there just as much as anywhere.   Instead of getting people out of slums, we should get the slums out of people.[4]

Jesus said "Blessed are the poor," and "The poor shall never cease out of the land."   Yet here we are engaged in the absurd[2] effort of trying to eliminate what cannot be eliminated.[7]   Moreover, it *should* not be eliminated, for the presence of those less fortunate than ourselves in this world brings out the best in us. When we give to our favorite charity, we are sharing part of our best selves.   But we should not ever forget that charity begins at home.

1. Undefined Terms

No clear communication is possible if we do not know what our words mean. Since words, unlike mathematical symbols, are not fixed in value but constantly changing, a writer who hopes to be understood must frequently pause to define his terms. A complete definition may be impossible (such a simple, everyday word as *property*, for example, is subject enough for a book), but the writer should at least provide a working definition—some indication of which of a word's various possible meanings he is using. In the essay under discussion, for example, the word *myth* seems to be used in its secondary and derivative sense of "something untrue," but it could also have that richer meaning suggested by Mark Schorer: "Myths are the instruments by which we continually struggle to make our experience intelligible to ourselves." Does the writer have this meaning in mind as well as the more obvious meaning? We cannot know, for he has not told us.

Other problems of definition occur throughout this essay. Just what is meant by "poor people," and in particular by the phrase "all the poor people in the world"? That's a large number of poor people, and of different kinds of poor people—people with plenty of food and no money as well as people in danger of starvation, young people with big debts but bright prospects as well as old people with no debts but no prospects either. Which of these people is the writer talking about? All of them? But surely some are happy, some unhappy; some interested in help from abroad, some not. Is he talking about only some of them? Then which ones?

And what about that word *unhappy*? It is hard enough to define happiness in the abstract; it is far harder to say with assurance whether someone else is or is not "happy." Is happiness the same as pleasure? Then what about those Christian martyrs who claimed to find ecstasy in their self-sacrifice—so much so that the early church inveighed against the seeking of martyrdom? Are brides happy, as the greeting cards say? If so, are the fainting fits, cold sweats, and panic that often accompany a bride to the altar part of her happiness? To see the concept in these terms is to see the word *unhappy* as mixed and relative, connected to the human condition, and not as absolute.

What should our writer have done? Probably he should have said, early in the paper, something like this: "By happiness I do not mean bliss or uninterrupted satisfaction, but simply a feeling that things are going reasonably well." This is no formal definition of happiness, but it is a good working definition for our writer's purposes. It will make his argument clearer to his readers, and his competence to expound it more apparent.

Obviously, most of the words in any essay have more than one possible meaning, and no one stops to define them all. How far should a writer go in defining terms? He should define all key words in his argument whose definition is not self-evident—words like *unhappy,* on which the argument of "An American Myth" pivots. He should define any other abstract terms—*myth, the poor*—that are not clear in context. He should define or explain all strange words. In the interests of style, he should present his definitions as gracefully and unobtrusively as possible; but if the claims of precision and the claims of grace conflict, the former should prevail.

2. Name-calling

Name-calling is an appeal to prejudice by false or invidious labeling. Words have connotations: some are neutral, some favorable, some unfavorable. A few years ago there was a popular parlor game in which people were asked to describe a given condition successively in the first, second, and third persons with increasing acerbity as the focus shifted away from themselves: "I am intelligent, you are clever, he is a smart aleck"; "I am enjoying myself, you should slow down, he is dead drunk." It is an old trick to place what you dislike in a class of things that all reasonable people dislike, and the writer of this essay has indulged it freely. Obvious examples are his use of the words *deadbeats* and *hopheads* to describe people on relief. Are there no old women, no cripples, no unemployed who would work if they could? Three other instances of name-calling in the essay, not all of them nouns, are indicated by the same number.

3. Inadequate Sampling

One of the commonest errors in amateur argument is that of generalizing from too small a sample. The writer of "An American Myth" claims to "prove" his thesis by citing what happened during one year in India. But it does not follow from that one instance (see 5 below) that the poor are happy if left alone or even that they riot and start wars whenever anyone gives them a little wheat. Even the one instance itself leaves something to be desired. What part of India are we talking about, for example, and what was the connection between the wheat and the outbreaks of violence? Not only is this instance no proof of the general case; it is itself unacceptable as evidence.

Another error in sampling appears in the list of countries— Turkey, Syria, Egypt, and so on—that the author provides. At first glance this list seems impressive; the author has been around and seen things. But then doubts creep in. Has he seen enough to make generalizations about "all poor people"? Of course not. Has he even really *seen* what he says he has seen? Looking and seeing are two different things, as different as tourism and research. "Personal observation" could mean occasional glances out the back window of the embassy limousine. Is that a big enough sampling to make generalizations about the poor in the Middle East and Mexico? Few would think it was.

4. Equivocation

To equivocate is to use a term in two or more senses without making the shift in sense clear. In "An American Myth" the most obvious equivocation is the play on the word *slums* in the next-to-last paragraph: "Instead of getting people out of slums, we should get the slums out of people." This sounds fine, but what does it mean? The argument rests on our equating run-down areas like Harlem or Watts with an internal psychological condition of which we know only that it is offensive to the writer. Can such disparate things be equated? Almost certainly not. But they are equated here anyway by the equivocal use of the word *slums*. Similarly, the word *manure* in the first paragraph is used simultaneously to mean filth and fertilizer.

There is also another and opposite kind of equivocation, in which different words are used for essentially the same thing, so that what is one thing in nature is made to appear two. A clever mystery novel was once published in which everything depended on the identity of one narrator, "I," with a "Mr. Taylor" frequently mentioned by another narrator; the reader was allowed to infer the twoness of this onesome right up to the last sentence of the book. Most such equivocations, however, are less deliberate. Thus the writer of "An American Myth" distinguishes between *aid*, which is no good, and *charity*, which is good. But what is foreign aid except charity on a large scale? If our writer objects to one and supports the other, let him speak of small-scale and large-scale charity, or of public and private aid. To do otherwise is to transform a difference in degree into a difference in kind.

5. Post Hoc Reasoning and Non Sequitur

If one of two associated events happened before the other, it may be wrongly argued that the first caused the second: *post hoc ergo propter hoc*, "after this, therefore because of this." Thus Philip Wylie writes of the effect of giving the vote to women: "Mom's first gracious presence at the ballot-box was roughly concomitant with the start toward a new all-time low in political scurviness, hoodlumism, gangsterism, labor strife, monopolistic thuggery, moral degeneration, civic corruption, smuggling, bribery, theft, murder, homosexuality, drunkenness, financial depression, chaos, and war." The implied assumption is that votes for women caused all the trouble. Wylie's facetious intent is plain, but this same fallacy is frequently found in more serious arguments. In "An American Myth," for example, the appearance of riots in India and "Yankee Go Home" signs in Egypt after these countries received American aid shipments does not prove that the aid *caused* the riots and the signs. Maybe it did, but the case is yet to be proved; our author provides no evidence whatever.

Post hoc is closely related to a more general fallacy known as *non sequitur*, "it does not follow." It is a good idea to be careful in using words like *because, since, thus*, and *therefore*. "I bought Lucy a Christmas present because I like her better than Eileen" is a *non sequitur* unless it has been established that you were in a position to buy only one present.

In the following dialogue from the film script of Jean Renoir's *Grand Illusion* there is a veritable escalation of *non sequiturs*:

THE LOCKSMITH: A good-looking blonde . . . big blue eyes. . . . An angel! Well, three days later I had to go and see the doctor. Don't trust a blonde!

ROSENTHAL: The same thing happened to me with a brunette.

MARÉCHAL: You can't trust anyone!

Based on an utterly illogical connection between hair color and venereal disease, the argument leaps from two unfortunate experiences to the supremely illogical conclusion that no one can be trusted. "Thinking" of this sort is all too common. The author of "An American Myth" is guilty of just such thinking when he claims that cutting off American aid would be a boon to its present recipients. How can he predict so simple and universal an outcome from so complex a set of conditions?

6. False Disjunction

To be caught on the horns of a dilemma is to be forced to choose between two equally undesirable alternatives. A dilemma is an either-or situation. If we take the highway, we will encounter traffic; if we take the bypass, we will be on a rough road. If we vote Republican, we will get a reactionary; if we vote Democratic, we will get a leftist. We must choose—or so at least we are told. But are these the only alternatives, and are they accurately and honestly defined? Often they are not. In "An American Myth," for example, we are told that everyone on relief is either a deadbeat or a hophead. A moment's thought will demolish this assertion. Elsewhere we have a subtler disjunction: between leaving the poor alone and trying to give every poor family television sets, two cars, and a house in the suburbs. If this is the choice we must make, there is much to be said for the author's recommendation that we leave the poor alone. But are these really the only alternatives? Surely the most starry-eyed dreamer favors more modest and realistic benefits for the roadless and suburbless peasant farmers of India.

The worst disjunction of all in this essay is the persistent separation of the poor ("they" or "these people") from the writer and his audience ("we" or "the rest of us"). This kind of simplification is one of the ways of prejudice. If one can somehow regard another person as a thing or a statistic, one is relieved of the necessity of understanding him, sympathizing with him, treating him with respect. According to the United States government, a family of four with an income of under $3,980 a year is poor. According to our writer, such a family is not only poor but radically different, which is tantamount to claiming that the $2 difference between $3,979 and $3,981 is some sort of unbridgeable chasm. F. Scott Fitzgerald was experimenting with the same distinction in reverse when he remarked to Ernest Hemingway, "The very rich are different from you and me." We like Hemingway's answer: "Yes," he replied. "They have more money."

7. Argument to Authority

Writers who have no evidence for their views often resort to citing some authority whose pronouncements they assume the reader will accept as sufficient. How do you know there is no serious smog problem in the city? Mayor Schultz says so. How do you know that the Chinese Communists are evil? General Baker says so, and he has spent thirty years in the Far East. This is all very well if the so-called authority does in fact know what he is talking about, but he may not. Especially in matters as complex and controversial as the smog problem and the future behavior of China, a discriminating reader is likely to want something more convincing than the opinion of Mayor Schultz or General Baker.

The all-time champion in the list of authorities cited, ranking just above Aristotle and J. Edgar Hoover, is the Bible. If the Bible says something, it must be true, or so millions of Christians have believed. Thus, in "An American Myth," we find Jesus cited to support the argument that it is pointless to talk about eliminating poverty. A deeply religious person might be swayed by this argument; but most people today would find the use of Jesus's name here a way of removing the discussion of poverty from the rational to the emotional level.

8. False Analogy

The writer of "An American Myth" is particularly addicted to the fallacy of false analogy. Consider, for example, his claim that some of the loveliest flowers grow on manure heaps. This is intended to suggest not only that some of the loveliest people come from slums, which may be true, but (as is clear from the context) that these people are lovely *because* they live in slums, which is doubtful. The intended analogy may be stated as follows: Slums are to the growth of lovely people as manure is to the growth of lovely flowers. As we have seen, the force of this metaphor depends heavily on equivocation in the use of the word *manure*.

The analogy between poor people on welfare and zoo animals is equally false. Basically it asserts that poor people and zoo animals are the same in one particular: if they are given the necessities of life and not forced to work for them, they will grow lazy and decadent. But zoo animals have no choice; they cannot hunt their food, they must eat what they are brought or starve. And as for people, some of the most energetic people in history, from Plato to John F. Kennedy, have not been deterred from achievement by having the necessities of life assured them from birth. The writer might reply that the very poor are different from John F. Kennedy, but that, as we have seen, remains to be proved. It would seem more likely on the face of it that they are different from zoo animals.

A discussion of false analogy in another context will be found in Chapter 7, pp. 118–119.

9. Undocumented Assertion

"An American Myth" is full of undocumented assertions. We must again and again ask this writer questions. How do you *know* what you say you know? How do you *know* that the poor in Egypt and those other countries don't feel pain the same way you do? How do you *know* what our policy makers think about slums? These generalizations appear here sometimes as premises and sometimes as conclusions, but in either case they are for the most part inadmissible. This writer has not learned much about evidence or its use. Slums are no worse than any other place once you get used to them, he says. How close has he been to one? We gather that he has frequented embassies, not slums. If he knows nothing about them from this kind of experience, then what other kind of experience is he drawing on: interviews, polls, books, other authorities? He does not tell us.

Bacon once wrote, "If we begin with certainties, we shall end in doubts; but if we begin with doubts, and we are patient with them, we shall end in certainties." A serious inquirer may take either path and find truth at the end, but not our writer. Beginning with certainties, and heedless of the most obvious objections, he proves (to himself) what he wants to prove and ends where he began. Whatever appeal this method may have, there is no truth in it, and less learning. Truth is a matter of keeping your mind open and adjusting what you think to accord with what you learn, a matter of weighing all the evidence you can find before deciding where you stand. The more evidence you invoke, no matter which way it points, the better your judgment is likely to be.

There is another undocumented assertion that runs through "An American Myth": the assertion of the writer's superiority. This is implicit rather than explicit and thus not strictly a logical fallacy in the sense of this chapter, but it is more damaging to his credibility than many of the other fallacies discussed in these pages. Indeed, it invites attention to them, since people are quick to look for flaws in snobs.

10. Argument ad Hominem and ad Populum

An argument that directs its appeal to the emotions rather than to the mind—to the pride, prejudice, cupidity, or private interests of the audience rather than to its reason—is called an argument *ad hominem* (to the man) or *ad populum* (to the people). One of the great *ad populum* arguments in our literature is Antony's funeral oration in *Julius Caesar*; such twentieth-century demagogues as Lenin, Hitler, and Senator Joseph McCarthy have done almost as well. The *ad hominem* argument is a staple of the television commercial: you, being a man of taste and discrimination, will of course want to smoke *our* brand of cigar or use *our* soap. Indeed, it is a soft-soap argument, the appeal of flattery to our soft spots or blind spots. In "An American Myth" the reader is repeatedly invited to see himself as part of an elite "we" who send wheat to India, who subsidize the poor, who pay the country's taxes. The writer instinctively feels, and he is right, that to the extent his readers identify with this "we" they will accept the separation between "we" and "they" on which his argument depends.

One flaw in "An American Myth" that has not been explicitly singled out for comment is the suppression of contrary evidence. This is not so much a logical fallacy as a moral failing, and perhaps not so much a moral failing as a strategic error. In writing exposition, there is no purpose in being dishonest; the whole point of writing an essay is to determine what is relevant to your subject and to let all relevant evidence have its impact. The writer of "An American Myth" did not so much knowingly suppress facts as choose to ignore facts that would not support his case. The resulting argument was (and usually is) less effective than it would have been if the writer had introduced and discussed the evidence he ignored.

The ten fallacies enumerated in this chapter, and the dozen-odd others discussed in books on logic, have a peculiar characteristic: they tend to merge into each other. Thus the manure-heap image is an instance not only of false analogy and equivocation, but of name-calling, false disjunction, and undocumented assertion. The appeal to Jesus is not only an argument to authority but an *ad populum* argument, not to mention an instance of "poisoning the wells," a logical fallacy in which the other party, though not demonstrably dishonorable, is deprived of all opportunity to reply with honor, as in the celebrated question "Have you stopped beating your wife?" It is also a fair case of suppressed evidence, since Jesus had a few remarks on the other side of the question as well, notably "Go and sell that thou hast, and give to the poor."

Most of the other examples discussed above could also be classified under two or more of the fallacy headings. What does this mean? It means, as we might expect, that illogicality is more a general state of mind than a series of particular fallacies with neat little names. Far from being the monster of unreason that our bill of particulars makes him out, the author of "An American Myth" is just a slightly more than ordinarily sloppy thinker, a slightly more than ordinarily hasty writer, and a slightly more than ordinarily passionate partisan. The way to avoid logical fallacies is to stop and think. Are you telling the reader no more than you can prove? Are you telling him everything he has to know if he is to judge matters for himself? Have you used words unequivocally and defined your terms? Are your premises clearly related to each other and to your conclusion? In a word, have you been honest and thorough? If you have, you have probably also been logical.

3

TONE

Tone is the quality that conveys a writer's attitude, and perhaps something of his intentions. "When you say that, smile!" said Owen Wister's cowboy to the stranger; unless the words came with the right tone, they were fighting words. Our culture hangs together partly because we know its idiom, know what tone to adopt in given situations. It also hangs together because at least some of us have an ear for tones that lie below the surface: the malarkey in the politician's promises, the hostility in the peace lover's sermon, the lie in the advertiser's "truth."

What is true of speaking is equally true of writing. In every written statement there is an implied voice, a tonal quality that reveals the writer's attitude toward his subject matter and toward his audience. Is he objective, angry, contemptuous, indifferent, amused, cynical, ironic, sentimental? The list of possible tones is almost endless. Indeed, a one-word description can rarely do justice to the tone of a piece of writing, for the tone can be as subtle and complex as the personality of the writer.

Here is a scientist writing for students of science: "Proteins are long-chain molecules built up of hundreds of molecular subunits:

the 20 amino acids." The tone is calm, unimpassioned, neutral; the writer's purpose is not to urge or persuade, but simply to put known quantities together into an objective description, and that purpose governs his attitude both toward his subject and toward his audience. If the same scientist were addressing a lay audience, his tone might be quite different. Here is the biologist Loren Eiseley writing for a popular audience on "How Flowers Changed the World":

> Before the coming of the flowering plants our own ancestral stock, the warm-blooded mammals, consisted of a few mousy little creatures hidden in trees and underbrush. A few lizard-like birds with carnivorous teeth flapped awkwardly on ill-aimed flights among archaic shrubbery. None of these insignificant creatures gave evidence of any remarkable talents. The mammals in particular had been around for some millions of years, but had remained well lost in the shadow of the mighty reptiles. Truth to tell, man was still, like the genie in the bottle, encased in the body of a creature about the size of a rat.

What makes the difference in tone? The fact that Eiseley, though objective in the sense that he never departs from what biologists accept as true, has another motive as well: the desire to be vivid and entertaining. Adjectives with immediate visual appeal like *mousy* and *lizard-like*, familiar turns of speech like *some millions of years*, familiar analogies like the genie in the bottle, all indicate that this author is writing to stimulate the interest and imagination of readers who know little about his subject. If he had addressed a professional audience in such terms, he would have seemed patronizing if not ridiculous.

KINDS OF TONE

It is impossible, as we have indicated, to list all the possible tones of voice a writer might use. They are as various as human temperaments and moods. But some tones are frequent enough in student writing, and give enough trouble, to be worth a few words.

Invective

Invective is name-calling, the expression of undisguised anger or passion in writing.   Here is a letter to a college newspaper, lamenting the treatment a speaker received at the hands of a crowd:

> In any community—even an academic community, I sup-
> pose—there will always be those fearful, ignorant, sadistic
> people who feel their smelly little existence to be somehow
> threatened by ideas different from their own.   Usually,
> though, the university tradition of free inquiry manages to
> keep their neurotic tendencies toward anti-intellectual,
> sheep-like orthodoxy and violence in check, at least until
> they get out of college.
>
> But now I watched a mob of these mental pygmies whose
> sick and unpatriotic intolerance had found a seemingly
> "legitimate" outlet in two-bit patriotism.   They threw various
> objects at ——— and then ducked behind each other (that's
> the old American way for you!).

Writers of invective in no way disguise their righteous indignation; they are not calm analysts but passionate partisans indulg-
ing (with apparent relish) their moral outrage.   This kind of
writing is rarely effective.   An angry writer usually has one of
two effects on his readers.   If they agree with him, his lack of
restraint embarrasses them: all right, they think, but why carry
on so?   If they do not agree, his lack of restraint confirms them
in their disagreement: loudmouths, after all, are never right.   A
soft answer turneth away wrath; a loud answer incurreth contempt.   Be wary of invective.   Even if people happen to be
"mental pygmies," they will not thank you for telling them so.

Invective for comic or satiric effect is another matter; witness
its appeal to gifted writers of all eras, from Rabelais to Shaw.
The Irish are among its most gifted practitioners, as in this genial
harangue by the artist Gulley Jimson in Joyce Cary's novel *The
Horse's Mouth*:

> "And what is a government individually, a hatful of prophets
> and murderers dreaming of bloody glories and trembling at

the grin of the grave. I forgive it, the belly-ripping abor-
tionist, the batter-brained, cak-handed, wall-eyed welsher,
the club-foot trampler, the block-eared raper that would sell
its sister for a cheer, the brick-faced hypocrite that would
wipe art and artists off the face of the earth as it would skin
an orange, and cut the balls off the genius of the Lord to
make a tame gee-gee for the morning Park. I forgive it,"
I said, as we got on to the bus. "I forgive government, with
all its works, because it can't rise out of its damnation, which
is to be a figment."

"That's rather strong," said a gentleman in shammy-gloves,
opposite.

And so it is, partly because Cary, like all good writers of
comic invective, has managed to avoid both the Scylla of boorish-
ness and the Charybdis of empty buffoonery. If you try the
form, remember that its essence is exaggeration, not pure inven-
tion; keep it funny, but keep it within shouting distance of the
truth.

Exhortation

Exhortation is close to invective. It is the voice of the preacher
or moralist, hammering home his values and opinions. Its intention
is to persuade, admonish, or incite. The exhorter wants you to do
or believe something, and he is forthright in telling you what. Here
is Philip Wylie on the subject of war:

There is no other way to look at war than as the final proof
of the infantilism of man—the revelation of his inherent lack
of civilization, his serfdom to his instincts, and, therefore, his
failure to achieve adulthood. War proves how wholly dependent we are upon the instinctual plane for our motives
and what a thin tissue our repressive brain—our reason—has
stretched between us and other animals.

Although a step beyond mere invective, this passionately opin-
ionated statement contains as much heat as it does light. Note
the unqualified assertions ("there is *no other way* to look at war,"
"war *proves*") and the denunciatory tone ("infantilism," "serfdom
to his instincts"). This writer is not sitting down to reason with

you; he is letting you know what's what.   As the reader, you are placed in the irritating position of being talked at: Wylie is doing all the speaking and you all the listening.   A writer's tone says a great deal about what he thinks of his readers—whether he considers them intellectuals or boobs, reasonable men or fanatics, friends or enemies.   Be careful not to insult your readers unless that is your intention.

Exhortation need not be so strident.   In "The Moral Equivalent of War," William James took an antiwar position in many ways similar to Wylie's, but listen to the difference in tone:

> It is plain that on this subject civilized man has developed a sort of double personality.   If we take European nations, no legitimate interest of any one of them would seem to justify the tremendous destructions which a war to compass it would necessarily entail.   It would seem as though common sense and reason ought to find a way to reach agreement in every conflict of honest interests.   I myself think it our bounden duty to believe in such international rationality as possible.

We are here a long way from invective; James keeps his temper, does not raise his voice.   He is practicing some of the reasonableness he preaches, and in doing so he is tacitly saying to the reader, "You are the kind of person who can be reached by reason."   Note the qualifications ("it would seem," "reason ought to");   our assent is invited, not commanded or presumed.   Such language tells us that we are being regarded as ladies and gentlemen, not as people who have to be browbeaten or yelled at. Is James's approach as effective as Wylie's?   Probably more so. When James's article appeared in 1910, some thirty thousand copies of it were distributed, and it has been often reprinted since.   It is still one of the most honored arguments against war in our literature.

Narrative

Narrative does not overtly argue or editorialize, but simply presents a set of events or conditions.   Consider the following paragraphs from Edward Loomis's story "Wounds":

A rifle bullet striking bone hits with a fine hardness, followed instantly by a numbing shock; and then down you go.

When it happened to me, I felt my left leg for blood, thinking to gauge the wound, but could not do it, for the blood was running imperceptibly in my heavy trousers already soaked with the rain. I moved the knee, where the bullet had hit, and said to the man ahead of me: "I think maybe I'm hit, by God! Now what do you think of that?"

There is no editorializing here, save in the selection and arrangement of details. If any argument against war is implied, that argument must be put into words by the reader. In effect, the writer of narrative creates a kind of vacuum for the reader's emotions to fill. "How awful!" the reader might exclaim, precisely because the author has not so exclaimed, has not taken the words out of the reader's mouth. The tactic of dispassionately presenting material that speaks for itself is one of the most powerful at the writer's command.

Satire

Satire is a form of ridicule aimed at correcting some folly or abuse. Here, for example, is part of a satirical book review by Thomas Reed Powell. After lamenting that most books on the Constitution of the United States "are very hard to read" and make you "think very hard all the time," Powell goes on to say:

The new book which Mr. Beck has written about the Constitution is a very different kind of book. You can read it without thinking. If you have got tired trying to read the other kind of books, you will be glad of the nice restful book that Mr. Beck has written. It runs along like a story in a very interesting way. Most of the story is about how the Constitution got made. This is really history, but it is written in a very lively way like a novel, with a great many characters, almost all male, and plenty of conversation and a very exciting plot. . . . Besides the story there are many quotations from Shakespeare, Beethoven, Horace, Isaiah,

Euripides, Beard, and other famous men. Many of these quotations are quite old, but some of them seem fairly new.

The book is made ridiculous. Why? Because by pretending to be a fool who admires it, Powell persuades us that no one but a fool *could* admire it, and hence that it must be a foolish book. As his satirical device, Powell has adopted the tone and tastes of a twelve-year-old. Note the incidence of the schoolboy word *very,* the jumbled chronology that puts Isaiah after Shakespeare and the historian Beard cheek by jowl with Euripides, the writer's simpleminded taste in novels (which he reads because they are lively, have exciting plots, and are above all easy), and the devastatingly feeble "seem fairly new." The writer is clearly immature, half-educated, and uninteresting; a book he likes must be awful.

Satire, more than most other tones, requires a sensitivity to the tone of others. Indeed, in parody, which is what Powell is writing, the satirist actually takes the tone of the person or piece of writing that he is satirizing—pompous, childish, inarticulate, or whatever. Although satire can be biting, it is just as often gentle: fun to write and fun to read. Unlike invective, satire usually invites the reader in and asks him to join the fun.

Irony

The dictionary defines irony as "a sort of humor, ridicule, or light sarcasm, the intended implication of which is the opposite of the literal sense of the word." This is an imperfect definition. Irony is by no means always funny, nor is it the same as sarcasm; sarcasm comes from a Greek word meaning "to tear flesh," a kind of direct assault, as when one says, "You think you're pretty damned smart, don't you?" One thing is said and another meant, but there is no real deception. Irony, by contrast, is oblique, subtle, and indirect in its working; the deception is not just a gimmick but an essential part of the writer's message.

It is the last part of the dictionary definition that gets to the heart of the matter. Irony always sets up a tension between opposites: between the ideal and the real, the seen and the unseen, the literal and the implied, the achieved and the intended. This duality must always exist. An elementary form of it was displayed some years ago by a San Francisco entrepreneur who marketed 29-cent cans of "fresh air" to be sent as gifts to people in Los Angeles. The directions on the can went something like this: "Punch a small hole in the top and inhale slowly. Do not gulp the air; breathing air can be habit-forming. Increase your intake by degrees. Ten cans a day can be safely consumed. If excessive euphoria is experienced, see your doctor." Where is the irony? In the contrast between the giver's ostensible motivation, benevolence, and his actual motivation, self-congratulation; and in the receiver's awareness of that contrast.

This is a low form of the genre, hardly more than a practical joke. At the other extreme is Jonathan Swift's famous "Modest Proposal," which sets forth in sober, businesslike language a proposal that the children of Ireland be slaughtered and used as a source of food for that starving land. The irony here comes from Swift's implied message: that even the most outrageous brutalities must now seem commonplace alongside the horrors wrought by England's exploitation of Ireland. He is ostensibly saying to the English "As a conscientious student of English administrative practice, I have come up with a plan that I think you will admire." He is in effect saying "You are monsters." The tension between the literal proposal and its implied meaning generates a terrific heat.

In desperate situations, irony sometimes seems the only possible mode of redress. Most Negro jazz has irony at its base; thus, for example, Louis Armstrong's classic "What Did I Do to Be So Black and Blue?" plays profound changes on the cliché "black and blue." Lenny Bruce's quip "Toilet, you're lucky you're white!" evokes the Negro problem in five words. In the following exchange reported in the *New York Times* between a South African judge and a political prisoner up for retrial, the prisoner is aware that any expression of dissatisfaction with his lot will be taken as evidence of criminal revolutionary sentiment:

"You have no objection to being ordered around by whites?"
"I have become satisfied to such an extent that my health keeps improving."
"Are you satisfied with your wages?"
"I have never complained—not on a single day."

"Do you want better wages?"
"No, your worship."
"Are you satisfied with your house?"
"It's a very beautiful house."
"Are you satisfied with the pass laws?"
"Yes, entirely."

Who could be taken in by this irony? If the judge was, he was a fool. If he wasn't, he was powerless to act, since the prisoner's words were scrupulously inoffensive. The judge was caught in that ironic situation known as the double-bind; there was no way he could win.

Similar circumstances evoked a celebrated piece of irony from Sigmund Freud. In May 1938, after intense harassment by the notorious Nazi secret police unit known as the Gestapo, the 82-year-old Freud was at last granted an exit visa from Vienna on the condition that he sign a document attesting that his treatment by the Germans had been irreproachable. He asked permission to add a few words below his signature, and this being granted, he wrote: "I can heartily recommend the Gestapo to anyone."

Irony can take many forms. There is dramatic irony (where a theater audience or a reader knows something a character does not know), there is Socratic irony (the pose of ignorance that Socrates assumed to bait his opponents), and there is verbal irony —some forms of which we have illustrated. Irony is one of the sharpest instruments of criticism available; thanks to its unique balance between intelligence and feeling, it can probe into the deepest aspects of existence. The ironic tone is not easy to master, but it is worth the effort.

ERRORS IN TONE

Tone is what establishes the rapport between writer and reader, the emotional premises of their relationship. But often a writer, without intending to adopt any particular tone, alienates his reader through sheer inadvertence, clumsiness, or insensitivity. The writer of "An American Myth," the essay discussed in Chapter 2, has made just such an error in tone; he sounds like a snob, and his readers react accordingly. In our remarks on invective and exhortation we pointed out some other pitfalls to be avoided; in the following pages we discuss still others.

Sentimentality

If irony is difficult for the beginning writer to master, sentimentality is difficult for him to avoid. By sentimentality we mean not just maudlin or gushy writing, but the whole range of counterfeit emotions. Here is a football player describing a visit to a hospital for crippled children:

> When I held Gracie in my arms, I knew then the meaning of the phrase "Strong legs run that weak legs may walk." She was about seven years old, and when I picked her up and held her close to me I could hear her heart beat, and when she smiled she brought tears to my eyes in spite of myself. I somehow knew, as I held her, that this was the happiest moment of her life. And seeing her suffering, I was filled with rage at all those ungrateful bums in Harlem and Berkeley who were out rioting and raising hell because they didn't think they were getting enough for nothing out of this life.

In a class discussion of this paragraph, one student put her finger on something puzzling: "I don't see how the writer could be so full of love in the first part of the paragraph and so full of hate in the last." When asked if the hate in any way discredited the love, made it seem fake or insincere, the class was almost unanimous in saying yes. What the class detected was the presence of sentimentality.

Sentimentality is often defined as "emotion in excess of the fact," the fact being a human situation—the death of a loved one, the election of a president, the birth of a baby—that legitimately evokes emotion. The sentimentalist squeezes more emotion out of such an occasion than discriminating people regard as proper or decent. He enjoys the emotion for its own sake, as a kind of narcotic, and he does not shrink from the stalest clichés when the fit is upon him. He invokes the patter of tiny feet, the love of a good woman, silver threads among the gold—all those prefabricated phrases that evoke stock emotional responses. During a recent political campaign a commentator reported a candidate's speech in these terms:

> He got his first rafter-ringing response by coming out four-square for the Declaration of Independence and the Constitution. He rated another salvo for saying he would not bend before the breeze or run with the tide. . . . And [he] talked tough about sending out the Marines to win back our respect. "History shows us what happens to appeasers," he said as the militant ladies in the audience beat their white gloves together.

That candidate knows the tricks of the sentimentalists. He is talking from the emotions to the emotions with no mediation from the mind. Sentimental clichés defeat the possibility of thought. What specific policies does our candidate believe in? He does not tell us, and those ladies with the white gloves, being sentimentalists themselves, do not ask him.

Sentimentality is a way of not facing reality; it prettifies things rather than seeing them as they are. The sentimentalist believes not in love, but in "true love," an ideal absolute that exists only as a fantasy and has nothing to do with real relations between real people. What he hates above all else is the complexity, ambiguity, and mess of actual life. "All idealization makes life poorer," wrote the novelist Joseph Conrad. "To beautify it is to take away its character of complexity—it is to destroy it." This insight is beyond the sentimentalist's comprehension. He will say, with Edgar Guest, that "It takes a heap o' livin' to make a house a home," but he will not include in that "livin' " the dirty diapers, the family quarrels, or Grandpa's addiction to bourbon. He does not care about "livin' " in any real sense; he lives in a world of wish fulfillment and sees what he wants to see.

Holden Caulfield, in *The Catcher in the Rye*, describes the classic type as he observes a woman sitting next to him in the movies. Although the film is (to use one of Holden's favorite words) hopelessly "phoney," the woman is crying her eyes out; and the phonier the film gets, the more she cries. This action would seem to indicate a kindhearted woman, whatever one might think about her taste. But Holden wasn't fooled; for sitting next to her was a small boy who, throughout the show, was bored and had to go to the bathroom. She wouldn't take him, but told him to shut up and behave himself. Holden comments: "She was about as kindhearted as a goddam wolf. You take somebody that cries their goddam eyes out over phoney stuff in the movies, and nine times out of ten they're mean bastards at heart. I'm not kidding."

Holden is perfectly right; moved by the secondhand suffering on the screen but indifferent to her boy's real distress, this woman is a mean bastard without even knowing it. So is Françoise, the cook of Proust's *Swann's Way*, who weeps over the childbirth symptoms she reads about in a medical book while ignoring a fellow servant in the agony of labor. Proust supplies a telling comment: "The sufferings of humanity inspired in her a pity which increased in direct ratio to the distance separating the sufferers from herself." Scratch a sentimentalist and you will usually find a person capable of cruelty, or at least an unlovely indifference to the distress of others.

This brings us to the illustration we began with. It was probably not just chance that brought hate and love into such uneasy juxtaposition in that football player's theme, but something more fundamental in his life, some deep-lying feeling of resentment or insecurity. His words described what he wished he felt or thought he ought to feel, not what he did feel. Sentimentality is a pretense, a masquerade, a protective device; it pretends to be full, but it is empty. As John Galsworthy said, "Sentimentalism is the working off on yourself of feelings you haven't really got."

Pomposity

The following passage is from an address given by a dean at an American university. He is welcoming the freshman class:

> I would like to welcome you to X——— University and to express the hope that your educational work will be most productive and rewarding. I am sure you will find that members of the University community are most willing to

help you receive the maximum benefit from the curriculum
and to have an enjoyable and satisfying learning experience
at X———. . . .

This program, which is designed to facilitate learning, involves the imparting of knowledge through research. To
maximize learning, the University has made provision for
small classes, close student-faculty contacts, high-quality instruction, and personalized education.

What is wrong with this passage? Simply that when we hear
language like this we don't believe a word of it, and we don't
believe the speaker believes a word of it either. The dean is
welcoming the freshmen, but he doesn't say so: he says he "would
like to welcome" them. He presumably hopes they will get a
lot out of their work, but he doesn't say so: he says he "would
like . . . to express the hope." This formal double-talk, this
reluctance to be simple and straightforward, is the antithesis of
communication. What sort of welcome or helpfulness is there
in words like *program* and *personalized education* and *learning
experience*? This is language for computers, not people.

Anybody trying to be friendly or personal or even human in
language like this is fighting a losing game. It is a language in-
sisting that one *not* be personal; it is remote, it translates personal relations into abstractions. So when someone talks or
writes this way, we dismiss him as not only boring but insincere. A sincere writer would care more about making us understand him.

Young people are less given to pompous writing than older
people, except perhaps to the extent that they seek to gain their
seniors' esteem. Yet for one reason or another, many young
writers have a desperate fear of being themselves in their writing.
In conversation or in personal letters they may be relaxed, but
when they go before a wider audience they put on a mask. Here
is part of a report by an education student on an experiment in
which music was piped into the corridors of a high school:

The hypothesis, therefore, is that music can reduce the intensity dimension of the student so that he remains in the range
of the effectiveness along the continuum. By remaining

within the range of his greatest effectiveness he should be able to maximize his rewards and thus possess a positive attitude toward school.

Language like this cannot be read; it must be translated. What this seems to mean is: "Students seem calmer and happier when the music is on, and do better work." But one cannot be sure.

Highbrowism

Highbrowism is close to pomposity as an error in tone, but it is usually more deliberate. The pompous writer indulges in "fine writing" out of insecurity, which leads him to a false notion of his own dignity and the dignity of the written word. The highbrow writer has a different motivation: he wants to show off. He cannot resist letting his teacher and classmates know that he is up on the latest fad or theory. His theme may begin as follows:

> "The Love Song of J. Alfred Prufrock" is a vision of the relativism of our time. "I should have been a pair of ragged claws" is but a distant paraphrase of Rilke's "Der Panther" and its "weiche Gang geschmeidig starker Schritte." To understand both works one profits immensely by an acquaintance with the Existentialist vision of Jean-Paul Sartre in "The Root of the Chestnut Tree" and Camus in "The Myth of Sisyphus."

What is wrong with this passage is not that Rilke, Camus, and Sartre are irrelevant, but that they are dragged in by the ears, introduced for self-advertising reasons rather than for what they contribute to the discussion.

The writer who cares about his readers will either suppress allusions of this sort or take care to explain them fully; he will be interested less in impressing than in instructing. To revert to our image of distance, the good writer does not widen, but narrows, the distance between himself and his readers. The frequent use of unexplained allusions is a manifest error in tone.

Flippancy

Flippant writing is writing that takes a serious subject lightly. Flippancy is a fault comparable to whistling in church or making jokes about wooden legs to a cripple; it can be forgiven in the very young, but it is seldom appreciated. Here is a sample from a freshman theme:

> I thought themes on what I did last summer went out with model T's, but since they didn't, I'll dig right in, for there's no point in flunking out of this school before I've given it a whirl (or vice versa). I'll tell you what I did last summer: I worked in a canning factory. And I'll tell you what I did in that canning factory every chance I got (which wasn't often): I sat on my can.

Most teachers will react to themes like this with bored tolerance. Sometimes writing like this can be funny, but usually it fails of its own ingenuousness. Good writing takes time and effort. Flippant themes usually come from an unwillingness to accept the challenge of an assignment, and they are judged accordingly. This is a pity in the case of our young canner, who clearly has a way with words. A little more effort, a little more restraint, and he might have written something effective and genuinely amusing.

Some writers seem to think that whatever emerges from their gut is sacred and should be recorded without modification for posterity to ponder. Their teachers rarely agree, and hence a conflict arises—one only partly related, to be sure, to the question of tone. Here is the beginning of a theme on the assignment "Is it ever permissible to break a law?"

> I started to think. I thought, questions like that don't turn me on. I mean, how do you answer questions like that, when those questions don't really exist? I moved on to what was important. What was important was the music, and the music told me all about law that I needed to know. I just took the hand of that music and it led me right between the

cliffs of right and wrong. It led me out, man, and it didn't matter whether the law said it was right or wrong.

Flippancy aside, this kind of psychedelic free-associating is of no use to anyone. Writing should be intelligible to as many people as possible. This writing is in a private lingo; it may mean something to the writer's friends, but it says nothing to anyone else. Is the writer trying to say something meaningful about the limits of the law? Then let him say it in words we can understand, and in a tone that invites our attention.

Tone is an expression of the relationship that exists between writer and reader, of the assumptions they share. The tone we use in discourse is a reminder of the kind of people we are, at least at the moment of speaking. If a conversation begins with "Listen, you son of a bitch," it is one sort of conversation; if it begins with "Is there anything I can do to help?" it is another sort. The same thing happens in writing. No matter how sure we are of our opinions, it is elementary courtesy and good sense to acknowledge the reader's existence, the possibility of his disagreement, the potential value of his criticism. No matter how indifferent we may be to our readers, it is elementary courtesy to put them at their ease. Unless we are bent on mayhem, it is elementary good sense to establish a basis for mutual respect.

PART 2
TECHNIQUE

4

PARAGRAPHS

Before you start to write, you must know your subject and your audience, you must have your material ready, and you must make your basic strategic decisions. But all this is not enough: you must also develop a talent for writing itself, an ability to reach and hold your readers. That is where technique comes in. Technique may be defined as a mastery of the psychology and the mechanics of good writing; it is what clears the static off the line from writer to reader. Always there is the reader to think of—the elusive reader with his unknown capacities and incapacities, his sophistication and his ignorance, his prejudices and his susceptibility to distraction. The pitfalls are many. Make what you write too long, and he will be bored; make it too short, and he will be confused by your omissions; add a comma, choose a word carelessly, and he may misunderstand you; get a fact wrong, misspell a word, and he may write you off as an ignoramus.

There is still another pitfall: make him work too hard, and he will give you up for the boob tube. The educated American today is accustomed to skillful writing—in newspaper stories and magazine articles, in national advertising, and even on network television, where scarcely a sentence is uttered that has not first been written down and revised to exacting standards by a professional writer. To be sure, much of this writing is shallow and unmemorable, devoted to conveying routine news or selling detergents; but for better or for worse it has taught the educated American reader to expect economy, clarity, and directness in what he reads. To get a hearing from readers so conditioned, you must not only say what you mean, but say it well.

The next five chapters are concerned with the technique of writing effectively. In Chapters 4–7 we progress from larger units of thought to smaller ones: paragraphs first, followed by sentences, then words, and finally an important special use of words, namely imagery. Chapter 8, "Mere Writing and Good Prose," shows how the lessons of Chapters 4–7 are applied in practice.

ASPECTS OF THE PARAGRAPH

Paragraphs are not just hunks of prose marked by indentations; they are the basic units of thought out of which an essay is composed. They are building stones, parts of a larger whole. Though we shall necessarily in this chapter discuss paragraphs without reference to their context, they are in fact inseparable from that context. To put this another way, the problem is not so much to write an effective paragraph, let alone a dazzling paragraph, as to write your paragraphs in such a way as to make an effective— and integrated—essay.

The Thesis and the Thesis Sentence

Being a single unit of thought, a paragraph often contains a topic sentence or thesis sentence in which the thought in question is stated in capsule form. Not every paragraph contains a thesis sentence as such, but every good paragraph contains a thesis. In this paragraph from the magazine *Ramparts*, the thesis (of both the paragraph and the essay) is stated with unusual explicitness in the first sentence:

It is the thesis of this essay that the reasonable man has become the enemy of this society at this time. His reason has been soured by compromise and his moral conscience traded for a conscience of conciliation. The capacity to ask fundamental questions appears to have been lost. The criticism of the war, in the mass media and in Congress, has been generally marginal and directed to practical, tactical techniques. The worst thing that reasonable men seem capable of saying about our attempt to control another people's destiny is that it is not working out very well; if we were winning, it would no doubt be considered a good war.

Here, by contrast, is a paragraph from Thoreau's *Walden* in which the thesis is not explicit but implicit:

Why should we be in such desperate haste to succeed and in such desperate enterprises? If a man does not keep pace with his companions, perhaps it is because he hears a different drummer. Let him step to the music which he hears, however measured or far away. It is not important that he should mature as soon as an apple-tree or an oak. Shall he turn his spring into summer? If the condition of things which we were made for is not yet, what were any reality which we can substitute? We will not be shipwrecked on a vain reality. Shall we with pains erect a heaven of blue glass over ourselves, though when it is done we shall be sure to gaze still at the true ethereal heaven far above, as if the former were not?

Thoreau's rhetorical questions, metaphors, and poetic style require more of the reader than the *Ramparts* passage; we are asked not just to follow a line of argument, but to participate imaginatively in the writer's meaning. Yet the single idea, the thesis, is there as surely in this paragraph as in the other. Can we phrase a thesis sentence? How about "A man should be allowed to mature at his own rate and in his own way"? It misses the charm and persuasiveness of Thoreau's words, but it gives us his kernel of meaning.

Unity and Coherence

Every good paragraph has two qualities: unity and coherence. It has unity in the sense that it is about a single subject, and coherence in the sense that its sentences fit together to make a connected whole. A simple way to test for these qualities is to write in one sentence the thesis of an essay and then do the same for each of its successive paragraphs. Your series of thesis sentences should give you in brief form the basic argument of the essay. If it does not, the essay probably suffers from logical gaps, irrelevancies, or padding. Further scrutiny of the thesis sentences should tell you where the trouble is and what kind of change would make things better.

Length

The following paragraph is from a review of pornographic films by David Denby:

> Going to these theatres produces a heavy depression hard to shrug off: the shabbiness of the material settles on the audience like ash, and prurient fascination struggles against distaste at oneself for not being out in pursuit of the real thing. At ordinary bad movies one can talk back to the screen, create an instant community of wise guys and complainers, and have a good time that way; at dirty movies a muttered complaint would destroy the concentration of a hundred men lost in the pornographic trance, a unique state of being which requires silence, isolation, and passivity. And even if one gives oneself over to the trance, the movies often fail to justify their only excuse for existence: keeping the viewer aroused. In Steven Marcus' excellent study of Victorian pornography, *The Other Victorians*, the author remarks, "Language is for pornography a bothersome necessity; its function is to set going a series of non-verbal images, of fantasies—and if it could dispense with words it would. Which is why, one supposes, the motion-picture film is what the genre was all along waiting for." But actually, words are more effective: they outline a situation, and then release the imagination to fill it out with ideal shapes and acts. Pictures imprison one in the actual; the imperfections of human forms,

the clumsiness of the actors, the ugliness of the lighting and shooting—all eliminate the freedom of fantasy and depress desire.

Although this paragraph carries its length with considerable grace, it is a fairly big block of prose and some readers would find it hard going. Can things be made easier for them? Why not begin a new paragraph with the third sentence? The first two sentences are concerned with the audience's reaction to such films; all the rest have to do with whether words or pictures are more erotically stimulating. Since two shorter paragraphs as proposed would each be as unified and coherent as the original long one, nothing would be lost by the change.

How long should a paragraph be? The only general rule is that it should be long enough to convey one more or less complex thought, and not so long as to alienate or stupefy its readers. Very short paragraphs are no better than very long ones. A series of one- and two-sentence paragraphs (a favorite strategy in political speeches and witty newspaper columns) suggests that the author is presenting a series of one-liners designed to evoke bursts of applause or laughter rather than a message to be considered and understood as a whole. An occasional one-sentence paragraph may be useful as a transition to a new line of thought, or for dramatic effect; but short paragraphs as a class should be left to the politicians and journalists, who have their own reasons for using them.

One exception, of course, is in written dialogue: convention decrees that each successive speaker's remarks, however brief, are given a separate paragraph.[1]

Transitions

What ties the sentences of a paragraph together? Sometimes transitional words and phrases (*moreover, thus, on the other hand, in retrospect*, etc.), sometimes coordinating conjunctions (*and, but, for, or, nor*). Sometimes the repetition of a key word or idea: for example, *trance* in the middle of the Denby para-

---

[1] Another exception is a paragraph like this one, where one sentence exhausts the subject.

graph above, or the idea of depression in the first and last sentences. Sometimes a vivid image or analogy that connects things up: for example, Thoreau's *drummer* or Denby's *ash* simile. Sometimes the examples supporting a generalization or a generalization climaxing a series of examples. Sometimes nothing more than the rhythm of the writer's excitement, or of the reader's interest. Much is made of so-called transitional devices by some teachers, but few writers consciously use such devices as a way of constructing paragraphs. In our view, the idea comes first, the writing follows, and the transitions from sentence to sentence are generated strictly as by-products of the writer's effort to make the reader see exactly what he means.

Indeed, the best writers make sparing use of routine transitional words and phrases in linking their sentences together. Such words and phrases are not bad in themselves, but when used to excess they make a paragraph seem full of hinges, like a trick floor at a carnival; it hangs together but is hard to walk on. If you know what you want to say, your ideas will jump from sentence to sentence like electric sparks, or flow like an underground stream. If your thought makes a coherent unit, transitions will be no problem.

Transitions between paragraphs follow the same general rules as transitions within paragraphs. If the ideas of two successive paragraphs are properly related, the transition between them will be clear and obvious. If the transition causes difficulty, the two ideas are no doubt faultily related; perhaps an intervening paragraph, or some different tack altogether, is needed to make the argument work. Some beginning writers give up when this happens and hope the difficulty will not be noticed. Even if it is not, the confusion it causes will be: a reader may not know where he has left the road, but he knows when he is in a swamp. There is no substitute for getting your ideas in a clear sequence before you begin to write, whether with an outline (see p. 235) or simply by hard thinking. When transitions between ideas are logical, transitions between paragraphs are no problem.

Variety

Another way of tying a paragraph together is to use different kinds of sentences in composing it. One possibility, illustrated in the paragraph from Thoreau, is to mix interrogative and imperative sentences with declarative ones. Other devices are just as effective. Follow a short sentence with a long one. Vary the subject-predicate-object form; begin some sentences with an introductory phrase or a subordinate clause. Don't have all compound or all complex or all simple sentences; have some of each. These rules, like all rules, are made to be broken by masters—the final arbiter is the taste and judgment of the writer—but it is well to be aware that one can bore as much by the sameness of one's style as by the dullness of one's thoughts.

We had thought to add a word of warning against the paragraph consisting of one monster sentence. But consider this paragraph from Norman Mailer's *Presidential Papers*:

It is not that Los Angeles is altogether hideous, it is even by degrees pleasant, but for an Easterner there is never any salt in the wind; it is like Mexican cooking without chili, or Chinese egg rolls missing their mustard;[1] as one travels through the endless repetitions of that city which is the capital of suburbia with its milky pinks, its washed-out oranges, its tainted lime-yellows of pastel on one pretty little architectural monstrosity after another, the colors not intense enough, the styles never pure, and never sufficiently impure to collide on the eye, one conceives the people who live here—they have come out to express themselves,[2] Los Angeles is the home of self-expression, but the artists are middle-class and middling-minded; no passions will calcify here for years in the gloom to be revealed a decade later as the tessellations of a hard and fertile work,[3] no, it is all open, promiscuous, borrowed, half bought, a city without iron, eschewing wood, a kingdom of stucco, the playground for mass men—[4] one has the feeling it was built by television sets giving orders to men.

Here is variety enough, detail enough, rhythm enough, to keep all readers aboard till the end of the ride. But is this *one* sentence? Only in the most technical sense. If periods were put in at 1, 2, 3, and possibly 4, we probably would not notice much difference—perhaps only a slight slowing down in our reading speed. Which punctuation is better? It is a matter of taste. If you can write paragraphs this good, you can go ahead and punctuate them any way you like.

Emphasis

Emphasis in paragraphs, as in sentences, is achieved less by raising one's voice than by the skill with which one's thoughts are marshaled. An occasional one-line paragraph may be emphatic; three in a row, or even three in a given essay, will be seen as a tedious straining for effect. An occasional exclamatory sentence can shock or excite, but strident or self-congratulatory exclamations like "I went through hell that day!" or "It was a *tremendous* experience!" will irritate the most sympathetic reader. A little shrieking goes a long way, whether the emotion is pain or rapture.

On the whole, we think coherence is the key to emphasis. Nothing underscores like clarity; nothing hammers a point home like a compelling reasonableness. Once again we come back to the importance of a coherent overall argument. However lucid and adroitly constructed a paragraph may be, if it does not hang together with the whole essay, it will hang separately.

OPENING AND CLOSING PARAGRAPHS

Opening Paragraphs

The opening paragraph of a story or essay sets the tone of what follows and the level of the reader's expectations. If an essay is to attract and hold readers, its opening paragraph must be inviting; it should make people want to read on, to follow wherever the writer leads. Too many student essays begin with dull paragraphs like the one on pp. 138–139 below, which in promising nothing but further dull paragraphs will lose nine readers out of ten. By contrast, consider this opening paragraph of an essay by Kenneth Burke dealing with the writers Thomas Mann and André Gide:

> When Gustav von Aschenbach, the hero of Thomas Mann's *Death in Venice*, was about thirty-five years of age, he was

taken ill in Vienna. During the course of a conversation, one keen observer said of him, "You see, Aschenbach has always lived like this," and the speaker contracted the fingers of his left hand into a fist; "never like this," and he let his hand droop comfortably from the arm of a chair. It is with such opening and closing of the hand that this essay is to deal.

This is an excellent beginning. The image of that opening and closing fist piques our curiosity and makes us eager to see how it is applied to Mann and Gide. Burke has caught our attention; we want to read on. The paragraph has a further virtue: it is short. In writing as in speaking, when you are out to capture an audience it is a good idea not to be long-winded.

Sometimes a writer wants merely to suggest his topic in the opening paragraph, to tease us into attention rather than to declare his theme unambiguously. The opening sentence of an article by Paul Ehrlich makes use of a perennially effective device, the prophecy of future catastrophe expressed as historic fact: "The end of the ocean came late in the summer of 1979, and it came even more rapidly than the biologists had expected." Another classic come-on opener reserves its punch for its final sentence, as in this paragraph by Roy Bongartz:

They used to teach kids back in the Thirties that Americans were all alike—or at least were supposed to be all alike —and there was this monumental pretense that racial and religious differences did not actually matter. This false game of course made no breach in the walls the Wasps built around themselves, but it did damp down the minorities, who tried to dilute their identities—even dyed their hair or trimmed their noses—so as to look, or feel, a bit more like Doris Day or John Wayne. But that old sham has been blown to bits by Power of various colors, first Black, and then Brown (Mexican-American) and Red (Indian). Now here's another: the Superjew.

The one characteristic all these examples have in common is that they make us ask on our own the very question the writer proposes to answer. How are Gide and Mann like open and closed fists? What happened to the ocean in the 1970's—or what will happen if our indifference persists? What on earth is a Superjew? After a good first paragraph we can hardly wait to read the second.

Closing Paragraphs

An essay should be a package with a string around it, not a gathering of fragments. In your closing paragraph, do not simply summarize what you have already said. We have heard it once and do not want to hear it again; what we want to know now is what to make of it, what you think it adds up to. Your closing paragraph should reveal in some fresh light what the essay has been driving at all along, or perhaps open our eyes to something new. It should not clobber our minds with repetition.

A good example is the closing paragraph of the sample research paper presented on pp. 240–253. Another is this paragraph from a student essay on E. M. Forster's "What I Believe":

> The "aristocracy of the sensitive, the considerate, and the plucky" is, then, at the very heart of Forster's thinking. It is an attractive aristocracy in its way: cultured, non-violent, good company. But what a private and limited aristocracy it is, and how far from the struggle for life's necessities! None of its members would be comfortable in industry or politics, or even at a football game. No black leader from the ghetto—however sensitive, considerate, and plucky— would seek to become a member. It is an aristocracy of the leisured and the well-off, a limitation that excludes most of mankind.

The first sentence serves as a transition from what has gone before. The second switches the focus from description to evaluation, and the last four make the writer's point.

KINDS OF EXPOSITORY PARAGRAPHS

The two main kinds of prose writing are narrative and expository. Narrative paragraphs tell a story, or part of one; since we are not concerned with fiction as such in this book, no examples are given. Expository paragraphs describe or explain something, or contribute to an explanation or an argument. They take many forms, of which four are discussed in the following pages.

Description

In describing something, be it an action or a landscape or a person or a thought, a writer always does one basic thing: he chooses a set of particulars, of details, that to his mind add up to a satisfactory picture. A scientist will normally choose the particulars most likely to convey his scientific findings without distortion; his appeal is to the intellect. A creative artist, aiming perhaps to evoke an impression or mood—the beauty of the flower rather than the dimensions of its petals—will usually emphasize particulars that appeal to our senses, as in this paragraph from Vladimir Nabokov's *Lolita*:

> Oh, I had to keep a very sharp eye on Lo, little limp Lo! Owing perhaps to constant amorous exercise, she radiated, despite her very childish appearance, some special languorous glow which threw garage fellows, hotel pages, vacationists, goons in luxurious cars, maroon morons near blued pools, into fits of concupiscence which might have tickled my pride, had it not incensed my jealousy. For little Lo was aware of that glow of hers, and I would often catch her *coulant un regard* in the direction of some amiable male, some grease monkey, with a sinewy golden-brown forearm and watch-braceleted wrist, and hardly had I turned my back to go and buy this very Lo a lollipop, than I would hear her and the fair mechanic burst into a perfect love song of wisecracks.

Description need not be objective, as the paragraph by Norman Mailer on p. 59 demonstrates. It can be favorable to its subject or unfavorable, depending on which details the writer chooses to include and which he chooses to omit. Some of the funniest descriptions make no pretense to objectivity, as in this paragraph by Gore Vidal:

Ronald Reagan is a well-preserved not young man. Close to, the painted face is webbed with delicate lines while the dyed hair, eyebrows, and eyelashes contrast oddly with the sagging muscle beneath the as yet unlifted chin, soft earnest of wattle soon-to-be. The effect, in repose, suggests the work of a skillful embalmer. Animated, the face is quite attractive and at a distance youthful; particularly engaging is the crooked smile full of large porcelain-capped teeth. The eyes are the only interesting feature: small, narrow, apparently dark, they glitter in the hot light, alert to every move, for this is enemy country—the liberal Eastern press who are so notoriously immune to that warm and folksy performance which Reagan quite deliberately projects over their heads to some legendary constituency at the far end of the tube, some shining Carverville where good Lewis Stone forever lectures Andy Hardy on the virtues of thrift and the wisdom of the contract system at Metro-Goldwyn-Mayer.

Deduction and Induction

When a paragraph (or an essay) begins with a general statement and moves to the particulars supporting it, we call that method of ordering deductive, from the Latin *deducere,* to lead out or away. When, on the contrary, a paragraph or an essay moves from particular facts or details to a general statement, we call its order inductive. Deductive paragraphs, consisting of a thesis sentence followed by further sentences illustrating or supporting its thesis, are the more frequent, but inductive paragraphs can be equally effective.

The *Ramparts* paragraph quoted on p. 55 is a deductive paragraph; the Mailer paragraph is another. Here is a good example of a deductive paragraph from Alvin Toffler's *Future Shock*:

This startling statement [that history is "speeding up"] can be illustrated in a number of ways. It has been observed, for example, that if the past 50,000 years of man's existence were divided into lifetimes of approximately 62 years each, there have been about 800 such lifetimes. Of these 800, fully 650 were spent in caves. Only during the past 70 lifetimes has it been possible to communicate effectively from one lifetime to another—as writing made it possible to do. Only during the past six lifetimes have masses of men ever seen a printed word. Only during the past four has it been possible to measure time with any precision. Only in the past two has anyone anywhere used an electric motor. And the overwhelming majority of all the material goods we use in daily life today have been developed within the present, the 800th lifetime.

Since the inductive paragraph is harder to compose, or at least comes less naturally to the beginning writer, several examples may be helpful. Here is an inductive paragraph beginning with a question and ending with an answer, from George Wald's "A Generation in Search of a Future":

How real is the threat of full-scale nuclear war? I have my own very inexpert idea, but realizing how little I know and fearful that I may be a little paranoid on this subject, I take every opportunity to ask reputed experts. I asked that question of a very distinguished professor of government at Harvard about a month ago. I asked him what sort of odds he would lay on the possibility of full-scale nuclear war within the foreseeable future. "Oh," he said comfortably, "I think I can give you a pretty good answer to that question. I estimate the possibility of full-scale nuclear war, provided that the situation remains about as it is now, at 2 percent per year." Anybody can do the simple calculation that shows that 2 percent per year means that the chance of having that full-scale nuclear war by 1990 is about one in three, and by 2000 it is about 50-50.

Here are two more representative examples, the first from *Newsweek*, the second from Dwight Macdonald's *Memoirs of a Revolutionist*:

"Last fall we were still interested in politics," confides a 23-year-old history student in Prague. "Then we cared about what was happening to our comrades. But today everybody is interested in saving his own skin and nothing else." That comment may well serve as a benediction for Czechoslovakia's once proud student movement after a bitter year of vicious purges by the hard-line Communist regime that replaced the liberal government of Alexander Dubcek. The tale offers a depressingly vivid illustration of what a government can do to its universities—and to the youthful spirit of reform—when repression becomes official education policy.

———

I remember when Franco's planes bombed Barcelona for the first time what a thrill of unbelieving horror and indignation went through our nerves at the idea of hundreds—yes, *hundreds*—of civilians being killed. It seems impossible that that was less than ten years ago. Franco's air force was a toy compared to the sky-filling bombing fleets deployed in this war, and the hundreds killed in Barcelona have become the thousands killed in Rotterdam and Warsaw, the tens of thousands in Hamburg and Cologne, the hundreds of thousands in Dresden, and the millions in Tokyo. A month ago, the papers reported that over one million Japanese men, women, and children had perished in the fires set by a single B-29 raid on Tokyo. One million. I saw no expression of horror or indignation in any American newspaper or magazine of sizable circulation. We have grown calloused to massacre, and the concept of guilt has spread to include whole populations. Our hearts are hardened, our nerves steady, our imaginations under control as we read the morning paper. King Mithridates is said to have immunized himself against poison by taking small doses which he increased slowly. So the gradually increasing horrors of the last decade have made each of us to some extent a moral Mithridates, immunized against human sympathy.

The great virtue of the inductive paragraph, as these examples make plain, is that it builds to a climax. Like a skillful speaker or a Fourth of July fireworks show, it saves its major statement for the end.

Classification

Classification is the breaking down of a subject into its component parts. Here is part of a paragraph from Loren Eiseley's *The Immense Journey*:

That food came from three sources, all produced by the reproductive system of the flowering plants. There were the tantalizing nectars and pollens intended to draw insects for pollenizing purposes. . . . There were the juicy and enticing fruits to attract larger animals, and in which tough-coated seeds were concealed, as in the tomato, for example. Then, as if this were not enough, there was the food in the actual seed itself, the food intended to nourish the embryo. All over the world, like hot corn in a popper, these incredible elaborations of the flowering plants kept exploding.

This ordering is clearly deductive: the reader is told that there are three, or four, or five items to be discussed, and the items are thereupon discussed. Most readers are grateful to have this sort of road map. The writer must of course take care, if he has promised three items, to deliver three, and not two or four.

Classification can also be negative, defining a term by what it is not or by how it differs from the familiar or the expected. Here is a paragraph from an essay by Irving Howe defining "The Idea of the Modern":

The kind of literature called modern is almost always difficult to comprehend: that is a sign of its modernity. To the established guardians of culture, the modern writer seems wilfully inaccessible. He works with unfamiliar forms; he chooses subjects that disturb the audience and threaten its most cherished sentiments; he provokes traditionalist critics to such epithets as "unwholesome," "coterie," and "decadent."

It is worth noting that the paragraph following this begins with the sentence: "The modern must be defined in terms of what it is not."

Comparison and Contrast

Comparison and contrast are among the most effective means of introducing, defining, or clarifying something. If a reader has never seen or heard an English horn but is familiar with the oboe, a comparison of the two instruments may be the best way of telling him what an English horn looks and sounds like. Similarly, in describing a sonata, a writer may find it useful to contrast it with another sonata, or with a concerto by the same composer.

Two effective uses of contrast follow. In the first, James Baldwin contrasts his American habits of mind with those he has acquired in Europe; he tentatively accounts for the difference by another contrast, between Europe's long experience in dealing with artists and America's shorter one. In the second, Stokely Carmichael contrasts Stokely the unreflecting boy with Stokely the enlightened man, and by implication the black experience of the 1940's with the black experience today.

> The American writer, in Europe, is released, first of all, from the necessity of apologizing for himself. It is not until he is released from the habit of flexing his muscles and proving that he is just a "regular guy" that he realizes how crippling this habit has been. It is not necessary for him, there, to pretend to be something he is not, for the artist does not encounter in Europe the same suspicion he encounters here. Whatever the Europeans may actually think of artists, they have killed enough of them off by now to know that they are as real—and as persistent—as rain, snow, taxes, or businessmen.
>
> ───
>
> I remember that when I was a boy, I used to go to see Tarzan movies on Saturday. White Tarzan used to beat up the black natives. I would sit there yelling, "Kill the beasts, kill the savages, kill 'em!" I was saying: Kill *me*. It was as if a Jewish boy watched Nazis taking Jews off to concentration camps and cheered them on. Today, I want the chief to beat the hell out of Tarzan and send him back to Europe.

Definition

Description, classification, comparison and contrast—these and many other ways of ordering are ways of defining as well. Every writer needs to define his terms, to provide working definitions as he develops his theme or argument. What are we talking about? What does it look like? How did it develop? Where is it found? What are its parts? These are just a few of the questions that can lead to paragraphs of definition. Here is such a paragraph by Mark Schorer in an essay on the nature of the novel:

> When we speak of technique, then, we speak of nearly everything. For technique is the means by which the writer's experience, which is his subject matter, compels him to attend to it; technique is the only means he has of discovering, exploring, developing his subject, of conveying its meaning, and, finally, of evaluating it. And surely it follows that certain techniques are sharper tools than others, and will discover more; that the writer capable of the most exacting technical scrutiny of his subject matter will produce works with the most satisfying content, works with thickness and resonance, works which reverberate, works with maximum meaning.

A paragraph of definition need not say everything there is to be said on its subject; if necessary, it can be supplemented or qualified later in the essay. That is what has happened here. Clearly we will need to know a lot more about "technique" before we understand what Schorer means by the term. This paragraph, his second, is only a start; as the essay moves on, other working definitions will finish the job.

There are many other kinds of paragraphs, but the other ordering principles sometimes invoked—exclusion, syllogistic order, cause and effect, and so on—seem to us either matters of common sense or so specialized as to be unhelpful. Indeed, we see ordering principles in general simply as a convenient way of sketching the range of paragraph types, not as a way of consciously constructing paragraphs. Writers do not organize their paragraphs by principle, but by what they have to say. Get your message straight and your paragraphing will take care of itself.

JUDGING A PARAGRAPH

Here is a paragraph from a student paper. Is it a good one?

Young people have always been rebellious, anxious for change. Presented with a group of problems they are not responsible for, they have a great urge to change things, to make a better world. They have not yet met with the discouraging realities of life and the accompanying loss of idealism. In college one is presented with a unique opportunity to voice views without the fear of recrimination that people with a fixed place in the community have. There is relatively little to lose because no roots have been set down. The college student is not tied to his college as the ordinary citizen is to his community. He has a sense of detachment which may give him the feeling that he can bring about great changes and certainly allows him to attempt this without fear.

The first question to ask is this: Is there a single idea that governs the whole paragraph and makes a unit of it? Can one state it as a thesis sentence? How about "Young people, especially college students, are rebellious because they have less to lose than their more established elders"? Since all seven sentences relate in some way to this idea, it is fair to consider the paragraph a unit. But now comes the second question: Is the paragraph coherent? Here one encounters difficulties. The first three sentences are about young people in general, the last four about college students. Is a connection established between these two worlds? None that can be put in words. The reader is supposed to infer a connection, but can only guess what the writer intended.

This brings us to our third question: Is the reasoning in the paragraph, or the way evidence is presented, sound and convincing? It is not, primarily because the generalizations of the first three sentences are too broad to be defended or, really, understood. Not all young people are rebellious; some are timid, some are indifferent, and some like things just the way they are. And not all rebellious young people are out to make a better world; some are simply neurotic, and some are juvenile delinquents. As for the claim that young people "have not yet met with the discouraging realities of life," what about young people in war-torn Vietnam or famine-ridden India? What people are we talking about, anyway? All young people or only some, and if some, which ones?

As the paragraph stands, then, it has a kind of unity, but little coherence. If the writer had begun by saying "Many young Americans are rebellious today" and otherwise qualified his opening remarks, the paragraph would be better, but since its details are nowhere specific and its point is not clear, it would still be boring and vaguely irritating. With all its defects remedied, the paragraph might read like this:

> In America most young people are brought up to believe in change—to believe that next year's model will be better than this year's, that the new math will supplant the old, that because people are growing taller they must be growing better as well. These illusions are reinforced by the behavior of many American adults, who trade in their cars, their jobs, even their wives and husbands, for new models in the recurrent expectation that the new ones will bring happiness. Small wonder that college students are such active seekers of change. Not only are they encouraged by the training and the example of their elders, but they are uninhibited by responsibility to a profession, a family, or a community, and unsobered by the recollection of their own past errors. In theory, at least, they are the perfect revolutionaries.

The revised paragraph has expressed much the same general idea as the original, but its generalizations are rooted in reality, its details are concrete and alive, and its final sentence makes the writer's message clear. And this is the point we have made throughout this chapter: If you have something to say and really want to say it, the chances are that your paragraphs will shape themselves. The person who is full of his subject almost *has* to communicate it clearly and convincingly. That motive in itself tends to be a shaper of good paragraphs.

5

SENTENCES

In this chapter, we are concerned with writing at the sentence level, and in particular with choosing the most effective wording from among two or more equally correct alternatives. The aggregate of such choices amounts to a writer's style. Style in this sense has little to do with the rules of grammar; good style is impossible without good grammar, but the two are by no means synonymous. Grammar and syntax (see Chapters 9 and 10) are matters of precision, style a matter of grace. Poor grammar or syntax may puzzle a reader or mislead him; poor style will irritate him or put him to sleep. Under the impact of awkward or leaden writing, the reader's brain becomes first overtaxed, then inefficient, and finally stupefied. Good writers try to spare their readers this distress by the practices set forth in this chapter.

BASIC PREFERENCES

Most good writers agree on five basic preferences:

1. Prefer verbs to nouns.
2. Prefer the active to the passive.

3. Prefer the concrete to the abstract.
4. Prefer the personal to the impersonal.
5. Prefer the shorter version to the longer.

Prefer Verbs to Nouns

New nouns and noun compounds pour into the language daily like so many boulders into a river, until one wonders if they will someday dam the flow forever. From electronics and space technology alone we have thousands of new names for things, ranging from simple compounds like *thermostress* and *countdown,* through contrived acronyms like *sonar* and *laser,* to sodden six- and seven-noun strings like *nozzle gas ejection ship attitude control system.* The effect of these nouns is to displace verbs. We do not begin *to count down* (verb); we begin the *countdown* (noun). We do not have a system by which gas *is ejected* through nozzles *to control* a ship's attitude (two verbs); instead, we have the monstrosity cited above (seven nouns), from which our only hope of delivery is the equally unacceptable acronym NGESACS.

Indeed, the mere proliferation of new nouns is less alarming than the increasing tendency to overuse all nouns, new and old alike, at the expense of verbs, which give language most of its life and movement. Fifty years ago it would have been natural to write *McCormick also invented a machine for picking corn;* today we incline to write *Another of McCormick's inventions was a mechanical cornpicker.* Fifty years ago, *This book tells you how to promote local sports without spending much money;* today, *The subject of this book is low-budget sports promotion techniques.* The modern versions are heavy and lifeless. Not only have the verbs given way to nouns, but the nouns themselves have lost their color: *corn* is buried in *cornpicker, sports* hangs grayly on a clothesline between abstractions, *money* has disappeared.

One finds writing of this sort everywhere. Scientists and technologists are perhaps the worst offenders, government officials the second worst, but no large class of writers is free of the disease. Remember our muffin-mouthed school principal in Chapter 1? Here is a history professor (nouns and pronouns italicized):

The Allen-Hamilton-Shippen *connection* represented for the Proprietary *party* a *leadership* comparable to *that* of the Pemberton-Logan-Norris *combination* of the *Quakers*, though the *former* exhibited less *unity* and *effectiveness* in *politics*.

There are ten italicized nouns and pronouns in addition to the six proper names, or five nouns for each of the sentence's two verbs. The proportion is too high, and the sentence is heavy-footed. The nouns can easily be cut to two, and the verbs increased to three:

Allen, Hamilton, and Shippen served the Proprietary *party* much as Pemberton, Logan, and Norris served the *Quakers*, but were less unified and less effective politically.

Here is a sentence from an academic report with its nouns italicized: "There has necessarily been a *tendency* on the *part* of *researchers* to continue *studies* with *equipment* now approaching *obsolescence*." As rewritten to cut down the nouns: "*Researchers* have necessarily gone on using obsolescent *equipment*." Here is an Army dispatch: "The *enemy* has had no *opportunity* to assemble *forces* in sufficient *quantity* to mount an *offensive* against *Danang*." As rewritten: "The *enemy* has failed to assemble a big enough *force* to attack *Danang*."

Nouns are of course indispensable; the problem is to avoid using them at the expense of livelier words. A sentence with too many nouns—and "too many" may usually be defined as one more than is strictly necessary—takes slightly more effort to read than it is worth. Multiply this extra effort by six or eight paragraphs and you have a fatigued reader, which is to say no reader at all.

Prefer the Active to the Passive

Verbs in the passive voice tend to yield unnecessarily dull sentences, as the following examples show:

She was not told by anyone.
No one told her.

Words are seen as bricks in an edifice of beauty.

Shelley sees words as bricks in an edifice of beauty.

A fair decision was rendered difficult by the judge's evident bias.

The judge's evident bias made it hard for him to decide fairly.

All three active versions are more forceful and direct. Moreover, there are secondary advantages. In the first example, the active saves two words; in the second, it makes the subject, Shelley, explicit; in the third, it makes for lighter and less formal language. Such advantages are common in switching from passive to active.

Another difficulty of the passive is that it avoids placing responsibility. It presents no subject, no actor, only the action and its object. Typical is the following murky recommendation from a government report: *It is urged that special study be given to the question of how the positive values in migrant life can be exploited in improving the teaching of the migrant child.* Urged, given, exploited by whom? We can only guess. Here are two sentences from student themes:

Frost's work contains much symbolism, symbolism that is strongly felt.

Pathos is aroused at Andrea del Sarto's meek submission to his wife.

By whom, the reader wonders, is Frost's symbolism strongly felt? By Frost? By his readers? By the writer? Whose pathos is aroused in the second example, and by whom or what? The answers to these questions make a difference, but there is no knowing what they are from the agentless passive construction.

To be sure, the passive has its legitimate domain. Sometimes the subject of a verb is irrelevant or too complex to identify: *He will be released from prison tomorrow / Two majors were promoted to lieutenant colonel / For we were nursed upon the self-same hill.* The point is not to avoid the passive altogether, but to use it sparingly. Use the active, with its superior vigor and directness, when you can; use the passive only when the active is clearly inconvenient or unidiomatic.

This rule has a corollary: Prefer the action verb to the linking verb, and the more forceful action verb to the less forceful. Linking verbs are the dozen or so verbs that take noun or adjective complements (predicate nouns or adjectives, as opposed to direct objects); the main ones are *be, become, look, seem, appear, sound,* and *feel.* These pallid verbs, especially *be,* are flourishing as never before in this golden age of nouns. Where once people said *George drives well / George drives a bus,* we now say *George is a good driver / George is a bus driver;* an action verb, *drive,* has dwindled into a noun, leaving the field to the linking verb *is. Is* supplies no motion to a sentence; it is inert, a kind of equals sign between nouns. No writer, of course, can avoid *is* and *are, was* and *were,* but good writers are always on the lookout to replace them with verbs of greater impact. The following alternative versions of a single sentence are listed in order of increasing effectiveness:

Passive

> It has been decided that a 10 percent tax increase is necessary.

Active, linking verb

> Our conclusion is that taxes must be increased 10 percent.

Active, action verb

> We have decided on a 10 percent tax increase.

Active, more forceful action verb

> We propose to increase taxes 10 percent.

Verbs are the wheels of writing; as they move, so moves the message they carry. If all the verbs in a paragraph are forms of *be* and *have,* the wheels will move slowly.

Prefer the Concrete to the Abstract

Concrete nouns stand for things. They are words like *hog, heart, helicopter, Harry*: specific designations for specific entities. Abstract nouns stand for ideas. They range along a spectrum from near-concrete words like *housing* through relatively simple concepts like *sympathy* and *difficulty* to more general terms like *situation* and *socialism,* and on to the formidable abstractions of modern scholarly discourse. At the extreme, we find such sentences as this one, the work of a doctoral candidate in philosophy: *From the standpoint of the historical development of empirical observation in scientific inference, it is worth noting De Morgan's acceptance of a subjective viewpoint in probability.*

Writing that runs heavily to abstract nouns is hard to read, partly because such nouns tend to be long and lifeless, partly because they take the tamer sort of verb (abstractions never *kick* or *ogle* or *revere* each other; they *cause* or *refer to* or *consist of* each other), but above all because they require the reader to invest time and effort in translating the writer's generalities into particulars. To be sure, some writing is slow going for the reader because it deals with genuinely difficult or complex matters; but much more is slow going solely because the writer did not know how to make his meaning immediately clear.

Abstractions are general, intangible, elusive. The human mind works best on particulars: on tangible, finite units. The *poor need better housing* is a simple enough sentence, but no two people can truly agree on its meaning until *better housing* is defined in terms of number of units, size of rooms, rental rates, and so on, and until *the poor* are defined as a particular class of people—for example, families of four or more persons living in New York City with an annual family income of under $3,980. Similarly, *Tom is brave,* or *The situation is desperate*, makes no sense without particulars. For example, we may know that Tom is brave because he stood up against a bully or saved a child from a fire; the situation may be desperate because enemy tanks are only a mile away, or because Dad cannot find a job.

In short, to make sense of abstractions we must see them in concrete terms. The beginning explanation of Einstein's theory of relativity is commonly made in terms of two trains: to a person on Train A, the apparent speed and direction of movement of Train B will depend on which directions the two trains are in fact moving in, and at what speeds. Complexities like De Morgan's "subjective viewpoint in probability" must be explained in similar concrete terms if we are to understand what they mean.

Some writers mistakenly feel that abstractions lend tone to writing, that they are more dignified than everyday words like *cat* and *dog*. Others use abstractions to avoid committing themselves to particulars—which means, in effect, to avoid the kind of careful thinking and articulation of thought that goes into all good writing. In both cases, the results tend to be vague and irritating. The following sentences from student themes illustrate this point:

> Other lessons were absorbed through his experiences.

> Attitudes and opinions resulted from these environmental occurrences.

> There is no way to overcome the situation of racial relationships.

The first writer seems to mean simply *He learned other lessons as well*; the second seems to mean *He got his ideas from what he saw and heard*; the third seems to mean *There is no way to end racial tensions*. Note that we say "seems to mean"; in none of the three cases can we be sure. It is as if the writer had tried deliberately to keep us guessing. Not only must a reader strain his mind to interpret such unexplained abstractions in concrete terms, but he must move on to the next sentence uncertain whether his interpretation of the previous one is correct.

In general, specific concrete details make for clearer communication; and the more specific, the clearer. Here are our three defective sentences made clear by the addition of details:

> He learned even more from talking with the lumberjacks.

> All he knew about Glasgow was what he could see from his window and what his nurses told him.

> Tensions between whites and blacks are inevitable in a mixed neighborhood.

Whatever the original writers meant, they would have done better to explain their meaning in concrete terms like these. Tell your readers what you mean in words they can understand. If you don't, you will lose the attention of most of your readers and confuse and irritate the few who stay with you.

Prefer the Personal to the Impersonal

Sentences with people in them make more interesting reading than sentences without people. Most sentences have people in them in the nature of things. Others have no people and no room for any: *The water was six feet deep/Transistors have replaced vacuum tubes.* Our concern here is with a third class of sentences, those that can go either way: that is, those whose meaning, though it involves people to some extent, can be expressed clearly and idiomatically either with or without a personal noun or pronoun. Our advice is to put the people in.

The point is illustrated in the following pairs of sentences. In each pair the first is perfectly acceptable but the second is slightly better:

It was necessary to get some sleep.
The boys had to get some sleep.

The drug would be lethal if it were swallowed.
The drug would kill anyone who swallowed it.

What was the casualty count?
How many people were hurt?

It is also a good idea to replace abstractions like *membership,* when used of people, with concrete nouns like *members,* which sounds more human than anything ending in *-ship.* In each of the following pairs, the second sentence is the more effective:

The leadership was completely replaced last summer.
The leaders were all replaced last summer.

The medical profession considers the practice unsafe.
Doctors consider the practice unsafe.

The police department soon had the crime wave under control.

The police soon had the crime wave under control.

The principle extends to more formal writing as well. Here is a passage from a preface to a book of readings:

Literary criticism as such did not seem useful for the purposes of this book. This is not to denigrate the art of criticism, but only to suggest that literary criticism, to be properly appreciated, must be accompanied by the texts it examines.

Here is the same passage livened up by the addition of people:

I decided against including literary criticism in this book, not because I have anything against it, but because readers cannot properly appreciate a critic's ideas without first reading the works he is discussing.

Prefer the Shorter Version to the Longer

Other things being equal, the shorter of two versions is the better. To be sure, other things *must* be equal—that is, the shorter version must convey the same information as the longer, and convey it just as clearly. *The tables were arranged in quincunx fashion* is shorter than *Four tables formed the corners of a square and the fifth was in the middle,* but the longer version will be clearer to most readers. Again, *according to Marcel* is shorter, but may be much less helpful, than *according to the Catholic existentialist philosopher Gabriel Marcel.* Readers for whom *Marcel* would have been enough will not be troubled by the extra words, and other readers will be glad to have them. It is basic good sense (not to mention courtesy) to explain matters that may be unfamiliar to your reader. To put this another way, brevity becomes desirable only after the reader's potential discomforts have been attended to.

The idea of keeping things short is not to reduce all writing to three-word sentences, but to eliminate the redundancies and dead words that so often clog the pipes. Why write *It was Harry that did it* when you can write *Harry did it?* Why write *There is a lot for us to talk about* when you can write *We have a lot to talk about?* What do the extra words add besides deadweight? A few further illustrations may help:

> It was clear to Havlicek on what basis the request for his resignation had been made.
>
> Havlicek knew why they wanted him to resign.

> The fact that Susan had made up her mind to leave college was distressing to her parents.
>
> Susan's decision to leave college distressed her parents.

> As a result of the labor policies established by Bismarck, the working class in Germany was convinced that revolution was unnecessary for the attainment of its ends.
>
> Bismarck's labor policies convinced the German working class that revolution was unnecessary.

In each of these pairs, the shorter version is only about half the length of the longer. Savings of this order are fairly common in editing first drafts written at full tilt. But smaller savings are also worth making:

> There was nothing for Alice to do.
>
> Alice had nothing to do.

> Banks in England are more helpful than banks in this country.
>
> English banks are more helpful than ours.

> It is predicted in the report that many polluted lakes will be pollution-free by 1980.
>
> The report predicts that many polluted lakes will be pollution-free by 1980.

Of our last eight examples of unnecessarily long sentences, no fewer than five begin with *It is, It was, There is,* and *There was.*

No other sentence opening is at once so conducive to excess wordage and so alluring to novice writers, perhaps because it staves off for a few seconds the necessity of coming to grips with what the sentence must actually say. These so-called expletive (literally "filling out") openings are not bad in themselves; indeed, they may yield impeccably brief and idiomatic sentences (*There were too many of them* / *It is hard to find*) or an emphasis not attainable more economically (*It was my fault that we lost*). But perfectly acceptable sentences of this sort are at least equaled in student writing by unnecessarily flatulent sentences along the lines of our five examples. In editing your first drafts, keep an eye out for expletive openings; probably two out of three such sentences can be effectively shortened.

Shortening a sentence often improves it in terms of one or more of the other four basic preferences as well. The Havlicek revision, for instance, dispenses with three abstract nouns, replaces a linking verb with an action verb, converts a passive construction to active, and adds some people (*they*); these changes, plus a halving of the word count, make a conspicuously better sentence. In the Susan example, and in two of the three shorter examples that follow it, action verbs replace linking verbs. In the Bismarck example, a passive construction becomes active and the nine nouns of the original are reduced to five. Conversely, nearly all the changes recommended under our four earlier headings—that is, changes to make sentences less noun-ridden, more active, less abstract, and more personal—had the additional effect of making the sentence shorter. Clearly the five rules are interrelated, and each reinforces the others.

We conclude this section with a horrendous example of academese from a recent book on juvenile delinquency:

> Contemporary economic perquisites and differential standards have an important conscious and unconscious effect upon the individual's expectation of what he considers to be his right. If the degree of social permissiveness generally sanctioned for attaining pleasures and status is not adequately available to the less economically or culturally favored, the deprivation begets resentment.

The passage violates every one of our five rules. It is sodden with nouns, twelve of them, all but one abstract. Though none of its four verbs is passive, only one, *begets*, has any motion. Its only human component, if human is the word, is a faceless social unit called *the individual.* It is at least a dozen words too long. One can only guess at what it means. Not only does such writing offend the ear and stun the mind; it separates the writer from the specifics that were his original point of departure, in this case the pressure of poverty and powerlessness on flesh-and-blood people.

Our first advice to a beginning stylist is to be honest and unpretentious; our second advice is to learn the five preferences listed on pp. 72–73 and learn to apply them in practice. They are the very foundation stones of style.

EMPHASIS

Word Order

In writing, as in speech, most sentences mirror the natural sequence of ideas in the mind whenever no particular emphasis is sought: subject—object—circumstances—afterthoughts. Emphatic sentences, by contrast, are a matter of deliberate artifice. Typically, the chief element to be emphasized is placed at the end; the lesser elements precede it, setting the stage for the main act.

Compare the following versions of the same incident, the first in natural word order, the second with the word order changed to emphasize *sister*:

> I started at the noise and looked up guiltily. My sister stood there in the doorway.

> I started at the noise and looked up guiltily. There in the doorway stood my sister.

Although, as this example suggests, the word or statement to be emphasized should come at the end of the sentence if possible, you can get the same effect, with somewhat diminished intensity, before a semicolon, a colon, a dash, or even a comma. The emphasis comes from a sort of echo in the moment of silence signaled by the punctuation mark. The stronger the punctuation, the longer the moment; the longer the moment, the more impressive the emphasis. In the emphatic versions of the sentences that follow, the emphasized elements (in italics) come before a period, a semicolon, and a comma, respectively:

Unemphatic

Ellen had her first sight of the sea at 24, after living in Kansas all her life.

Emphatic

At 24, after living in Kansas all her life, *Ellen had her first sight of the sea.*

Unemphatic

He was skinny and weak when I first knew him; today he must weigh 200 pounds.

Emphatic

When I first knew him, *he was skinny and weak*; today he must weigh 200 pounds.

Unemphatic

Lincoln was such a man, it is said.

Emphatic

Lincoln, it is said, was such a man.

Although the emphatic versions here seem better than the unemphatic in getting the emphasis where it belongs, the emphatic treatment is by no means always to be preferred. Most unemphatic sentences are inoffensive, and many are eloquent. The best writing mixes the two kinds.

Coordination and Subordination

There is, however, one kind of unemphatic sentence to guard against. That is the compound sentence: the sentence of two or more clauses joined by coordinating conjunctions, usually *and* or *but*. Sentences of this form have neither the potential elegance and strength of the simple sentence, nor the possibilities of emphasis afforded by the complex sentence.   They have an inherently boring symmetry: *John played baseball, and Mary went to the movies.*   An occasional sentence of this sort is fine.   A sprinkling of them makes for writing that is blander than necessary.   A preponderance of them is fatal to good prose.

Lazy writers like the compound sentence because it covers all possibilities without committing itself to any.   Does *He was rude and she was angry* mean that his rudeness made her angry, or were their reactions simultaneous, or what?   The writer who uses *and* this way saves himself the trouble of deciding and specifying which of these relationships he means, if indeed there is any relationship at all.   Here are two typical compound ramblers:

> I don't think I ever actually talked to him, *but* he was the ultimate symbol of authority, *and* the mere sight of him used to fill me with physical terror.

> The play is very funny *but* it is also sad, *and* one is never allowed to forget the theme.

In the first, there is no *but* or *and* relationship worth the name. Properly reorganized, the sentence becomes two sentences with no conjunctions at all: *He was the ultimate symbol of authority; the mere sight of him used to fill me with physical terror. I don't think I ever actually talked to him.*   The second sentence needs subordination of the less important ideas to the more important one: *Funny as the play is, one is never allowed to forget the underlying sadness.*   Both writers, by reaching mechanically for their old friends *and* and *but*, have obscured the true relationships between the elements they are relating.

Before you connect two clauses with *and*, stop and think.   Is there really any *and* connection at all?   Do we need *and* in a sentence like *Steve was a hero-worshiper, and his hero was Che Guevara,* or would a semicolon or a period be enough?   Even if there is a legitimate *and* connection, is the *and* construction the best possible, or is one idea in fact subordinate in meaning or importance to the other?   Which is better, *Mary went away, and John was unhappy,* or *After Mary went away, John was un-*

happy? Most good writers would vote against *and* in both these examples. Write *and* in your first draft if you must, but in editing get rid of as many *and*'s as you can.

In Chapter 4 we discussed how to write effective paragraphs by varying sentence types—simple, compound, and complex; declarative, interrogative, and imperative—and by varying sentence lengths. Readers interested in the present discussion of emphasis at the sentence level may want to review this discussion, which appears on pp. 58–59.

SOME JARRING CONSTRUCTIONS

So far we have been concerned with ways of making writing more lively; in this section we shall consider ways of making it less irritating. Writing can be irritating in many ways: it can be perverse, superficial, dishonest, cryptic, boring, cute. Bad grammar is irritating, so is bad syntax, and so are the various forms of dull writing discussed earlier in this chapter. Our concern here, however, is exclusively with the minor irritations produced by clumsy sentence structure in sentences otherwise perfectly acceptable.

We shall consider five irritating constructions: (1) the breaking up of auxiliary verb constructions by obtrusive adverbial phrases; (2) the subordination of one *that, who,* or *which* to another; (3) the following of one *but* or *however* with another; (4) the excessive repetition of the same sound in a single sentence or phrase; and (5) false telegraphy, that is, leading the reader to suppose a sentence has one construction when in fact it has another.

Obtrusive Adverbial Phrases

In an auxiliary verb construction like *were doing, have done, has been done,* a simple adverb usually goes between the auxiliary and the verb (*We have always done what we could*) or between the two parts of the auxiliary (*It has often been done that way*). The same placement works well enough for a short adverbial phrase (*We have at least done what we could / It has more often than not been done that way*). It does not work at all well, however, for a phrase longer than three or four words, or for a word or phrase of any length that is set off by punctuation. The following examples of obtrusive adverbial phrases progress from least to most irritating:

> The point had been *angrily and almost hysterically* made.

> The explorers of this terrain have, *as yet,* been few.

> A parallel has—*justifiably, I think*—been drawn between Ivy Compton-Burnett and Jane Austen.

> I could see that I was *one way or the other* going to have to spend the evening with Charley.

> The nations of the Third World have, *in the fifteen years since the Bandung Conference,* looked in vain for a leader and a program.

The first sentence will pass as it stands but would be improved by joining the verb to its auxiliary: *had been made angrily and almost hysterically.* The word order of the second sentence is fine; all that is needed is to delete the commas, which give *as yet* a seemingly pointless and thus irritating emphasis. In the third sentence the emphasis given by the dashes is proper enough, but it comes at the wrong place. Joining the verb to its auxiliary improves things immensely: *has been drawn—justifiably, I think— between.* In the last two sentences the adverbial phrases are simply too long to be placed as they are. The solution is to move them: *I could see that one way or another I was going / In the fifteen years since the Bandung Conference, the nations.* Auxiliary verb constructions are only one of the many victims of the obtrusive adverbial phrase. The standard simple-verb constructions are equally vulnerable, as these examples show:

> The miniskirt is *in the eyes of the fashion industry* a dead issue.

> How many minority group members are *by actual count of the Census Bureau or its state counterparts* on welfare?

> Gambetta's indifference destroyed, *if we can believe Denis Brogan,* what hope there was of a reconciliation.

Each of these italicized intruders—and most adverbial phrases and clauses longer than three or four words—should be put at the beginning of the sentence.

Double That

The irritation caused by the double-*that* construction should be plain from the following examples:

> The *Times* editorial said *that* Alston was afraid *that* he would be fired.

> It was the National Council *that* made the prediction *that* no Republican would be elected.

> Professor Aaron is the one *who* introduced the poet *who* won second prize.

Sometimes you can repair this construction by simply dropping one of the two relative pronouns: *The* Times *editorial said that Alston was afraid he would be fired.* Where *said* is the main verb, another option is *according to*: *According to the* Times *editorial, Alston was afraid that he would be fired.* Sometimes the construction can be fixed only by rewriting: *The prediction that no Republican would be elected came from the National Council.*

The double-*that* construction creeps into the work of skilled writers as well as novices. One even encounters triple *that*'s, as in these sentences by Jerome Bruner and George Wald, respectively, from passages quoted in earlier chapters:

> There still lingers the innocent Christian conception . . . *that* it is something *that* we have done or failed to do as individuals *that* creates a rather Protestantized and private unhappiness.

> Anybody can do the simple calculation *that* shows *that* 2 percent per year means *that* the chance of having . . . full-scale nuclear war by 1990 is about one in three.

Note that the objectionable double- or triple-*that* construction always involves the subordination of one *who, which,* or *that* clause to another: *X says that Y thinks that Z is true.* Where the second *that* is not subordinate to the first, there is nothing to object to; thus we might rewrite Wald's sentence acceptably as follows:

> According to a simple calculation *that* anybody can do, 2 percent per year means *that* the chance of having . . . full-scale nuclear war by 1990 is about one in three.

And where two relative clauses are related in a coordinate rather than a subordinate fashion, the repetition of *who, which,* or *that* after the coordinating conjunction is not only acceptable but usually preferable, as in the following sentences:

> The report confirmed *that* her father was too ill to work *and that* her mother was crippled.

> It held a small, irregularly shaped vase, *which* no one at that time could place *but which* Paddock later identified as of Mixtec origin.

Deleting the second *that* would make the first sentence slightly ambiguous: did the report specify her mother's condition, or does the information come directly from the writer? Deleting the second *which* would make the construction of the second sentence less immediately clear.

Double But

The double-*but* construction jerks the reader's mind back and forth from *but* to *but* like the eyes of someone watching a tennis game. *However, yet, nevertheless,* and other action-reversing words are as irritating with *but* as another *but* would be. Some examples:

> She wanted to go, *but* her father would not let her, *but* then he changed his mind.

Earl, *however*, hung back, *but* no one even noticed.

I was good at translation, *though* my pronunciation was only fair; *however*, I did well on the test.

To repair such a construction, get rid of at least one *but* or *however*. As with the double-*that* construction, this is sometimes simply a matter of dropping one word of the pair: *Earl hung back, but no one even noticed.* More often, rewriting is necessary:

At first her father refused to let her go, *but* later he changed his mind.

Even *though* my pronunciation was only fair, I was good at translation and did well on the test.

The objection to the double-*but* construction applies only when each *but* introduces or governs a complete clause, as in the examples above. In particular, it is a bad idea to begin two successive sentences with *but* or the equivalent, as is done in the following passage from a student paper:

This line of criticism has so far only penetrated the periphery. *But* in the next few years it will undoubtedly be one of the main areas of interest to students of science fiction. *However*, some things stand out at first glance.

Repetition of the Same Sound

Still another kind of doubling irritation has nothing to do with such logistical problems as the nesting of *that* within *that* or the zigzagging of *but* after *but*. This kind comes strictly from the excessive repetition of the same sound within a limited number of words. The repeated sound is typically a suffix or a preposition, as in the following examples:

For a painter, he works remarkab*ly* quick*ly*.

The other spy was equal*ly* bad*ly* treated by the Algerians.

According to the latest inform*ation,* accommod*ations* are available only to people with reserv*ations.*

The thing *to* do was *to* change his strategy *to* adjust *to* the new situation.

Some *of the* parents *of the* members *of the* club could not be reached.

None of these sentences is impossible, but each can stand improvement. Why not *he is a remarkably quick worker* in the first sentence, and *just as badly* in the second? In the third, *information* can be changed to *word* and *accommodations* to *rooms* or whatever. The end of the fourth can be edited to *was adjust his strategy to the new situation,* the beginning of the fifth to *Some of the club members' parents.*

False Telegraphy

Some sentences confuse the reader by telegraphing one construction and delivering another. Here are a few examples:

To Germany, France, England, and Russia are natural enemies.

Reports reached the dean of students arrested for throwing firecrackers at the Governor's limousine.

Mr. Hastings, the vice-chairman, and General Benton were absent.

I said that Tuesday was impossible, not every Tuesday.

In the first sentence, the reader infers a series of four; this does not work, and he has to read the sentence carefully to discover that it breaks after *Germany.* In the second, the reader mistakenly makes a unit of *dean of students.* In the third, is Mr. Hastings the vice-chairman or are they two different men? In the final sentence, the writer means "I said [that] that [particular] Tuesday was impossible, not [that] every Tuesday [was impossible]." The most adroit reader would have trouble extracting this meaning from the sentence as it was written.

False telegraphy is easy enough to fix; the problem is to spot it. It helps if you can put your paper aside for a while between first draft and final typing. After a day or so, you can approach your own writing as another reader might, critically and with a fresh eye. If you find a sentence baffling at first—however momentarily—so will other readers, and revision is accordingly in order.

HOBSON'S CHOICES

Thomas Hobson was an irascible Englishman of Elizabethan times who rented horses to travelers on the condition that they take the horse he chose for them or none at all. His horses were a sad lot, and "Hobson's choice" has accordingly come to mean a choice between alternatives all of which have serious drawbacks.

Confronted by a Hobson's choice between a technically correct sentence that sounds awkward and a good-sounding sentence that is technically deficient, many students resignedly opt for one or the other without reflecting whether there may be some third alternative that is neither awkward nor unsound. Consider the following sentences:

Either you or I (*are*) (*am*) wrong.

There was a furor about the Undersecretary of (*State*) (*State's*) not being invited.

Willie Mays was as good an (*outfielder*) (*outfielder as*) or better than Joe DiMaggio.

"Th' expense of spirit" is one of the best, if not the best (*sonnet*) (*sonnets*) ever written.

Bohr thought of Einstein as much as a friend (*as*) (*as as*) a teacher.

In each of these sentences, the first alternative listed is the more natural or unobtrusive, but is technically defective; the second is better technically, but is rhetorically ugly. A Hobson's choice, then, but with one important difference: Hobson's customer had to choose between the alternatives offered him, and we do not. Why confine ourselves to the possibilities in parentheses? Why not rewrite the sentence to get around the difficulty?

Either you are wrong or I am.

There was a furor when people learned that the Undersecretary of State had not been invited.

Willie Mays was at least as good an outfielder as Joe DiMaggio.

"Th' expense of spirit" is one of the best sonnets ever written, maybe even the best.

Bohr thought of Einstein not only as a teacher, but as a friend.

Don't just give up and allow an awkward sentence to stand. Except, perhaps, in the higher reaches of science and technology, ideas can always be expressed in sentences that are simultaneously grammatical and graceful. If a sentence is intractable on its own terms, choose other terms. If you find yourself wound up in a construction you cannot handle, choose another construction, one you are more at home with. The language is flexible; it has many ways of saying what you want to say. Why run into a wall that you can as easily walk around?

6

WORDS

Thirty years ago American textbooks spent many pages correcting some five dozen classical diction errors: *lay* for *lie*, *he don't* for *he doesn't*, *principle* for *principal*, and the like. Some of these errors and confusions are rarely encountered today. Others persist, not only among the educationally underprivileged but among college students with a good background in high school English. Brief discussions of the most troublesome of these questions will be found in the Index to Current Usage, pp. 266–308. Here we shall confine ourselves to questions of a more general nature.

USING THE DICTIONARY

Diction begins with the *dictionary*, a word that for some reason makes many students wince. As the following discussion shows, there is nothing impenetrable about the way information is arranged in a dictionary. Most of the conventions not illustrated in the sample entry we discuss below are no harder to decipher than the ones discussed, and the rest are easily mastered with the help of the brief explanations at the front of every dictionary.

The entries for the word *delay* shown below appear in *Webster's Seventh New Collegiate Dictionary*. The first entry, **¹de · lay**, is for the noun (*n*); the second, **²delay**, is for the verb (*vb*). The dot between *de* and *lay* in the first entry indicates that *delay* may be divided at this point if it comes at the end of a line. The notation \di-'lā\ is the standard pronunciation; the exact weight of *i* and *ā* and the meaning of ' are explained on the dictionary's endpapers. The information in brackets is the standard derivation of the word: through the Middle English verb *delayen* from the Old French *delaier*, a compound of *de-* and *laier*, "to leave," which in turn derived, through its alternative form *laissier*, from the Latin verb *laxare*, "to slacken." By convention, when there are separate entries for the noun and verb forms (or whatever) of a single word, the word-break, pronunciation, and derivation indications are given only once.

The entry **²delay** has two major divisions, *vt* and *vi*. *Vt* stands for "verb, transitive," the kind of verb that takes a direct object: *He delayed his decision / The soldiers delayed the train*. *Vi* stands for "verb, intransitive," the kind of verb that does not take an object: *Even when urged to hurry, they delayed*. Two derivative forms, the noun *delayer* and the adjective *delaying*, are listed without definitions, since their meaning can be unmistakably in-

---

¹de·lay \di-'lā\ *n* **1** **:** the act of delaying **:** the state of being delayed **2 :** the time during which something is delayed
²delay *vb* [ME *delayen*, fr. OF *delaier*, fr. *de-* + *laier* to leave, alter. of *laissier*, fr. L *laxare* to slacken — more at RELAX] *vt* **1 :** to put off **:** POSTPONE **2 :** to stop, detain, or hinder for a time ~ *vi* **:** to move or act slowly — **de·lay·er** *n* — **de·lay·ing** *adj*
syn DELAY, RETARD, SLOW, SLACKEN, DETAIN, mean to cause to be late or behind in movement or progress. DELAY implies a holding back, usu. by interference, from completion or arrival; RETARD applies chiefly to motion and suggests reduction of speed without actual stopping; SLOW and SLACKEN both imply also a reduction of speed, SLOW often suggesting deliberate intention, SLACKEN an easing up or relaxing of power or effort; DETAIN implies a holding back beyond a reasonable or appointed time
syn DELAY, PROCRASTINATE, LAG, LOITER, DAWDLE, DALLY mean to move or act slowly so as to fall behind. DELAY usu. implies a putting off (as a beginning or departure); PROCRASTINATE implies blameworthy delay esp. through laziness or apathy; LAG implies failure to maintain a speed set by others; LOITER and DAWDLE imply delay while in progress, esp. in walking, but DAWDLE more clearly suggests an aimless wasting of time; DALLY suggests delay through trifling or vacillation when promptness is necessary

ferred from what precedes. Finally, two separate synonymies are given, one for the transitive *delay* in its second sense, the other for the intransitive. Synonymies are one of the most useful features of the modern dictionary, discriminating as they do between near-synonyms like *illusion* and *delusion, postpone* and *defer, show* and *demonstrate,* alternatives that most of us find it hard to choose between without expert guidance.

The boldface numbers indicate the various definitions of a word. In *Webster's Seventh* and most other dictionaries, the sequence of definitions is strictly historical: that is, sense 1 of a word is neither necessarily better (in any way) nor necessarily more often encountered than sense 2, but simply entered the language earlier than sense 2. The historical examples on which most such decisions are based are presented in the greatest of all dictionaries, the *New English Dictionary on Historical Principles* (1884–1928), reissued in thirteen volumes in 1933 as the *Oxford English Dictionary* and known familiarly as the OED. Approximately one-fifth of the OED entry for *delay* and its derivatives is shown on the facing page.

College students rarely have occasion to consult the OED, and many can go for months at a time without consulting its nearest American equivalent, the 2,662-page, 13-pound, 4-inch-thick *Webster's Third New International Dictionary* (1961), with its 450,000 entries and its controversial hands-off approach to status labels. Your own abridged dictionary, whether *Webster's Seventh* or another, should be sufficient for most uses.

A dictionary will answer a thousand questions if you will only ask them: on spelling (*indispensible* or *indispensable?*), on pronunciation (*boo-kay* or *bo-kay?*), on word breaks (*plea-sure* or *pleas-ure?*), on definitions (what does *strophe* mean?), on the choice of words (*compulsory* or *obligatory?*), on the choice between different forms of a word (*dwelled* or *dwelt?*), on levels of usage (can I call someone a *hophead* in a term paper?), on any subject having to do with the form, meaning, and status of words. And not only ordinary lowercase words either, since most dictionaries include geographical names, personal proper names, common abbreviations, and other material, either in the main alphabetical sequence or in separate sections at the end. The dictionary may not be the liveliest book around, but to a writer—

1. *trans.* To put off to a later time; to defer, postpone. † *To delay time*: to put off time.

c **1290** *S. Eng. Leg.* I. 87/30 And bide þat he it delaiȝe Ane þreo ȝer. **1297** R. GLOUC. (1724) 513 Me nolde nouȝt, that is crouninge leng delaied were. **1393** GOWER *Conf.* III. 290 For to make him afered, The kinge his time hath so delaied. **1489** CAXTON *Faytes of A.* I. xxii. 68 To delaye the bataylle vnto another day. **1586** B. YOUNG *Guazzo's Civ. Conv.* IV. 181 b, Delaie the sentence no longer. **1594** WEST *2nd Pt. Symbol.* Chancerie § 140 Who .. with faire promises delaied time, and kept the said C. D. in hope from yeare to yeare. **1611** BIBLE *Matt.* xxiv. 48 My Lord delayeth his comming. **1737** POPE *Hor. Epist.* I. i. 41 Th' unprofitable moments .. That .. still delay Life's instant business to a future day. **1821** SHELLEY *Prometh. Unb.* III. iii. 6 Freedom long desired And long delayed. **1847** GROTE *Greece* I. xl. (1862) III. 433 He delayed the attack for four days.

b. with *infin.* To defer, put off.

a **1340** HAMPOLE *Psalter* vi. 3 How lange dylayes þou to gif grace. **1611** BIBLE *Ex.* xxxii. 1 When the people saw that Moses delayed to come downe. **1799** COWPER *Castaway* v, Some succour .. [they] Delayed not to bestow. **1847** TENNYSON *Princ.* iv. 88 Delaying as the tender ash delays To clothe herself, when all the woods are green.

† **c.** With personal object: To put (any one) off, to keep him waiting. *Obs.*

1388 WYCLIF *Acts* xxiv. 22 Felix delayede hem. **1512** *Act* 4 *Hen. VIII*, c. 6 § 2 If .. the same Collectours .. unreasonably delay or tary the said Marchauntes. **1530** PALSGR. 510/1, I delaye one, or deferre hym, or put hym backe of his purpose. **1639** DU VERGER tr. *Camus' Admir. Events* 88 It was not fit shee should delay him with faire wordes. **1768** BLACKSTONE *Comm.* III. 109 Where judges of any court do delay the parties.

2. To impede the progress of, cause to linger or stand still; to retard, hinder.

1393 GOWER *Conf.* III. 261 Her wo to telle thanne assaieth, But tendre shame her word delaieth. **1634** MILTON *Comus* 494 Thyrsis! whose artful strains have oft delayed The huddling brook to hear his madrigal. **1709** STEELE *Tatler* No. 39 ⁋ 4 Joy and Grief can hasten and delay Time. **1813** SHELLEY *Q. Mab* II. 197 The unwilling sojourner, whose steps Chance in that desert has delayed. **1856** KANE *Arct. Expl.* II. xv. 161 To delay the animal until the hunters come up.

3. *intr.* To put off action; to linger, loiter, tarry.

1509 HAWES *Past. Pleas.* xvi. lxix, A womans guyse is evermore to delaye. **1596** SHAKS. *1 Hen. IV*, III. ii. 180 Aduantage feedes him fat, while men delay. **1667** MILTON *P. L.* V. 247 So spake th' Eternal Father .. nor delaid the winged Saint After his charge receivd. **1850** TENNYSON *In Mem.* lxxxiii, O sweet new-year delaying long .. Delaying long, delay no more.

b. To tarry in a place. (Now only *poetic*.)

1654 H. L'ESTRANGE *Chas. I* (1655) 3 Paris being .. in his way to Spain, he delaid there one day. *a* **1878** BRYANT *Poems, October*, Wind of the sunny south! oh still delay, In the gay woods and in the golden air.

c. To be tardy in one's progress, to loiter.

1690 LOCKE *Hum. Und.* II. xiv. § 9 There seem to be certain bounds to the quickness and slowness of the succession of those ideas .. beyond which they can neither delay nor hasten.

any writer—it is by far the most useful. Keep one on your desk, and use it.

CONNOTATION

Connotation and Denotation

The meaning of a word has two aspects, denotative and connotative. A word's denotation is what it literally means, as defined by the dictionary; its connotation is the associations it evokes. These associations may be of several types. Some are simply echoes of one of the word's other established meanings: it is for this reason that the Tenth Commandment's injunction not to covet our neighbor's ass evokes snickers today. Others are historical associations: *escalate,* for example, formerly a neutral word coined to describe the motion of an escalator, took on connotations of planned violence with its application by journalists and others to American policy in Vietnam. Still others are social: thus *square,* in the sense of a person seen as offensively conventional, carries a connotation of rejection by the young.

The meaning of connotation may be illustrated by contrasting two sentences from the same paragraph of *Education at Berkeley,* the report of a faculty committee issued following the first student disturbances at the University of California:

> The search for genuine experience leads also to experimenting with non-addictive hallucinatory drugs.

> This desire for instant poetry, instant psychoanalysis, and instant mysticism is a further form of escape from hard work.

The first sentence is standard expository prose; its words mean what the dictionary says they mean. In the second something quite different is going on. Not only is *instant* a surprising modifier of activities that we normally think of as contemplative and introspective, but it calls to mind instant coffee, instant cake frosting, and other such ersatz offerings of the modern supermarket. By modifying *poetry, psychoanalysis,* and *mysticism* with a word that not only denotes an unsuitable speed but connotes a doubtful level of quality, the authors are denigrating the students' views; they are saying that these spoiled kids want to know life's greatest experiences with no more work or waiting than it takes to warm up a TV dinner. The connotations of *instant* in this sentence carry almost the whole burden of the authors' critical intent.

Thus, by astute manipulation, a new combination of words creates a new idea, a new impression, a new meaning. Human experience and history and literature are always doing this to words. *Collaborator,* from *co-* (with) and *labor* (work), once meant simply one who worked together with someone else; later the word came to be restricted largely to literary work, and still later it acquired the unpatriotic connotation of working willingly with one's country's enemies. Thanks in part, perhaps, to the Women's Christian Temperance Union, *temperance,* which once meant nothing more than moderation in speech and conduct, has come to connote not only abstinence from liquor but an offensively high-minded moral strictness.

Euphemism is another force for change, especially when it comes to unglamorous or undignified jobs. Dogcatchers in some New Jersey towns have rebaptized themselves *animal custodians*; writers and editors of technical matter in the aerospace industry are commonly called *publications engineers*; and Gowers reports an English butcher with a sign reading *Meat Technologist. Undertaker,* which originally meant nothing more than one who undertakes an assignment, came by euphemism to mean one who prepares the dead for burial; after acquiring negative connotations from this association, it was discarded by sensitive American undertakers in favor of the tonier *mortician,* which in turn acquired the same connotations as *undertaker* (not to mention the scorn normally accorded transparent euphemisms by outsiders) and has subsequently been replaced by *funeral director. Employment* itself, once a euphemism for job or work, has apparently become a dirty word in California, where the former Department of Employment has been renamed the Department of Human Resources Development.

Many euphemisms never achieve public recognition, let alone dictionary status; our meat technologist, for example, presumably found no imitators, and the world seems equally resistant to recent efforts by American advertisers to substitute *bathroom paper* for toilet paper and *motion discomfort* for airsickness. Others go on to lose their euphemistic connotations and become fully accepted in their new sense. Thus *mistress,* once a euphemism for paramour or concubine, is now the customary word for a woman having an affair with a married man; *liquidation,* since being used by Hitler and Stalin as a euphemism for murder, carries this meaning along with its others; and *senior citizen* as a euphemism for old person, despite widespread denunciation by citizens senior and junior, is accepted by most dictionaries as Standard.

Connotation and the Dictionary

Time and accident corrode words, change them, encrust them with connotations. The dictionary sometimes spells these connotations out, either by adding them as new denotations ("**square** . . . 8:** a person rejected for conventionality or respectability"), or by adding qualifying phrases to existing denotations ("**collaborate 1:** to work jointly with others esp. in an intellectual endeavor"), or by labeling a word slang, substandard, archaic, or what have you.

More often, however, the dictionary is no help. *Webster's Seventh,* for example, gives no hint that the second meaning of *suggestive* ("tending to suggest something improper or indecent") has all but routed the first and neutral meaning ("giving a suggestion," "full of suggestions"); and it does not even mention the heavy sexual connotations acquired in recent decades by *provocative.* Its definition of *gamesmanship,* "the art of winning games by doubtful expedients without actually violating the rules," gives no idea of the sardonic, post-Christian, under-the-Bomb connotations of this word and such allied compounds as *brinkmanship* and *one-upmanship.* When it comes to new words and new combinations and uses of old words, the ponderous process of lexicography is no match for the lightning leaps of the language. The best and most recent dictionary can scarcely keep abreast of denotation, let alone of connotation.

Though the dictionary can sometimes help, then, the main burden of getting connotations straight falls squarely on the writer's experience and observation. No advice is possible or necessary here except to keep your eyes and ears open. If you don't know exactly what a word means but think it may give offense, you presumably refrain from using it in a conversation with your girl friend's mother. Do the same in your writing. Try to use only words whose connotations you feel confident you understand. If you are moved to use other words as well—and of course you will be and should be—see who else is using them and how they are being used, in conversation, in lectures, in what you read. There is no need to use them in writing until you have made them your own.

THE CHOICE OF WORDS: STATUS

Standard and Non-Standard English

One of the most important aspects of connotation is status. A word's status has no necessary connection with its meaning: there are "respectable" words for nonrespectable things, and nonrespectable words for respectable things. For example, in the sentence *I was snowed,* the word *snowed* has the perfectly respectable meaning "overwhelmed," perhaps by someone's good looks or suave approach. And yet the connotations of *snowed* make it less than perfectly respectable; it is a teen-age word, suitable for casual teen-age conversation or a letter to a friend but too colloquial for formal writing. *Overwhelmed* has the opposite connotation; one rarely hears the word spoken, but it is acceptable in formal use as *snowed* is not. One word is acceptable spoken English, at least for teen-agers; the other is acceptable written English.

How do such distinctions come about, and what are we to make of them? They come about naturally rather than artificially. New words are introduced into the language to denote new things, new ideas, new shades of meaning; and immediately people face a choice between the new word and whatever word or phrase was used to express roughly the same idea before. Some new words are accepted immediately: *television* is an example. Others are accepted after a brief struggle with an existing equivalent (*radio* versus *wireless*) or with an alternative new word or form (*automation* versus *automatization*). Still others spend years in colloquial status before they win formal acceptance: the word *swamped,* in the sense "overwhelmed with work," ran this course many decades ago. Finally, some words—for example, the names of such ephemeral dances as the *frug* and the *watusi*— never rise beyond colloquial status and ultimately drop from the language altogether.

At any given time, then, the language consists broadly of two kinds of words, those acceptable for formal use and those acceptable for informal use only, plus a borderland of words on probation. By formal use we mean primarily serious expository writing, though the term extends to public speaking, business letters, conversations with eminent men, and so on. Whether a word is acceptable or unacceptable for formal use is determined by a consensus of educated persons, as evidenced in what they write and read. Formerly, dictionaries signaled this consensus by status labels: Standard English was unmarked; non-Standard was marked *colloq., slang,* or the like, or left out of the dictionary as trivial, ephemeral, or vulgar. *Webster's Third* (1961) startled everyone by omitting these labels as too crude to capture the complexities of usage and too vulnerable to unpredictable changes in our language habits. But people wanted status labels despite these irrefutable arguments against them, and more recent dictionaries, notably the *American Heritage Dictionary* (1969), have not followed Webster's lead.

Non-Standard English as subdivided by *American Heritage* embraces four main status categories: NON-STANDARD, chiefly well-established errors like *disinterested* for *uninterested* and rusticisms like *anyways* and *ain't*; INFORMAL, words used in "the speech of educated persons when they are more interested in what they are saying than how they are saying it," e.g. *mad* for angry, *gripe* for complain; SLANG, words designed "to produce rhetorical effect, such as incongruity, irreverence, or exaggeration," e.g. *junkie* for heroin addict, *broad* for woman; and VULGAR, words like *shit* and *fuck*. All words in the first category can be dismissed as unacceptable in writing, except of course in dialogue, with which we are not concerned here. The other three categories are discussed at greater length in the following pages.

Contractions

Most authorities recommend not using contractions in writing except in dialogue. Where you would say *won't* or *I've*, they recommend writing *will not* and *I have*. We agree in general but make one important exception, to wit, where the full form sounds stilted we prefer the contraction: *They don't make cars the way they used to / Sometimes you just can't win / Let's face it.*

Abbreviations

The abbreviations *Mr.*, *Mrs.*, and *Dr.*, and the very recent form *Ms.*, are Standard preceding a name; do not spell out *Doctor*. Abbreviations and acronyms (*IBM, GHQ, UNESCO*) may be used in formal writing if three conditions are observed. First, make sure your readers know what they stand for, since abbreviations familiar to you may be Greek to others. When in doubt, spell things out the first time: *gross national product (GNP)*. Second, keep the incidence of abbreviations as low as you can, since pages bespattered with clusters of capital letters are uninviting. Write *United States* or *American* rather than *U.S.*, and *Soviet Union* rather than *U.S.S.R.* Write *electrocardiogram* rather than *EKG*; and before using *ICBM* for a second time, see whether plain *missile* will serve. Third, avoid headlinese. *LBJ* for *Lyndon B. Johnson, GOP* (Grand Old Party) for *Republican,* and *GM* for *General Motors,* however indispensable to headline writers, have no place in formal expository writing; the same goes for common-noun abbreviations like *P.O.* for *post office* and *TV* for *television.*

Shortenings and Simplified Spellings

"Shortenings" is the term used in Wilson Follett's *Modern American Usage* for words like *quote* (for *quotation*), *recap* (for *recapitulate* or *recapitulation*), *photo, exam, psycho, grad, lab,* and *prof,* all of which Follett properly considers unsuitable for formal writing. Some shortenings have become Standard; we no longer think of *bus* as short for *omnibus, coonskin* for *raccoon skin,* or *taxicab* for *taximeter cabriolet.* Those that have not become Standard should be avoided.

Another form of shortening is simplified spelling. Spelling reformers from the time of George Bernard Shaw and Theodore Roosevelt to the present day have affected such simplified spellings as *tho* and *thru;* advertisers have offered us *lo-cal* and *lo-fat* food and *u-haul* trailers; restaurants serve *donuts, ham 'n' eggs,* and *leg o' lamb;* teen-age girls fill their letters and diaries with *'cause, alrite,* and *tonite.* What slight appeal these forms may have soon wears thin; only a few, e.g. *rock 'n' roll* and *hi-fi,* have become Standard.

Clichés and Vogue Words

Clichés are commonly stale metaphors (see p. 124); vogue words are words or short phrases that have achieved prominence from their association with a public event or pronouncement, their conspicuous use by some arbiter of taste, or their capacity for solving certain problems faced by large numbers of speakers or writers, notably how to sound impressive at the least expense of time and thought. Some characteristic vogue words of the past twenty years are the low-level metaphors *framework* and *ceiling* and the noun-derived verbs *fault, trigger,* and *structure.* Both clichés and vogue words are typically Standard so far as denotation is concerned; their connotations are what make their status questionable.

A few vogue words go on to become permanent parts of the language in their vogue sense, but most soon lose whatever aptness may have initially commended them and linger on as clichés, overused by the hasty and misused by the uninformed. Everyone uses some vogue words, but good writers keep the number small by their habit of scrutinizing all but the simplest of the words they use for wrong connotations or shades of meaning. Must this reconsideration, they ask, be called an *agonizing reappraisal,* this family quarrel attributed to the *generation gap,* this rise in costs or productivity described as *escalation?* Hasn't the time come to give up *ceiling* and go back to *upper limit,* to give up *fault* and go back to *find fault with?*

There are vogue suffixes as well as vogue words, notably in

recent years *-ize, -type,* and *-wise.* Some words in *-ize* are clearly here to stay: *winterize, Americanize, tranquilize.* Others—among them *finalize, personalize,* and *slenderize*—have been accepted by Webster but are not used in formal writing by most educated people. Still others—*concertize, accessorize, moisturize*—are as yet too much even for Webster. A good rule for formal writing is to use only such words in this suffix as have no ready equivalent, and to coin no new ones.

As for *-type,* in such expressions as *hose-type apparatus* and *California-type sunglasses,* it should be restricted to dealer's catalogues, parts lists, the patois of supply sergeants and commercial travelers, and jocular evocations of the preceding. Good writers shun the construction as vulgar; bad ones embrace it as a way of sounding authoritative without the labor of fully articulating their meaning. The reckless addition of *-wise* to nouns to form adverbs (*saleswise, percentagewise, footballwise*) is a comparable affectation of the slovenly and the tin-eared, in whose keeping it may safely be left.

Slang and Vulgar Words

Whether out of in-group solidarity or from genuine inability to think of Standard equivalents, student writers often pepper their themes with current slang like *uptight* for antagonistic or conservative, *rip off* for rob or steal, and *out of sight* for wonderful. The effect is not so much vigorous as noisy and shallow. These are vogue words as surely as the kind just discussed—as ephemeral in their power to differentiate, as drearily indicative of a stereotyped world view, as prone to becoming clichés. Just as a word like *finalize* signals the routine-bound bureaucrat or Army officer, so a word like .*dig* for comprehend or enjoy signals the perennial sixteen-year-old.

An occasional well-chosen slang expression is all right, especially if no Standard equivalent comes to mind; but a lot of slang, like a lot of any other kind of cliché, is a sign that the writer's mind is not on his work. Use slang in speaking with your friends; everyone does. Use it if you like in your notes to yourself, as the writer of the research paper discussed in Chapter 13 and 14 used *pot* for *marijuana* on his note cards. But when you are performing for a serious audience, put away your tin piano and use the Steinway.

Vulgar words do not shock; they bore. Used well in dialogue, as in certain modern movies, they are indispensable in evoking character, and we may all rejoice that the former ban on their use in the arts no longer exists. But they have no place in expository prose, being at once overemphatic and maddeningly vague. What is meant by *The Chancellor's so-called "program" is a lot of liberal bullshit?* The writer clearly disapproves of the program, but we have not the foggiest notion why; what is worse, we get the impression that he himself cannot explain why and is raising his voice to hide his confusion.

Terms designedly offensive to a given race, sex, occupation, or other large class of people should also be avoided. No college student today would write *nigger* or *wop* as a simple synonym for Negro or Italian, but an astonishing number of students see nothing wrong with writing *queer* for homosexual or *pig* for policeman. *A visible tension built up between the pigs and the demonstrators,* writes a Japanese-American girl who sympathized with the demonstrators. But are policemen any more *pigs* than she is a *broad* or a *gook?* Disparaging terms like *pig* not only assert a doubtful claim to ethical superiority but implausibly impute evil characteristics to a whole class of which the writer can know at most a few members. Some writers seemingly use such terms to make it clear that they are on the side of the angels. If so, they have a different notion of angels from ours.

Status and the Dictionary

Dictionaries like *Webster's Third International* and *Webster's Seventh Collegiate,* which keep status labels to a minimum, offer a writer little help in distinguishing Standard from non-Standard. They omit vulgar words and label blatant slang, but offer no clue that a sentence like *Nixon's yapping about commies drives me nuts,* which no English teacher in the United States would accept, is other than impeccable English.

Dictionaries with status labels are more helpful. To take the sentence just cited, for example, the *American Heritage Dictionary* labels *yap* and *nuts* slang and *commie* informal. Yet the use of such labels raises almost as many questions as it answers. How, for example, did *American Heritage* draw the thin line between *booze, cop,* and *snappy* (informal) and *hooch, dick,* and *spiffy* (slang)? On what conceivable basis do they proclaim *schnook* Standard and *schlemiel* slang? *Nigger* vulgar, *dago* slang, and *yid* Standard? *Get away with* informal and *get by with* Standard? *Bite the dust* Standard and *kick the bucket* slang?

Sentences every bit as bad as our Webster example would be accepted as Standard by *American Heritage* definitions: for example, *The Indians laughed when that schnook Custer bit the dust* and *The D.A. put the screws to the chintzy bugger.* And what is more, seemingly irreproachable sentences are relegated by *American Heritage* definitions to "informal," i.e. non-Standard, status. *Whenever Harvey took her out, they went to the movies* is such a sentence; *You can rarely get away with shortchanging people* is another. If these sentences are non-Standard, the moon is made of green cheese.

Maybe *American Heritage* is just a poor dictionary, but we think not. The main problem, as noted above, is that dictionaries simply cannot keep up with the language: one looks in vain, for example, in the standard dictionaries of the early 1970's for *split* in the sense of departing in a hurry or *freak* as in *freak out* or *speed freak.* Nor can a dictionary label vogue words or other words whose use is essentially a matter of taste. *American Heritage* makes a game try with its "usage notes" (see example), the result of a questionnaire sent to a panel of 104 prominent writers, educators, and other public figures. But in a dictionary

---

Usage: O.K. (or *OK*) is especially appropriate to business correspondence and informal speech and writing, and usually inappropriate to expressly formal usage. In the following examples of general written usage, distinguished from the aforementioned, *O.K.* is termed most acceptable by the Usage Panel when employed as a noun (*his O.K. is considered a formality,* acceptable to 57 per cent) or as a verb (*to O.K. an arrangement,* acceptable to 42 per cent). As a predicate adjective (*all is not O.K. in their relationship*), it is acceptable to only 23 per cent, and as an adverb (*the radio was working O.K.*) to only 20 per cent. Many Panel members term *O.K.* acceptable in speech generally, however.

From *The American Heritage Dictionary of the English Language.* Copyright © 1969, 1970, 1971 by the American Heritage Co., Inc.

of some 75,000 entries only a few hundred at most can be discussed at this level of subtlety, and even for this few hundred a 1968 consensus may well be useless by 1972 or 1980. Yesterday's illiteracy (*presently* for *now*), yesterday's genteelism (*perspire* for *sweat*), yesterday's slang (*gobbledygook, joy ride, hippie*), is today's Standard. Who can doubt that some of today's non-Standard words will be Standard tomorrow?

In the end, the writer must choose. Even the distinction between Standard and non-Standard, important as it is, should not be made too much of. Vigorous writing has the accents and rhythms of speech; it should have, so far as possible, the words natural to speech. Slangy writing has its faults, but so has the other extreme: if the student who writes *I freaked out* offends the dignity of the reader, the student who writes *My reaction was intense to the point of excess* achieves an empty dignity at the expense of vigor.

We do not mean that you should simply define as Standard whatever words you feel comfortable with. If you feel that a certain non-Standard word *ought* to be Standard, that only stuffy people are against it, you may be right, and ultimately your opinion may help to form the subtle consensus that changes a word's status. But until that time proceed with caution. A distinction between words is like a statutory distinction: it may be unjust or obsolete, its repeal may be imminent, but while it is on the books a prudent person will not ignore it.

THE CHOICE OF WORDS: IDIOM

Idiomatic and Unidiomatic English

Idiomatic English is English as reasonably well-educated native speakers speak it. Unidiomatic English, by contrast, not only rings oddly in the ear, but also, by virtue of its departure from the familiar, unnecessarily taxes the understanding. Small departures from idiom may go unnoticed, especially if they are few. Large departures, or small ones in large numbers, make for the hardest kind of reading. Unidiomatic language is sometimes colorful—the authors cherish a Korean student's sentence, *He just like a monkey, he up and down the tree*—but in expository prose any pleasure it may give is soon lost in the effort to understand what is being said.

Native speakers of English have far less trouble writing idiomatically than foreigners who learn English as a second language. We do not have to learn, for example, when to say *the* and when to omit it in everyday expressions: we learn as children that people go *to the* movies but go *to* church, that people watch television but listen to *the* radio. There is no rational basis for these distinctions, just as there is no reason why an expression like *the heat of the battle* should have vanquished *the ardor of the combat* or *the passion of the struggle.* The language has simply come in the course of time to favor one form over another. The efficiency of this process is its own excuse. By learning the idiomatic forms of the more common expressions as children, we clear our minds of the many thousands of rejected alternatives with which the uncertain foreigner must grapple.

The difficulty comes with the less common expressions. Everyone knows that we say *bad weather* rather than *ill weather,* but should we say *bad omen* or *ill omen, bad tidings* or *ill tidings, bad health* or *ill health*? Should we describe Grandma as *kind, kindhearted,* or *kindly*? Does one *make, take,* or *reach* a decision? Does one differ *with* or *from* someone, and is one's view then different *from* or *than* his? More than one of these alternatives may be acceptable. What is important is not so much to find "correct" answers to questions of this sort as to ask the questions in the first place—that is, to have some sense of the alternatives and not settle for a lazy first stab.

The following sentences illustrate only a few of the many possible kinds of errors in idiom (corrections in parentheses):

Rousseau's argument was the opposite to Hobbes's. (*of*)

The need of action should have been apparent. (*need for;* or *necessity of*)

When we finished sweeping the sidewalk, we considered the job as done. (*considered the job done;* or *regarded the job as done*)

Most importantly of all, the Giants' shortstop was ill. (*important*)

She confessed to have seen neither accident. (*to having seen*)

The Tonkin Gulf Resolution made a mountain of a molehill. (*out of*)

Trivial as such errors are, they are irritating, and they are also hard to avoid. The only defense against them is attention. Read a sentence over. If it sounds wrong, even though you cannot say exactly how, switch to a more manageable construction. For example, if you are uneasy with both *opposite to* and *opposite of* in the first sentence, try *Rousseau and Hobbes presented opposite arguments*; if you are not sure what is wrong with *confessed to have seen*, try *confessed that she had seen*. No one alive has a complete mastery of English idiom at the *opposite to / of / from* level.[1] It is plain common sense to stick as much as possible to constructions that you know are idiomatic.

For more subtle questions of word choice—for example, between *kind* and *kindly*, between *informer* and *informant,* between *evoke, extract,* and *elicit*—the dictionary is often helpful, especially in its comparisons of near-synonyms, as given, for example, in the entry for *delay* discussed earlier in this chapter. Another useful book is a thesaurus, which gives synonyms and near-synonyms for all the most common nouns, verbs, adjectives, and adverbs. If you cannot think of precisely the right word but can think of a word meaning roughly the same thing, a thesaurus will probably lead you to the word you want.

A number of idiom questions that trouble students are discussed in the Index to Current Usage, pp. 266–308. In the rest of this section we shall consider the three idiom problems that in our experience, apart from the choice of prepositions, lead to the most errors in student writing: (1) choosing the idiomatic form of an adverb having two forms, (2) forming the comparative and the superlative correctly, and (3) using *the* properly before abstract nouns followed by *of.*

---

[1] If you want to be the first, the place to start is with Frederick T. Wood's *English Prepositional Idioms* (New York, 1967), which runs to 562 tightly packed pages.

Adverbs with Two Forms

Some adverbs have two forms, one ending in *-ly,* the other indistinguishable from the adjective form. This causes no problems when the two forms have radically different meanings, as with *hard/hardly* and *late/lately*; probably no one would write *turned down coldly* (in a cold manner) for *turned down cold* (totally). The difficulty comes when the two forms have essentially the same meaning, as in these examples:

Two days' supplies were lashed (*tight*) (*tightly*) to the mast.

The doctor told me to go (*slow*) (*slowly*) for a while.

We always travel (*light*) (*lightly*).

Butkus talked (*tough*) (*toughly*) but sensitively.

In the first two sentences either choice will serve, though in the second *go slow* is probably more idiomatic for this meaning (compare *go easy*). In the third sentence, *travel light* is a cast-iron idiom and *light* is accordingly the only possible word. The fourth sentence offers a Hobson's choice: *talked tough* is the established idiom, but *toughly* goes better with *sensitively*. The best solution here, as for all Hobson's choices, is to reword: *Butkus's remarks were tough but sensitive,* or what have you.

When both forms seem equally idiomatic, try looking them up in your dictionary, remembering that your concern is only with the *adv.* entries. If the dictionary doesn't help, either form is probably acceptable. The one thing not to do is reason that since you need an adverb and the *-ly* form is indisputably an adverb, that form is automatically preferable. This kind of reasoning yields unidiomatic English like *The car stopped shortly,* or even, from a student paper, *The honors came thickly and fast.*

Comparative and Superlative

Almost all adjectives and adverbs of one syllable form the comparative and the superlative in *-er* and *-est* rather than by adding *more* and *most.* Almost all adjectives and adverbs of three or more syllables take the *more* and *most* forms only; and the exceptions (*ignoble, unlikely,* and other negative forms of two-syllable adjectives taking *-er* and *-est*) can go either way. The problem accordingly comes down to two-syllable adjectives and adverbs. Of these, adverbs formed by adding *-ly* to adjectives invariably take *more* and *most*; the rest vary according to the whims of the idiom. We can write *earlier, narrower, oftener,* but not *earnester, suddener, distraughter*; we can write *commonest, cleverest, pleasantest,* but not *preciousest, carefreest, bizarrest.* How is one to know when to use *-er* and *-est,* when *more* and *most*?

The best answer is to consult a good unabridged dictionary. Webster's Third, for example, lists -ER/-EST after every word capable of taking these endings, and gives full forms where an *e* is swallowed (*later, freest*), where a consonant is doubled (*bigger, reddest*), where the comparative and superlative are irregular (*well, better, best; little, less, least*), and where the suffix form is not clearly dominant (thus ancient is "*often* -ER/ -EST" and *careful* is "*sometimes* CAREFULLER . . . CAREFULLEST"). Collegiate dictionaries tend to be less useful this way. *Webster's Seventh,* for example, makes no distinction between *quiet,* which can take *-er/-est,* and *constant,* which cannot, and states no preference between *yellower* and *more yellow.* Students who do not have easy access to an unabridged dictionary will have to rely on their ear in such matters, when in doubt using *more* or *most.*

Omission of The

The unidiomatic omission of *the* before abstract nouns followed by *of* is a development of the past forty years or so, and to our mind a deplorable one. Instead of *The discussion of politics was dangerous,* we now often find the truncated *Discussion of politics was dangerous*; instead of *Meyers opposed the extension of the draft,* we find *Meyers opposed extension of the draft.* Headline writing, with its premium on saving space, may be partly responsible, along with a mistaken notion, perhaps derived from a superficial analysis of Ernest Hemingway's style, that dropping articles, prepositions, and conjunctions automatically makes writing more forceful. Whatever its causes, this practice yields a kind of pidgin English that grates on the sensitive reader's ear. To the writer there can be only this advice: do not drop *the* casually, and when in doubt retain it.

A special case of this difficulty occurs in course names and the names of academic disciplines. Here one must distinguish between formal course and department names, which need not take *the*, and the names of subjects or lines of study. The following sentences, all of them correct, illustrate the distinction:

> Jane did especially well in Theory of Complex Numbers. (*course name*)
>
> Jane took several courses in *the* theory of complex numbers. (*subject*)
>
> He has a joint appointment in History and History of Art. (*department names*)
>
> At Yale *the* history of art is taught by a separate department. (*subject*)

When the subject and the department name are indistinguishable, add *the* and lowercase: *I am majoring in the history of art.*

THE CHOICE OF WORDS: PRECISION

In *Plain Words* (1954), Sir Ernest Gowers gives the three basic rules of good writing as follows:

> Use no more words than are necessary to express your meaning, for if you use more you are likely to obscure it and to tire your reader. In particular do not use superfluous adjectives and adverbs and do not use roundabout phrases where single words would serve.
>
> Use familiar words rather than the far-fetched, if they express your meaning equally well; for the familiar are more likely to be readily understood.
>
> Use words with a precise meaning rather than those that are vague, for they will obviously serve better to make your

meaning clear; and in particular prefer concrete words to abstract, for they are more likely to have a precise meaning.

The first of these rules, which has little to do with the choice of words as such, we have discussed elsewhere (pp. 80–82 and 137–140). The second, which had as its target a once numerous class of writers who used ornate words like *septentrional* and foreign expressions like *tête-à-tête* in preference to their plain English equivalents, need not detain us. The third, however, to "use words with a precise meaning rather than those that are vague," is as good advice to American students today as it was to the British bureaucrats of Gowers's time. Consider the following sentences:

The authorities took favorable action on the proposal.

Our whole program will be affected if any further difficulties develop.

The situation required Engel to seek financial help.

What have we been told? Vague, abstract words like *authorities, affected, develop,* and *situation* do not clarify meaning but obscure it. To some writers—notably those who are trying to deceive their readers, to sell them something, or to allay their anger —obscurity may have its uses. But to the honest writer there is no substitute for the precise word and the necessary detail. If *the situation* can be described, describe it. If *difficulties* means a cement workers' strike, or the likelihood of a riot, or too little money, say so. A certain decorum is conventionally observed in sex and bathroom matters; but these aside, your duty as a writer of expository prose is to say as well as you can exactly what you mean.

Be on the lookout especially for the colorless but insidious three- or four-word phrase that has elbowed out a perfectly good single word or shorter phrase of the same meaning: *climate of opinion* for *opinion; put within the framework of* for *relate to; in this day and age* for *today.* George Orwell, in his splendid essay "Politics and the English Language," is succinct on this point: "Prose consists less and less of *words* chosen for the sake of their meaning, and more and more of *phrases* tacked together like the sections of a prefabricated hen-house." He goes on:

> A scrupulous writer, in every sentence that he writes, will ask himself . . . Could I put it more shortly? Have I said anything that is avoidably ugly? But you are not obliged to go to all this trouble. You can shirk it by simply throwing your mind open and letting the ready-made phrases come crowding in. They will construct your sentences for you—even think your thoughts for you, to a certain extent—and at need they will perform the important service of concealing your meaning even from yourself.

In the end, we are back to brevity. To write effectively you must make every word count: not be abstract when concreteness is required, and not use three words where one or two will serve as well. The French philosopher Pascal once apologized to a correspondent for writing him so long a letter. "This letter is so long," he wrote, "because I have not had time to make it shorter." What he meant is plain: that to make one's meaning clear, time spent in pruning excess words and puncturing gassy ones is time well spent.

In the last three sections we have discussed the three main considerations affecting the choice of words: status, idiom, and precision. A word like *hangup* may be precise and idiomatic in context, but is unacceptable on status grounds. A word like *badly* is Standard and may be precise enough, but is unidiomatic after *feel*. A word like *modernization* is Standard and idiomatic, but may be insufficiently precise. Of the three qualities, the most important is precision. Making your meaning clear comes before writing idiomatically and using words of irreproachable status—provided, of course, you are not so unidiomatic or slangy that your meaning never gets through. If you have built your hen-house right, people will not worry much about an occasional flaw in the paint job.

7
IMAGERY

The comedian Shelley Berman once described a hangover in these terms: "My left eyeball has a headache, my tongue's asleep, and my teeth itch." The effect of this sentence depends upon images, in this case bizarre images. By attributing familiar sensations to unlikely parts of the body, Berman obtains some surprising effects. He not only makes us laugh, he gives us a new sensory experience (or the memory of an old one); we are not just told about the hangover, we feel it. Our response to this image is not the same as the actual physical experience, any more than grief felt in reading a story is the same as real grief; but it is a good approximation of reality. In imagination, we have had a hangover.

Images can do such things. They invite us into experience; they do not keep us at a distance, as mere definitions or explanations often do. They communicate the sounds, tastes, smells, sights, colors, and tactile feelings of life. Images are not just figures of speech, though they usually appear in this form; they are all those means whereby sensory experience is conveyed in language. Our senses do not report to us on "justice" or "beauty" or "the gross national product"; these abstract concepts are derived from thought, from ratiocination, rather than from direct experience. Images tell us about the smell of a flower, the beauty of a woman, the sound of music, the fear of death. They refer to that immediacy of experience where we live and move and have our being.

This is not to say that imagery is unconnected with abstract thought; on the contrary, it is often the best possible way to make difficult abstractions clear, especially to a lay audience. Thus an atomic physicist will say: "Just as a coal fire needs oxygen to keep it going, a nuclear fire needs the neutrons to maintain it." A biologist explaining spectroscopy to lay readers: "Just as in a crystal chandelier the sunlight is shattered to a rainbow, so in the spectroscope light is spread out in colored bands." A political analyst: "It is as sensible to combat communism by military means as to combat malaria by swatting mosquitoes." A great poet and moralist: "No man is an island entire of itself; every man is a piece of the continent, a part of the main."

The greatest of all English poets, seeking to convey the patriotism of the venerable John of Gaunt in *Richard II*, does so almost entirely in images. Gaunt, near death, speaks of the country he loves:

> This royal throne of kings, this scepter'd isle,
> This earth of majesty, this seat of Mars,
> This other Eden, demi-Paradise;
> This fortress built by Nature for herself
> Against infection and the hand of war;
> This happy breed of men, this little world;
> This precious stone set in the silver sea,
> Which serves it in the office of a wall,
> Or as a moat defensive to a house,
> Against the envy of less happier lands;
> This blessed plot, this earth, this realm, this England.

COMPARISON AND ANALOGY

Definition and Examples

Imagery evokes comparisons, implied or explicit. "He wormed his way into her good graces" sets up an implicit comparison between a man's insinuating tactics and the movement of a worm. "The batter fanned" compares the batter's futile swing to the motion of a fan, which touches only air. And so it is with the salesman's *broad-brush* categories, the data that are *fed in* to a computer, the ship that *plows* the sea, the market that *nosedives*, the housewife who is *snowed under*, the business that stays *above water*, the effort that gets *sandbagged*, the timid man who is *cowed*. All evoke comparisons with familiar acts or things.

It is useful here to distinguish between analogy and true comparison. "That man is a rat" is an analogy; "Hitler was a greater tyrant than Mussolini" is a comparison. In the first, two dissimilar things, a man and an animal, are being compared; in the second, two men are being compared. Analogies ask our emotional assent to similarities between two wholes: a man and a rat, war and hell, property and theft. Comparisons ask our intellectual attention to literal and particular similarities or differences. If I compare John F. Kennedy and Richard Nixon as statesmen, I will compare specific and parallel aspects of their statesmanship, such as their success in handling international affairs or in protecting civil liberties. But when Shakespeare asks in a sonnet "Shall I compare thee to a summer's day?" he has no literal or intellectual comparison in mind: to compliment his lady he wants us to think of the beauty, warmth, and luxuriance of summer, and to ignore the mosquitoes and the sunburn. The poet asks our indulgence and we grant it.

Analogies that are just and fresh not only delight but clarify, emphasize, instruct—even win arguments. The best are unanswerable. Mrs. Thrale once remarked to Samuel Johnson that a certain young woman would be terribly unhappy to hear of a friend's losing an estate she had long expected to receive. "She will suffer as much, perhaps," replied Dr. Johnson, "as your horse did when your cow miscarried." Montaigne quotes the witty reply of a Roman Stoic who was asked why Stoics sometimes became Epicureans out Epicureans never Stoics: "Plenty of capons are made out of cocks, but cocks are never made out of capons."

Misuses of Analogy

But analogy can be as tricky as it is useful. The Vietnam War, for example, was at one time widely justified by the so-called domino theory, which held that unless Chinese expansionism were stopped in Vietnam, the other countries of Southeast Asia would fall to the Communists like a row of standing dominoes when the first one is knocked into the second. "Domino theory" is a striking phrase, simple and visual; it reduces a most complex issue to terms a child can understand. But is the analogy true? Are nations really comparable to dominoes? Will they fall in the same mechanical way when pushed? Why didn't England fall like a domino before German pressure in 1940? If the analogy is false, the argument is false.

Does this matter? It depends on how the analogy is used. Literal truth is not always an issue. Shakespeare's sonnet is no less effective for the omission of mosquitoes, Dr. Johnson's remark no less compelling for his ignorance of the lady's true thoughts. A lawyer can be an "ambulance chaser"—that is, someone who makes capital of other people's disasters—without having ever chased an ambulance. And who cares if the man who defined a camel as "a horse designed by a committee" was harder on committees than they deserve?

The trouble comes when an analogy is presented as part of a logical argument, as the domino theory often was in the 1960's. If you use an analogy this way, as a building stone in a larger argument, you forgo the poet's right to indulgence; the analogy must be demonstrably sound on all relevant points, the stone able to bear the weight you put on it. Many faulty analogies pass for true, usually by suggesting that their two elements are literally comparable when they are not. Uncle Harry may be a rat, but it does not follow that he can live on an ounce of cheese a day. The only defense against this sort of thinking is the kind of dogged scrutiny illustrated in the following argument, where Julian Huxley is examining the assertion that God rules the universe:

> I believe this fundamental postulate to be nothing more than the result of asking a wrong question: "Who or what rules the universe?" So far we can see, it rules itself, and indeed the whole analogy with a country and its ruler is false. Even if a god does exist behind or above the universe as we experience it, we can have no knowledge of such a power; the actual gods of historical religions are only the personifica-

tions of impersonal facts of nature and of facts of our inner mental life.

SIMILE AND METAPHOR

Simile

Most figures of speech, and most of the examples given so far in this chapter, are either similes or metaphors. On a superficial level it is easy to disinguish between these two categories. A simile is an explicit comparison or analogy using *like, as, compared with,* or the equivalent. Here are some examples:

The gray chill seeped into him like water into sand.
WILLIAM FAULKNER

Almost without exception, the men with whom I worked on the assembly line . . . felt like trapped animals.
HARVEY SWADOS

Yet, when the mind looks out for the first time into this manifold spiritual world, it is just as much confused and dazzled and distracted as are the eyes of the blind when they first begin to see.
CARDINAL NEWMAN

She plays bridge with the stupid voracity of a hammerhead shark.
PHILIP WYLIE

The female body, even at its best, is very defective in form; it has harsh curves and very clumsily distributed masses; compared to it the average milk-jug, or even cuspidor, is a thing of intelligent and gratifying design.
H. L. MENCKEN

These similes serve in various ways to clarify, to give emphasis, to control the tone, and to support arguments. Faulkner's visual image makes us feel the penetration of the chill; one sensory impression is used to emphasize another. Swados and Newman use similes to clarify and back up arguments. Wylie and Mencken use them mainly for dramatic effect, to underscore their semi-comic invective. All these similes, and 99 percent of all success-ful similes, are short, simple, and clear. They make their point without straining, and are free from self-contradiction.

Beginning writers sometimes have trouble on this last point. The following examples from student themes show how one can go wrong:

> Macbeth struggled like a man in a whirlpool formed partly by nature, partly by the witches, and partly by his wife.

> The radio quiz show is like a vast technical jungle that is intent on making itself a pleasant form of gambling.

> Linda was beautiful, he thought, like a Spitfire or a DC-3.

The first two sentences show the imprecise and clumsy think-ing characteristic of this kind of error: the idea is lost in the strained and overcomplex image. In the third sentence, the in-tended analogy between a girl's beauty and the beauty of two classic airplanes is destroyed by the connotations of *spitfire* (is beautiful Linda a shrew?), and perhaps, at least among readers not familiar with the DC-3, by connotations of great weight as well (is beautiful Linda a *fat* shrew?). However clear and just these three images may have seemed in the writers' minds, they appeared out of focus on the written page.

Metaphor

In metaphor, *like* and *as* are omitted and the comparison is as-serted as an identity; the gap between the things compared is virtually closed. Instead of saying "He's like a jackass," we say "He's a jackass." Instead of saying "The raindrops are coming down *like* pitchforks," we say "It's raining pitchforks." George Orwell, in reviewing Salvador Dali's *Life*, writes: "Dali is even by his own diagnosis narcissistic, and his autobiography is simply a strip-tease act conducted in pink limelight." "*Like* a strip-tease act" would have been far less forceful.

A remark of James Baldwin, "I have discovered the weight of white people in the world," is a more complicated metaphor, one that works partly as a literal statement and partly as a play on words. White people, the oppressors, are *like* a weight on the Negro's back; but Baldwin is also using *weight* in the sense of weighty people who make weighty decisions, people with the power to push other people around. When Shakespeare wrote "the hearts that spaniel'd me at heels," he condensed what otherwise would have been a clause with a simile ("that followed me as spaniels follow their masters") to a single verb, and in so doing not only snapped our imaginations to attention, but voiced at the same time Antony's controlled contempt for his fickle followers. When Jesus spoke to the crowd in the Sermon on the Mount, he spoke almost entirely in metaphors, drawing upon their enormous dramatic power to drive home his meaning:

> Ye are the salt of the earth: but if the salt have lost his savour, wherewith shall it be salted? . . . Ye are the light of the world. A city that is set on an hill cannot be hid.

But metaphor is more than a way of decorating or enlivening language. It is a way of thought as well. Comparisons—not just between things as alike as Ann's hair and Sally's, but above all between things as unlike as rain and pitchforks, as wind and time, as men and salt—are part of the unending human effort to find unity in a universe of bits and pieces. "Like and like and like— but what is the thing that lies beneath the semblance of things?" asked Virginia Woolf. Whatever that ineffable "thing" may be, it will be expressed (if it is expressible at all) as a metaphor.

Poetry is especially devoted to this search for unity in diversity, and poets constantly use metaphor to probe into reality. "I can hear light on a dry day," says the poet Theodore Roethke. And again, as he recovers from an illness that is both physical and mental, "I'm sweating out the will to die." In the first metaphor, two senses, sight and hearing, are fused into one. In the second, two levels of meaning are joined: the physical "sweating" of the poet's fever and the figurative "sweating out" of his psychological crisis. "How can we know the dancer from the dance?" asks William Butler Yeats in the poem "Among School Children." The question gives us an unforgettable glimpse of the poet's vision of unity behind, and within, all experience.

The poet is not the only one who takes metaphor seriously. The "bandwagon approach" in advertising, the Iron Curtain in contemporary history, the Oedipus complex in psychology—all these terms are metaphors used as shorthand for more or less complex ideas. The distinguished scientist J. Bronowski asserts the value of metaphor for scientific thinking as well:

> All science is the search for unity in hidden likenesses. The search may be on a grand scale, as in the modern theories which try to link the fields of gravitation and electromagnetism. But we do not need to be browbeaten by the scale of science. There are discoveries to be made by snatching a small likeness from the air, too, if it is bold enough. In 1932 the Japanese physicist Yukawa wrote a paper which can still give heart to a young scientist. He took as his starting point the known fact that waves of light can sometimes behave as if they were separate pellets. . . . A schoolboy can see how thin Yukawa's analogy is, and his teacher would be severe with it. Yet Yukawa without a blush calculated the mass of the pellet he expected to see, and waited. He was right; his meson was found, and a range of other mesons, neither the existence nor the nature of which had been suspected before. The likeness had borne fruit.

People writing on political subjects have inclined heavily to metaphor from Aristotle to the present day. In the following passage Charles Frankel, a Columbia professor who served briefly in Washington as a minor official under the Johnson Administration, describes the difficulty of getting anything done:

> The government becomes like an immense, somnolent animal that cannot twitch its toe unless it first moves twenty other parts of its body. And before it can do that, it has to undertake a laborious task of self-inspection. It must notice that its tail is tangled in its rear legs and unwind it; it must cure its right front foreleg of the tendency to move backward whenever the left foreleg moves forward; and, at the end, it must probably take one extra foot, whose existence it had forgotten, out of its mouth. By the time it has finished this process, the animal is

often too tired to twitch its toe—if it can even remember that this was its original intention.

As a beginner, you may find it hard to think of yourself as in the same class with writers like Frankel. But you, too, will find metaphors virtually inescapable in any writing that strives seriously for clarity, vividness, or depth.

MISUSES OF METAPHOR

When metaphors are used well, they call attention less to themselves than to the meaning they carry. When they are misused, they are conspicuous and often absurd. Three errors in particular should be avoided: stale metaphor, mixed metaphor, and inappropriate metaphor. By stale metaphor we mean tired or dead images; by mixed metaphor, combinations of incompatible images; by inappropriate metaphor, images that are likely to make readers uncomfortable.

Stale Metaphor

Imagery, as we have seen, should evoke comparisons in which one element helps to clarify the meaning of the other. Some images, however, no longer have this power. "The field of medicine," for example, no longer calls to mind a piece of land. What was once a living image is now moribund, a chiché without grace or force. Yet such images hang on, and in the hands of thoughtless writers yield sentences like this: "Graphic arts first attracted his attention, but he was soon seduced by a more lucrative field." This writer has lost sight not only of what a field is but of what seduction is. Our language is full of such stock comparisons: "His mind is like a steel trap," "We got down to brass tacks," "Moving to Florida gave them a new lease on life." Some images of this sort have more force left than others, but they are all more dead than quick. Writers who habitually rely on such hoary phrases are letting dead people do their thinking for them.

Even worse are those weary old saws that many people confuse with wisdom. Take, for example, the old standby "Where there's smoke, there's fire." When Senator Joseph McCarthy claimed in

1950 that there were 205 Communists in the State Department, many people swore that there was truth in his assertion because —naturally—"Where there's smoke, there's fire." Yet in this instance it would have been truer to say "Where there's smoke, there's a smoke screen."

Mixed Metaphor

One trouble with old saws, as with dead images, is that their relative truth tends increasingly to be seen as absolute. A moment's thought dispels this illusion. If "Virtue is its own reward" and "Honesty is the best policy," why all the proverbs about prudence and discretion? If "A bird in the hand is worth two in the bush," what are we to make of "Nothing ventured, nothing gained"? If "Haste makes waste," why is it that "He who hesitates is lost"? Another trouble is that the residual force of a stale image may clash ludicrously with its new context. Thus we find sentences like "When he pulled up stakes, you could have knocked me over with a feather," or even "I'd give my right arm to be ambidextrous."

A person who writes this way has lost touch with what his words mean; he has used metaphors without remembering the pictures they were created to evoke. "The sole aim of a metaphor," writes George Orwell, "is to call up a visual image." If he was wrong to exclude the other senses, he was right to insist on the importance of the visual. The man who wrote "The house system must be geared into the whole teaching arm of the university" was not seeing straight, and consequently not thinking straight. Gears do not mesh into arms. A similar blindness afflicted Secretary of State Dean Rusk in this comment on Vietnam: "When all the frosting is off the cake, it boils down to this —when they keep coming at you, do you get out of the way or meet them?" The general superintendent of the Chicago public schools was not at his best when he wrote: "With limited resources at his command, each youth must meet and conquer his own Achilles' heel." Nor was President Nixon in May 1971, when he told reporters, "We have some cards to play and we intend to play them to the hilt."

Alas, these are not rare specimens to be chuckled at and forgotten. Here is a sampling of comparable howlers from student themes and exams:

> Since Kafka was imbedded in the ice of many frustrations, he naturally formulated ideas for dynamiting the ice.

> I have come to the point where I must cease casting anxious eyes about, wondering which path in life will be presented to me on a silver platter.

> The desire is monomaniacal, reaping, if not suicide, at least the stagnant, self-polluting backwaters of nihilism.

> What is a young man to do in this day and age, with the octopus of Communism spreading its testicles all over the face of the earth?

> But as soon as we draw back to define our own conclusions about these novels, a gnawing dissatisfaction, a vague worm of discontent, peeks its head above the back of the tapestry.

> Had Jude become a curate, he would have been able to ensconce himself in the pillows of thought, locating himself in an environment designed to cultivate and mature the intellectual seeds which Jude himself planted in his own mind.

> Lewis shows us her lion through a 3-D viewer, and we see that it is really paper and we are not impressed.

> Virginia Woolf secures her tunneling process to the concrete realities of color, shape, and mass on a very short rope.

By no means all mixed metaphors are as funny—or perhaps the word is screwy—as these. Indeed, the typical mixed metaphor is not funny at all, just slightly wrong, like these three from themes on Claude Brown's *Manchild in the Promised Land*:

> Our social taboos frown on the free give-and-take as Mr. Brown describes it in Harlem.

Many foundations of today's need for racial justice in America are echoed in Claude Brown's book.

The big question, which has been in the background for so long, has finally come to the surface.

Taboos do not frown, and foundations are not echoed; things in the depths may rise to the surface, but things in the background must come to the fore. The meaning of these sentences is reasonably clear, but their effectiveness is diminished by the use of metaphors that set off a buzzing in the reader's brain.

Sometimes, of course, metaphors can be deliberately mixed for humorous or other purposes. The student who wrote "Jane Austen is intent on carving her little piece of ivory until the blood runs" mixed a metaphor with happy results, as did W. C. Fields when he remarked, "There comes a time in the affairs of man when he must take the bull by the tail and face the situation." In *The Heart of Midlothian,* Sir Walter Scott has Reuben Butler, a dour old puritan, mix a metaphor with spectacular effect. Butler is referring to his son's fitness for the ministry:

I will make it my business to procure a license when he is fit for the same, trusting he will be a shaft cleanly polished, and meet to be used in the body of the kirk; and that he shall not turn again, like the sow, to wallow in the mire of heretical extremes and defections, but shall have the wings of a dove, though he hath lain among the pots.

Wyndham Lewis in *The Apes of God* got a suitably ironic effect by describing a character as possessing "fountains of energy, of the sort that do not grow on every tree." And we are indebted to a newscaster (who may not have been trying to be funny) for "The United Steelworkers will get down to brass tacks today."

Sometimes, too, well-known metaphors can be turned inside out to good effect. It has been said of Henry James, for example, that in writing at great length about small matters "he chewed more than he bit off." And Oscar Wilde once threw new light on the old biblical injunction by saying, "If a man smite thee, turn the other face."

Inappropriate Metaphor

Finally, there is the question of taste. As Keats once said, we hate writing that seems to have a "palpable design" upon us. We turn away from writing marked by excess, by too much spilling of emotion; we are annoyed, or provoked to laughter, by signs that the writer is working too hard. The excessive or tasteless use of metaphor can give this effect. Take this sentence: "The conscience of man takes precedence in the logistics of American action; it is the silk thread shining through the hair-shirt of our native literary search." Military images and images of sin vie for our attention; the metaphor is not exactly mixed, but it is too rich to swallow. In rejecting a metaphor of this kind, of course, a reader rejects the message as well.

Another kind of error in taste may be illustrated by the following horrendous prayer, which was reprinted in the *New Yorker*:

> At a meeting in the Benson Hotel to promote the Portland Open golf tournament, the following invocation was given by Rev. Lester Harnish, pastor of the First Baptist Church:
>
> "Oh God, in the game of life you know that though most of us are duffers, we all aspire to be champions with plenty of birdies or eagles.
>
> "Help us, we pray, to be grateful for the course—including both the fairways and the rough.
>
> "Thank you for those who have made it possible for us to tee off. Thank you for the thrill of a solid soaring drive, the challenge of the dog leg, the trial of the trap, the discipline of the water hazard, the beauty of a cloudless sky and the exquisite misery of rain and cold.
>
> "Thank you, O God, for Jesus Christ our pro, who shows us how to get the right grip on life, to slow down in our back swing, to correct our crazy hooks and slices, to keep our head down in humility and to follow through in self-control.
>
> "May He teach us also to be good sports who will accept the rub of the green, the penalty for being out-of-bounds, the reality of lost balls, the relevancy of par, the dangers of the 19th hole and the authority of our special rule book, the Bible.

"And Lord, when the last putt has dropped into the cup; the light of our last day has faded into the darkness of death; though our trophies be few, our handicap still too low and that hole-in-one still only a dream; may we be able to turn in to You, our tournament director, at the great clubhouse, an honest scorecard.

"Through Jesus Christ we pray, Amen."

No student would be guilty of such an effort. Yet it is not entirely unlike what many beginning writers try to do—or find themselves doing. It is easy, once a metaphor gets started, to keep it rolling; and it is almost always a mistake. Metaphor is like a beautiful motif in a symphony. Used with restraint, it gives the work meaning and depth. Used grossly or too frequently, or sustained too long, it cloys. Taste in these matters cannot be legislated or dictated; it must be felt. But when in doubt, remember the Reverend Lester Harnish and keep your metaphors short.

8

MERE WRITING AND GOOD PROSE

Learning to write is essentially a process of modifying the spoken language, with its natural redundancies and imprecisions, to meet the requirements of another medium. Our first serious efforts to write yield a kind of written talk, charming enough in its way but needing to be reconsidered, revised, perhaps condensed or expanded, if its full meaning is to come through. If the revising is left undone, or done badly, the result is mere writing, mere brushstrokes on the canvas. If the revising is done well—whether in the mind before writing, or after writing a first draft, or more commonly both—the result is good prose. In this chapter we will illustrate and describe these two classes of writing, and show how to go about converting the one into the other.

MERE WRITING

Two Examples

Let us begin with two paragraphs of admirable prose. Here is the poet and critic Yvor Winters:

> At the church I sat with the family, in a private room to the side of the pulpit. After the sermon I looked once more

into the casket. The black hair seemed not to have stirred. The face was not heavily wrinkled, but there were a few small wrinkles about the mouth and eyes. The skin was preternaturally and evenly white, and in the wrinkles there seemed a trace as of an underlying darkness, even and impenetrable. At the grave, a mile and a half outside of town, the ceremonies were brief, for a vile sleet had set in. The coffin was lowered; the last prayer was read; and the grave was filled with stones and mud. As we drove away, I looked back to see a huge mound of hot-house flowers, dark heavy green, and clear hard white and yellow, lying as if murdered in the colorless air, beneath driving sleet.

And here is the drama critic Kenneth Tynan:

Let me court peril with a generalization: that good drama, of whatever kind, has but one mainspring—the human being reduced by ineluctable process to a state of desperation. Desperate are the cornered giants of Sophocles; desperate, too, as they huddle in their summer-houses, the becalmed gentry of Chekhov; and the husband of French farce, with a wife in one bedroom and a mistress in another, is he not, though we smile at his agony, definably desperate? The clown in the haunted house and the prince on the haunted battlements have this in common, that their drama heightens as they are driven to the last ditch of their souls. How, in this extremity, will they comport themselves? It is to find out that we go to theaters.

Without pausing to examine what makes these paragraphs effective, let us go on to consider how a novice—whom we shall call Plotz for convenience—might have handled the same themes. Here is Plotz's hypothetical version of the Winters passage:

Sitting there with the family in the church, in a private room on the left side of the pulpit, was one of the most frustrating experiences of my life. After the sermon for some reason—though I didn't want to—I looked into the casket again. This was my first funeral, and I guess I was in a state of shock or something. His black hair looked just the way it did in real life, and so did the wrinkles on his face, but what especially got me was the chalky whiteness of the face. During the services at the grave, it began to sleet, and everybody hurried to get the ceremony over with. The coffin was lowered into the open grave, the last prayer was read by the minister, the grave was filled, and everybody hurried to drive away. Afterward, as I looked back at the grave, I saw some frozen flowers with the sleet pelting down on them.

And here is his version of the Tynan passage:

It seems to me that one way of describing the appeal that good drama has for an audience is to say that it typically shows the behavior of people who have been driven to desperation by extreme pressure in believable circumstances. And this goes for comedy, too: the main actors in a farce are typically just as desperate about trying to solve their silly problems as the main actors in a Shakespeare or Chekhov play are about trying to solve theirs. As the situation gets more desperate, the audience's feeling of involvement and tension increases. If the play is a good one, the audience is typically hooked by this time; it identifies completely with the main actor and wonders nervously how his desperate situation will be resolved. In the last analysis, the reason that people go to the theater is to observe the behavior of people more or less like themselves in extreme but believable situations.

Neither of these hypothetical versions is exactly bad. Both are free of the errors in grammar and spelling that mar much undergraduate writing, and both convey a reasonably clear message. Yet the writing in both cases is mere writing. Why? Perhaps the best way to get at the complex answer to this question is to appraise the two passages at three levels: first as paragraphs, following the criteria of Chapter 4; next in terms of their sentences, following Chapter 5; and finally in terms of their diction, following Chapters 6 and 7.

Paragraphs

A paragraph should make one clear point, and neither of these paragraphs does. The first one makes no point at all. This happened, that happened; I felt this way, I felt that way—whatever the writer is trying to tell us, it doesn't get across. The second, by contrast, makes too many points. To Tynan's original point about desperation Plotz adds two lesser ones: that dramatic situations must be "believable," and that increased dramatic pressure increases an audience's involvement. If these further points are worth making, they should be made in separate paragraphs. In this paragraph they simply confuse things.

Further, both of Plotz's paragraphs exhibit a bland sameness of sentence structure and sentence length. Four of the first paragraph's seven sentences are compound sentences in *and* and *but*, a form whose allure for the unskilled writer often leads to its excessive use. The second paragraph is better this way, yet its five routine declarative sentences are no match for Tynan's original, which leaps from imperative to declarative-interrogative to declarative and then back to interrogative again before coming to rest with a declarative. In sentence length and sequence the story is the same. Winters's original builds from short descriptive sentences at the beginning to a long, sonorous, reflective one at the end; Tynan's from long exploratory sentences at the beginning to short, brisk ones at the end. In Plotz's versions all the sentences are seemingly medium-length; there is no pattern, no movement.

Sentences

Just as Plotz's two paragraphs are defective as paragraphs, so are their sentences defective as sentences—not dramatically so, but in the small ways that differentiate mere writing from good prose. On pp. 72–73 we list five basic preferences on which good writers agree: prefer verbs to nouns, active to passive, concrete to abstract, personal to impersonal, shorter to longer. Plotz's writing could stand improvement along several of these lines, especially the last.

Compare, for example, Tynan's clause "their drama heightens as they are driven to the last ditch of their souls" with Plotz's corresponding sentence, "As the situation gets more desperate, the audience's feeling of involvement and tension increases." Tynan's wording is nothing special, but Plotz's is downright bland. In place of Tynan's personal subject (the embattled clown or prince) he offers an impersonal *situation* responded to by an impersonal *audience*; in place of Tynan's short and relatively concrete nouns *drama, ditch,* and *souls* he offers the polysyllabic abstractions *situation, audience, feeling, involvement,* and *tension.* Both versions are fourteen words long, but only Tynan has made his fourteen words pull their weight.

Similarly, Plotz's version of the Winters paragraph is no longer than the original, but some thirty of his words could be omitted without ever being missed. Do we really need the third sentence, which seems to lead nowhere? In the next-to-last sentence, do we really need "into the open grave" and "by the minister," and in the last sentence do we need "Afterward"? A good writer does not waste words establishing routine connections like this; he suggests them or leaves them to inference. Nor will he bother spelling out what readers can be presumed to know on their own or have been told already. Compare Tynan's ten-word final sentence, for example, with Plotz's corresponding sentence. The difference in length comes from Tynan's simply omitting the object of *find out.* The omission not only spares the reader a pointless redundancy, but gives Tynan's ending a snap that Plotz's lacks.

Diction

Plotz is probably young. "I guess I was in a state of shock or something" sounds like youthful confusion, not only about the possible state of shock but about the reader's probable interest in thoughts so ill-formed. *What got me* and *hooked* are informal expressions of the kind one finds in student themes, standard in speech but not Standard. The repetition of *I, my,* and *me* in the first passage (nine times here to only three in Winters) has a youthful ring, as does the repetition of the pet word *typically* in the second. None of these errors is serious in itself, but taken together they exhibit the characteristic imperceptiveness of mere writing. Any writer can make such slips, but a good writer would correct them.

Another thing we miss in Plotz's writing is the carefully chosen particulars that give the Winters and Tynan passages so much of their power.   The grave is no longer a mile and a half outside of town; for all we are told it may be in the churchyard itself, a distinctly different sort of place from Winters's dreary heath. The flowers are no longer hothouse flowers, no longer "clear hard white and yellow" with foliage of "dark heavy green"; no longer, in short, Winters's pathetic gladioli, florist-forced and chosen by family and friends in the traditional pale funeral colors, but flowers of no special kind or color.   In Plotz's second paragraph we find not "the becalmed gentry of Chekhov" and "the prince on the haunted battlements," not even *The Cherry Orchard* and *Hamlet*, but "a Shakespeare or Chekhov play"; not a husband shuttling frantically from a wife in one bedroom to a mistress in another, but "the main actors in a farce."   The loss of detail is one no reader can be expected to make up on his own.   Details are important: they give a message form and impact.   Only poor writers shun them, whether from caution, laziness, or the mistaken belief that it is more impressive to be general than specific.

Finally, Plotz's writing has no imagery whatever: nothing to match Winters's vivid image of the murdered flowers, nothing even at the modest level of Winters's simile "trace as of an underlying darkness" or Tynan's metaphor "last ditch of their souls."   Plotz's language never soars or dances, but clomps dully along until it stops.   A writer who shrinks from imagery has only one string to his bow: the flat statement.   When he plays we hear sound, not music.

In short, Plotz's two paragraphs, though unassailable on grammatical grounds and easy enough to understand, lack the perfections of technique.   As paragraphs they lack focus and movement; their sentences are too abstract and heavy with unnecessary words; their diction is sophomoric and monotonous.   Reading them is like hearing a football game over a car radio in a thunderstorm; the essentials come through if one is sufficiently attentive, but many of the details are lost and with them most of the pleasure of listening.   Despite the virtues of these paragraphs—and they have some—they are the work of an amateur, not good prose but mere writing.

EDITING

The Nature and Functions of Editing

The process by which you convert mere writing to good prose is called editing. All book publishers and magazines assign editors to manuscripts, and newspapers have editors to edit the raw writing of reporters for clarity and style. College students, having no such help available, must be both author and editor, both writer and rewrite man.

Editing takes time. If you leave yourself only two hours to write a paper and spend two hours writing it, you have a first draft, not a paper. You are better off if you leave yourself three hours and spend the third editing what you have written in the first two. Another thing editing takes is perspective: it is best done after an interval. Ideally, this interval should be several days or more—the Roman poet Horace recommended nine years —and should include time for pondering or researching the main troubles revealed in the first draft. If your schedule allows no time for such luxuries, shorten the interval, but try not to eliminate it. If you can separate writing and editing by as little as a night's sleep, or even a meal or a game of tennis, you will do a better job of editing than you would after no interval at all.

Finally, editing cannot be done well under pressure. You can sometimes bat out a first draft in hot haste; some people even write more fluently that way. But editing is another matter. In editing you have to ask yourself how well a sentence or a paragraph works, whether its meaning comes through, whether it can be made clearer and stronger, what kind of change might help. If you are not pressed for time or distracted, whatever you do will probably be for the better.

Editing has two functions: to correct and to improve. The first function has to do with errors of grammar, syntax, punctuation, and so on, and with basic clarity and consistency; these matters will be discussed in the following chapters. In this chapter we are concerned with the second function: with ways of making writing generally more effective. Mere writing, first-draft writing, may be errorless; it may also be clear. What it usually is not, and what editing seeks to make it, is readable. Mere writing can often be understood, but only good writing can be enjoyed.

Two Examples

We have given an example of editing at the end of Chapter 4, in the section entitled "Judging a Paragraph." We give two others here, beginning in each case with mere writing and ending with good prose. Here, to begin with, is a paragraph from a freshman theme about an essay by George Orwell:

> The descriptions in this essay are incredibly graphic. I was carried along from one beautifully written paragraph to the next, and I was horrified by some, disgusted by others, but I was always amazed by how close the writer's experience had been to mine. After I had finished reading this essay, though, I was in an exceedingly dismal state of mind, recalling how bleak my own childhood had been and realizing that others were the same.

One finishes this paragraph with irritation. Its adverbs are too frequent and intense, its two long sentences are poorly constructed, it lacks detail, and its messages conflict. The writer seems simultaneously impressed with Orwell's writing ability, disgusted and horrified by the incidents Orwell describes, amazed at the parallel with his own experience, and plunged into gloom by recalling that experience. Nonsense, says the reader: the mind is no such three-ring circus. One of these emotions we might have believed, or two in sequence; but not all four at once. Either the writer does not know what he thinks about Orwell's essay, or he dislikes it but thinks he had better pretend otherwise.

Let's get rid of these difficulties and see what happens. Let's bring on the circus acts one at a time, and leave the main act on longest. Let's cut down on the adverbs, tighten up the rambling sentences, and replace empty general words like *descriptions* and *experience* with specifics. With these changes made, our paragraph might look like this:

> Orwell's essay helped me to see my own boarding-school days in perspective. Crossgates and my school were very similar: the snobbery, the concern with money, the sexual anxiety, the obsession with sports. Perhaps all boarding

schools are like that; at all events, Orwell helped me to see for the first time that I had been one of many. Others were just as timid, just as withdrawn. Dozens of my schoolmates must have suffered as I did, and for as little reason.

This paragraph is not perfect prose, but it has risen above mere writing. It has authority: the writer has clearly understood Orwell's experience and related it to his own. It is spare: there are no gratuitous intensifiers like *incredibly* and *always*, no functionless words like *reading*, no ambiguous words like *others*. It offers details: not "the writer's experience," but snobbery, money, sexual anxiety, sports; not mere bleakness, but persecution for being timid and withdrawn. Finally, it has a rhythm or pace that puts the rambling original to shame.

On this last point, a word of advice: reading aloud can help. In matters of rhythm, or even in matters only tenuously connected with rhythm, the ear can sometimes hear what the eye cannot see—that a sentence is too complicated for a reader to take in, or too feebly related to another sentence, or ugly or pompous-sounding or just plain silly. If our freshman had read his Orwell paragraph aloud and listened to himself as he read, he might have rewritten his long, shapeless first sentence into something more easily grasped; and he might have toned down such overintense words as *disgusted* and *amazed*.

Reading aloud works best with a listener or two, since most of us are sensitive to criticism from others, including unspoken criticism, and since such criticism is likely to tell us more than our own biased promptings. Alternatively, of course, you can read the work aloud to yourself, or read it silently but try to sound the words in your mind. Whatever you do, if something sounds wrong—even if you don't know why—throw it out, replace it, edit it. Conversely, what your ear tells you is good probably *is* good. If something sounds exactly right when you say it, it will usually pass muster on paper.

Here is another paragraph in need of improvement:

There is not very much to be said in favor of the argument that the right to vote in elections should be dependent on residence in a community for a period of at least six months. The living patterns of the American people at the present time are not the same as those of fifty or a hundred years ago, at the time of the passage of the laws that established the six-month residence requirement.   There is more changing of residence today from one community to another; for example, some men are transferred from one city to another by the companies they work for, and many old people move to California or Florida when they reach retirement age.   It does not seem fair that people who move to new communities should have their right to vote taken away from them, and especially that they should be deprived of the right to vote in national elections.

In editing dull writing like this, the first thing to look for is what some professional editors call "fat": long phrases that can be cut out altogether, or replaced by a shorter phrase or a single word, with no loss of meaning.   Consider the first sentence.   Its first thirteen words can be replaced by the shorter and more direct phrase "It seems unjust," and two later phrases—"in elections" and "a period of at least"—can be simply deleted.   The second sentence is just as overweight.   "The living patterns of the American people" can be cut down to "American living patterns"; "at the present time" can be deleted altogether, since the time is perfectly clear from the context; and the sixteen-word final phrase can be cut to "when the residence requirement was established."   Changes like this give us a much leaner paragraph:

> It seems unjust that the right to vote should depend on residence in a community for six months.   American living patterns have changed in the hundred years since the residence requirement was first established.   People change residence more frequently today: for example, executives are transferred and old people move to California and Florida.   It seems especially unfair that people who move should lose the right to vote in national elections.

This is better, but still rather flat.   Some further changes, to bolster the argument and introduce variety into the sentence pattern, make it better still:

> Why should the right to vote depend on six months' residence in a community?   Things have changed since 1900:

the nation counts for more, the community for less. Every year thousands of executives are transferred, thousands of old people move to Florida, thousands of teachers and graduate students move to new universities. Why penalize these people? At least we should let them vote in national elections.

We started with 155 words, which we cut first to 70 and finally to 66. The editing has lost nothing worth keeping; indeed, as sometimes happens, new material has actually been added, with the result that the final version says more in 66 words than the original said in 155. Moreover, with the static suppressed, the message comes through more clearly. Our editing has cut away the fat and kept the meat.

Note also the changes in sentence structure. The four sentences of the original were all declarative; in the final version two sentences are interrogative. These changes help make the argument more direct and immediate, and for the first time give something of that sense of the writer's personality (rather a strident one, in this case) which is indispensable to style.

There is nothing absolute about these changes. Brevity is good, but a passage, as we have seen, can be too brief for its content; better a word too many than a word too few. Interrogative and imperative sentences should be used sparingly; less dramatic devices often serve as well. Above all, you should avoid unnatural changes. *The wind died down* may be unexciting, but *Down died the wind* is no improvement. If you cannot find a natural way to make a sentence shorter or snappier, let it stand and go on to the next one.

Editing at its best will correct obvious errors in spelling, punctuation, and so on, and eliminate the repetitions, awkward wordings, and bits of foolishness that often creep into first drafts. It will correct slips of tone. It will change unnecessarily long phrases like *was due to the fact that* to short ones like *happened because,* and short ones like *the maintenance of* to shorter ones like *maintaining.* It will fashion sentences of different lengths or kinds to lighten the going where it is otherwise heavy.

Too much to ask? Perhaps at first, but it gets easier, and it can even get to be fun if you have a first draft you respect and a good working knowledge of the basic principles of writing.

GOOD PROSE

In this chapter we have examined four samples of good prose, ranging from the merely competent voting-rights paragraph to the almost poetic paragraph by Yvor Winters. We have seen how these passages differ from clumsier treatments of the same material, and how editing can make the difference. We have seen in a general way what makes mere writing mere. Let us now try to summarize what makes good prose good.

In the first place, the *authority* that comes from knowing one's subject and one's mind. A good writer knows what he wants to say.

In the second place, *detail*. Not just flowers, but hothouse flowers of two specific colors; not just a farce, but a French bedroom farce with a wife in one bedroom and a mistress in another. Detail is a tricky quality, to be sure. Too many details make for tiresome reading, and a wrong or obtrusive detail may be worse than no detail at all. But the impulse to precision is central to good prose. The telling detail is the essence of descriptive writing.

In the third place, *economy*. A good writer pares away unnecessary blubber: abstract nouns like *situation* and *circumstances*, mechanical intensifiers like *very* and *really*, flabby phrases like *in such a way as to* and *in view of the fact that*, unnecessary connections and elaborations. Tynan does not say, "It is to find out *the answer to this question* that we go to theaters"; the italicized words are unnecessary, hence burdensome, all weight and no substance. Good writing is the right length for its content. What can be said in eighty words is said in eighty words, not a hundred.

Finally, *variety*, in the rhythmic sense. There is something in the human mind—in the reader's inner ear—that calls for a short sentence after several long ones, or a longer one after several short ones. Too many simple sentences set us to wishing for a complex sentence, and vice versa. The rhythms of prose are not the rhythms of popular music; steady repetition of the same beat after a point is not pleasing but irritating, and in the end stupefying.

That is all very well, you may say, but how does it translate into advice to the novice writer? Am I really expected to emulate the likes of Winters and Tynan, men of exceptional gifts and wide interests who have spent a lifetime writing? Maybe not, but with a little effort you can surely hope to match the competent expository prose of our revised Orwell and voting-rights paragraphs. If it takes you a while, you aren't the first. Writing is like playing tennis or playing the piano: doing it badly is the necessary first step to doing it well. The big thing to strive for is not virtuosity but competence: not to soar in one great bound to the heights of Milton or Ruskin, but to climb out of the swamp of mere writing onto the solid ground of good prose. If you can do that, you will have done all this book asks of you and all anyone could ask.

PART 3
MECHANICS

9

GRAMMAR

In Part 2 we were concerned with the art of writing effectively, with choosing which of various alternatives is *best*. In Part 3 our concern will be with the mechanics of writing correctly, with choosing which of various alternatives is *right*. The rejected alternatives of Part 2 were clumsy or irritating or confusing or substandard. Those of Part 3, though in many cases clear and straightforward enough, have been pronounced unacceptable—or permanently second-best—by the consensus of educated people. Part 2 dealt with choices; Part 3 deals with rules.

Rules in this sense should be seen not as a constraint on the writer but as a convention between the writer and the reader, a mutual agreement on details that clears the way for more important matters. A good writer depends on the rules of grammar, syntax, orthography, and punctuation the way a good general depends on the fundamentals of military strategy: he may violate them for good reason in occasional unexpected circumstances, but they remain the standard to which all his choices are referred. A writer of expository prose who repeatedly violates these rules by ignorance or design builds his house on quicksand. Whatever effects he may achieve, making his meaning clear is not one of them.

Since grammar and syntax are variously defined and understood, it may be well to begin by defining the two terms as we use them. A problem in *grammar*, by our lights, involves a choice between alternatives differing in number, gender, case, or tense. A problem in *syntax* involves a choice between different ways of relating two or more parts of a sentence to each other. Our concern in this chapter is with grammar.

NUMBER AND GENDER PROBLEMS

People (is) (are) my business

Everyone knows that singular subjects take singular verbs and plural subjects plural verbs. The difficulty lies in determining when a subject is singular and when plural, and sometimes in determining which of several words or phrases is in fact the subject. The present section will be confined to common sources of error and confusion, and will not pursue the more bizarre complications to which this deceptively straightforward-sounding rule gives rise.

When the subject is singular but a predicate noun is plural, stick strictly to the rule. All of the following sentences are correct:

My only *source* of support *was* my parents.
My *parents were* my only source of support.

The one *thing* the Allies lacked *was* troopships.
Troopships were the one thing the Allies lacked.

With a subject made up of two or more nouns linked by *and*, use a plural verb: *Wine, women, and song were Bao Dai's downfall.* There are exceptions—for example, *A year and six months was all they needed* / *Bread and butter is tedious fare*—where the compound subject, being essentially singular in meaning, takes a singular verb; but these exceptions are few. When in doubt, use the plural: *Rain and sleet were forecast for the week of the convention.*

With a subject made up of two or more singular nouns linked by *or* or *nor*, use a singular verb if the components are singular, a plural verb if they are plural:

Either Egypt or Israel *has* to back down.

The investigation did not reveal whether the pilot, the navigator, or the bombardier *was* responsible.

Neither the ranchers nor the miners *pay* this tax.

If some components are singular and some plural, you may face a nasty choice:

Usually the coaches or the manager (*gives*) (*give*) the signals.

When money is short, either the farmhouse or the crops (*have*) (*has*) to be mortgaged.

Neither the governor nor the Teamsters Union officials (*were*) (*was*) sympathetic.

Since each of the alternatives in parentheses has its drawbacks, the best thing to do is reword the sentence to avoid the number problem. This is often easy enough: *The signals are usually given by the coaches or the manager / When money is short, either the farmhouse or the crops must be mortgaged / Both the governor and the Teamsters Union were unsympathetic.* If no alternative wording can be found, make the verb agree with the nearest noun or pronoun component of the subject:

Either the Joint Chiefs or one of the field commanders *was* lying.

Has Socrates's question, or Hobbes's and Rousseau's questions, ever been satisfactorily answered?

Who takes (his) (our) (their) turn next?

Number difficulties may involve not only verbs but pronouns and nouns:

> The diary never said whether it was Sir Robert or his sister that hanged (*himself*) (*herself*) (*themselves*).

> The plan was for me or Ken to take (*my*) (*his*) (*our*) car.

> Either the linebackers or the free safety missed (*his cue*) (*their cue*) (*their cues*).

Sometimes you can solve this problem by spelling things out: *The plan was for me to take my car or Ken to take his / Either the linebackers missed their cue or the free safety missed his.* Sometimes you can solve it by rewording: *Either the linebackers or the free safety missed a cue.* If no better solution can be found, make the pronoun agree in number and gender with the nearest component of the subject, making this component plural if possible and masculine if there is a choice of genders:

> Either Paul or the *twins* left *their* baggage.

> One would never expect a nurse or a *doctor* to injure *himself* that way.

They each (have) (has) children of (their) (his) own

Each as a subject takes a singular verb; so do nouns modified by *each* and *every* and the nouns *anyone, anybody, no one, nobody, everyone,* and *everybody.* These words cause few problems with verbs; the trouble comes in determining the number and gender of any following nouns and pronouns. Good writers, faced by a choice among *Anybody can try this experiment for himself, Anybody can try this experiment for himself or herself,* and *Anybody can try this experiment for themselves,* choose the first. The convention here, according to H. W. Fowler's *Modern English Usage* (1926), is that "where the matter of sex is not conspicuous or important the masculine form shall be allowed to represent a person instead of a man." With a glance in the direction of the 1926 equivalent of Women's Lib, Fowler goes on to remark, "Whether that convention, with *himself or herself* in the background for especial exactitudes, and paraphrase always possible in dubious cases, is an arrogant demand on the part of male England, everyone must decide for himself (or for himself or herself, or for themselves)."

To the general preference for the singular with words like *each* several exceptions may be noted. First, when *each* modifies a plural noun or pronoun, it takes the plural: thus, whereas the singular is correct in *Each man here has a dollar* and *Each of us has a dollar,* the plural is correct in *We each have a dollar* and *We have a dollar each.* Second, *none,* unlike *no one* and *nobody,* can take either the singular or the plural. If your emphasis is on the individual components of the class of things that *none* refers to, use the singular: *None of these three books is worth reading.* If the components are more sensibly thought of in groups or batches, use the plural: *No letters have been received, and none are expected.* In borderline cases, most good writers use the singular.

Finally, when no combination of *each* or *every* can convey your precise meaning without sounding foolish, use the plural and hope for the best: thus *Some children raised their hands,* which does not tell how many hands each raised, is preferable to *Some children raised one hand each,* which is overexplicit and silly.

The coaches made their own (decision) (decisions)

Whether to use the singular or the plural with the plural possessives *their, our,* and *your* is not always easy to decide. Do we say *The prisoners went to their death bravely* or *went to their deaths bravely? We changed our mind* or *changed our minds?* The English language has no clear rules or patterns on this point, and in borderline cases either form will serve. A rough rule of thumb might be as follows: when the noun is concrete or tangible, use the plural; when it is highly abstract, or when a fixed idiom is involved, use the singular; in between these extremes, take your choice. Thus:

The two girls changed their dresses. (*Concrete.*)

The two girls changed their mind [*or* minds]. (*In between.*)

The two girls changed their religion. (*Abstract.*)

The two girls changed their tune. (*Idiom.*)

Of course, when there is only a single item in question, the singular is used: *We love our country.*

The jury (was) (were) served coffee

With collective nouns—words like *crowd, committee,* and *majority,* which are singular in form but plural in connotation—either singular or plural verbs may be used, depending on context. When in doubt, use the singular: *The crowd was dispersed by the police / The committee is unable to reach an agreement.* If you are not happy with either the singular or the plural, and there are times when you won't be, try a different wording that gets around the problem: *The onlookers were dispersed by the police / The committee members are unable to reach an agreement.*

Where *the majority* simply means *most,* use the plural: *Some agreed, but the majority were undecided.* Use the plural also with such ostensibly singular expressions as *a number of* and *a handful of* when they mean *some* or *many,* as they usually do: *A small number of people were present / A high proportion of Americans go to college.*

A word cannot be simultaneously singular and plural. This difficulty is exhibited in the following sentences, in which conflicting words are italicized:

The younger generation *has* no patience with legal restrictions; *their* law is action.

Two days *was* a long time, and what would happen when *they were* over?

Everyone from the Chinese restaurant *was* there, wearing *tuxedos* and evening *dresses.*

The first two sentences can be made consistently singular by changing *their* to *its* and *they were* to *it was.* In the third sentence, the plural is better: *All the people from the Chinese restaurant were there.*

Mathematics (are) (is) difficult

Some words are plural in form but singular in meaning. For most such words (*scissors, glasses, pants*) the plural is idiomatic. The chief exceptions are *news,* the names of certain diseases (*measles, mumps, shingles*), and words ending in *-ics* when used to designate a more or less formal body of knowledge or course of study: *Politics is the art of the possible / Ethics attracts modern philosophers more than logic.* In less formal uses the plural is more common: *His politics were dirty / Their ethics are questionable.* The Latin plural *data,* being singular in appearand and to some extent in connotation, increasingly takes the singular in modern usage and will someday be as singular as *agenda,* which has traveled the same road; at this writing, however, good usage still favors *data are.*

One of the boys (was) (were) absent

Watch out for the false association of verbs with nearby nouns that are not in fact their subjects. Number errors from this cause, which is sometimes called "attraction," are surprisingly common. The two following examples are wrong:

> The pattern of monetary and role allocations in schools *impose* rigid limits on managerial power.

> The ways and means of arriving at a workable treaty *remains* to be explored.

The subject of the first sentence is *pattern,* not *allocations* or *schools;* the subject of the second is *ways and means,* not *treaty.* Errors of this sort come from haste, and should not survive a careful editing.

In this connection, note that *with* and its compounds (*together with, along with*) do not act like *and* to make a subject plural. The following sentences are both correct:

> Del Vecchio and the two other rioters *were* fined $500 each.

> Del Vecchio, along with the two other rioters, *was* fined $500.

POSSESSIVE PROBLEMS

Forming the Possessive

To form the possessive, use *'s* for the singular (*John's hat, the dog's dish*) and an apostrophe only for the plural (*the ladies' bridge club, the Smiths' car*). For words that do not form the plural in *s*, notably *men, women,* and *children,* add *'s* for the plural possessive (*the children's toys, the alumni's wishes, the people's choice*).

Some singular common nouns and many proper names end in an *s* or *z* sound. Most of these, along with all names ending in silent *s* or *x* (*Descartes, Malraux, Illinois, Arkansas*), form the possessive in *'s* just like any other singular noun:

Henry James's novels	for appearance's sake
Essex's plot	Degas's paintings
our hostess's husband	Columbus's crew
in Jesus's name	Alcatraz's first warden

A few such words, however, notably ancient Greek and biblical names of three or more syllables ending in a *z* sound, become too awkward to pronounce with the extra syllable added by *'s* and conventionally form the possessive with the apostrophe only: *Aristophanes' comedies, Socrates' wisdom.*

No apostrophe is used in the possessive pronouns *his, hers, its, ours, yours, theirs,* and *whose.* Errors on this point, particularly *it's* for *its,* are common in student writing. *It's* means *it is* or *it has* and nothing else (*It's a rainy day* / *It's been fun*); *who's* means *who is* or *who has* (*Who's there?* / *Who's seen Mary?*). The forms *her's, our's, your's,* and *their's* do not exist. Note, by the way, that *whose* may be used freely in place of the awkward *of which* irrespective of whether it refers to a person or a thing: *the house whose garden we admired* is Standard English.

Misplaced Apostrophe

In some idiomatic phrases involving possessives, it is not immediately obvious where the apostrophe goes. Is it *state's rights,* for example, or *states' rights?* Is it *bull's-eyes* or *bulls'-eyes* or *bullseyes?* Is it *hornet's nest* or *hornets' nest, doctor's orders* or *doctors' orders?* Try your dictionary on questions like this, or better yet an unabridged dictionary. If you can find no pronouncement one way or the other, your best bet is usually the singular. In proper names, the plural is the more common: *Reserve Officers' Training Corps, Professional Golfers' Association.*

The practice of eliminating the apostrophe from what is properly a possessive form has become established in some proper names (*the Veterans Administration, the Artists Workshop*), and is now being extended to some common compounds as well (*teachers college, citizens group*). There is no warrant, however, for the wholesale elimination of the apostrophe in terms of this form. In particular, keep the apostrophe where dropping it would yield a nonexistent word like *mens or childrens.* For the same reason, take care to put the apostrophe where it belongs, not one letter away. It is *women's club,* not *womens' club; sheep's wool,* not *sheeps' wool; womens* and *sheeps* are not English words. The opposite error (*John Adam's presidency, the United State's viewpoint*) evokes nonexistent singulars: a president named *John Adam,* a country named *the United State.*

Beware of adding an apostrophe to a plural noun being used as an adjective: it is *physics test,* not *physics' test* or *physic's test.* And never use an apostrophe to form the plural of a word that has a perfectly good plural of the normal form. Errors of this sort are common on signs: *Strawberry's for Sale; We Charge Battery's.* On doorplates we may find *The Jones's,* implying that some sinister figure known as The Jones lurks within, rather than an innocent family of Joneses. This last error in particular smacks of illiteracy: if it creeps into a first draft, it should creep no further.

Unwieldy Possessives

When a choice between *s's* and *s'* yields two equally or almost equally unattractive alternatives, try to avoid the choice by rewording. Why make the difficult choice between *the metropolis's growth* and *the metropolis' growth* when you can say *the growth of the metropolis,* or *the growth of metropolitan Toronto?* Most words of over three syllables whether or not they end in *s,* and many three-syllable words ending in *s* or an *s* sound (*wilderness, residence*), take the *of* form much more gracefully than the apostrophe. An especially awkward possessive is *United States'*: *the United States' viewpoint* is not wrong, but might better be changed to *the American viewpoint* or *the viewpoint of the United States.*

Possessives of long phrases should also be avoided. *The man in the street's opinion* might just get by, but *the man in the fur coat's car* is too much; the *of* construction is better for both.

Compound Possessives

Short compound possessives of the form *John('s)* and *Mary's money* are harder to avoid. Whether to use *'s* after the last noun only or after each noun in the series depends on whether the possessors should be thought of as a unit or as separate entities. The following four phrases are correct:

> Mother and Dad's wedding anniversary
> Mother's and Dad's summer clothing

> Ed, Bill, and Charley's Bar
> Ed's, Bill's and Charley's responsibilities

OTHER CASE PROBLEMS

Apart from the possessive problems just described, case problems in English are few and are getting fewer. On the one hand, the generations of American farm boys and immigrant children who were exposed at home to the likes of "Me and her get along fine" have given way to the sophisticated television viewers who now fill our kindergartens. Today the basic rules of case in good spoken English are taken in early. On the other hand, teachers have reconsidered the old rules and discovered that some of the expressions they formerly condemned as ungrammatical are not so bad after all. Recent developments in linguistics and lexicography have also encouraged the abandonment of outworn grammatical formulas where they conflict with usage.

The result of all these developments has been a revolution in teaching and grammatical thinking. The fussy-sounding expressions *It is I* and *That is he* are no longer taught, and *Whom are you kidding?* is down to its last dozen defenders. Only a rare voice is still raised against T. S. Eliot's "Let us go then, you and I," on the ground, now generally considered irrelevant, that *I*, being in apposition to the objective *us*, should be the objective *me*. Many teachers no longer even object to *whom* in *They gave him men whom he knew could be trusted*, or to *who* in *Who are they talking about?* The argument against these sentences is sound and logical: it can be grasped, diagramed, explained. The argument for them is simply that this is what most people, including educated people, would actually say. With the triumph of *It's me* and *That's him*, both indefensible in classical terms, both rooted in usage, a new era has dawned.

We cannot yet say with any certainty what the case rules of that era will be, save for the obvious ones that give no one any trouble. Accordingly, in all matters of case (that is, in all choices between *I* and *me, he* and *him, she* and *her, we* and *us, they* and *them, who* and *whom*) our advice is simply to write what you would say—if, that is, you speak something like Standard English.

TENSE PROBLEMS

Foreigners learning English find the tenses difficult to master, but for native-born writers only three kinds of decision may be said to give trouble: between past tense and present in sentences like *She asked herself whether the law (is) (was) just*; between present and perfect in sentences like *He would have been glad to (go) (have gone)*; and between indicative and subjunctive in sentences like *If Reagan (was) (were) president, things would be different*. Although the subjunctive is technically a "mood" rather than a tense, the distinction has no practical effect.

The Past vs. the Present

In a clause following a past-tense verb or a verb in the conditional (*would* + verb), the verb should normally be in the past tense, not the present. The following sentences are correct:

She asked herself whether the law *was* just. (not *is*)

Professor Snyder explained what "atomic weight" *meant*. (not *means*)

One would think he *was* crazy. (not *is*)

The use of the past tense here is natural and idiomatic; the present tense, though not wrong, sounds unnatural. Note especially that the past-tense verb does not connote finality—in the second sentence above, for example, the choice of *meant* rather than *means* carries no suggestion that "atomic weight" means something different today. The present tense is preferable to the past only when the past would be patently awkward or misleading:

The dispute was over what freedom *means* in the Soviet Union.

The Senator explained what the Republicans stood for thirty years ago, and what they *stand for* today.

The Perfect

One verb in the perfect tense (*have* + verb) should not be subordinated to another: write *He would have been glad to go,* not *He would have been glad to have gone.* The following sentences are correct:

She would have given anything *to be chosen.* (*not* to have been chosen)

Gallman *has enjoyed being* Ambassador to Korea. (*not* enjoyed having been *or* enjoys having been)

It would have been easy for Myra *to make* her father happy. (*not* to have made)

The Subjunctive

The subjunctive offers few difficulties save to those who try to extend its legitimate domain. Its chief accepted uses today are as follows: (1) the use of *were* for *was* in clauses introduced by *if* and *wish* and expressing hypothetical rather than factual conditions (*if I were king* / *I wish I were dead*); (2) the omission of *should* in clauses introduced by verbs expressing will, command, or desire (*I move that the meeting be adjourned* / *I insist that my money be refunded*); and (3) the use of infinitive rather than indicative forms in half a dozen old-fashioned expressions, notably *come what may, be that as it may, far be it from me,* and *suffice it to say.*

Much ink has been spilled in defense of the subjunctive in category (1) against the incursions of the indicative; but *if I was king* and *I wish I was dead,* though not yet accepted as proper by authorities on usage, are gaining inexorably and seem likely to prevail. Category (2), by contrast, is of recent growth and very vigorous, in large part because the use of *should,* though perfectly correct and natural to many Englishmen, strikes Americans as softening the intended meaning. In English usage, *I insist that my money be refunded* and *I insist that my money should be refunded* mean the same thing. In American usage, the first means "Give it back," the second "By rights I should get it back." The first form, being in this interpretation more manly than the second, has prevailed.

Category (3) offers no problems. In fact, the subjunctive as a whole offers no problems except to writers with a flair for the archaic, that minority in every generation who are prompted by their fondness for an older prose or poetry (*If this be treason* / *What care I how fair she be?*) to revive a form that is as foreign to modern writing as the casual use of Latin. Here are two sentences from student themes:

> Whether his charge *be* true or false, it has the authority of his suffering.

> If these conditions *be* made, no man could qualify.

The first *be* should be *is,* the second *were* or *are.* In both cases, *be* was once correct but is no longer. One may regret the change, but one must respect it. As Fowler wrote nearly fifty years ago, those who traffic in archaic subjunctives run the risk, "first, of making their matter dull, . . . and lastly, of having the proper dignity of style at which they aim mistaken by captious readers for pretentiousness."

10

SYNTAX

Good syntax is a matter of arranging or grouping words for maximum clarity to the reader. A few typical sentences in which the words are not prop'y arranged will illustrate the chief problems discussed in this chapter:

> The first stanza is serious, straightforward, and sets the theme of the poem.

> Lying in the gutter, Hannah found her lost watch.

> Seymour's brother asked the pitcher if he could play third base.

> The town, which I grew up in, had only one school.

> Like the AMA plan, private groups were to allocate the subsidies.

The first sentence is unparallel; having established the pattern of a series of adjectives, the writer has veered off before completing it. The writer of the second sentence has improperly attached the phrase *Lying in the gutter* to *Hannah* rather than to *watch*. In the third sentence, there are three possible antecedents for *he*. The fourth sentence may conceivably be correct, but would probably prove in context to require not *The town, which* but *The town that*; the issue here is that of restrictive versus nonrestrictive clauses, a basic distinction in the use of English. The fifth sentence, illustrating one of the three "syntactical battlegrounds" with which we conclude the chapter, misuses *like* as a conjunction. Either it should begin *As in the AMA plan,* or it should end *the new plan called for the subsidies to be allocated by private groups*.

PARALLELISM

According to Blake, there are three main states: innocence, experience, and a higher innocence. Their major symbols are the child, the man, the woman, and Christ. No good writer will subject his reader to conundrums of this sort. A change to *the child, the adult, and Christ* is essential to make the two series parallel to each other, and hence coherently related to each other; failing this change, the reader will either move on perplexed to the next sentence or have to spend time sorting out the two series. Either way he will be irritated, and with justice.

Although failures of parallelism are rarely so striking, the principle is of the first importance in good writing. Things related to each other in parallel construction are clearly related; where the parallelism is faulty, the relationship may or may not be clear. And where any chance for confusion exists, some readers will surely become confused.

The basic requirement for a parallel construction is easily stated: What is true of one element must be true of the others. If one element is a noun, the others must be nouns; if one is a prepositional phrase, the others must be prepositional phrases; if one has a verb, the others must have verbs. There are two main kinds of parallel construction in English: the series of three or more elements (*red, white, and blue*) and the correlative pair (for example, *either/or*). In the next few pages we shall consider the most frequent departures from parallelism of both kinds, and the best ways of repairing them.

Series

The most common form of unparallel series is the one illustrated above: *The first stanza is serious, straightforward, and sets the theme of the poem.*   Here are two others of the same sort, both, as it happens, slips in current handbooks of English:

> Most uses of capital letters are conventional [*adjective*], easily understood [*adjective*], and cause [*verb*] no difficulty.

> She made more sandwiches [*noun*], more hot chocolate [*noun*], and scraped [*verb*] out the last of the pudding.

To correct the faulty parallelism, either make the three terms of the series syntactically identical (*Most uses of capital letters are conventional, easily understood, and easy to apply*) or abandon the series as such (*She made more sandwiches and hot chocolate, and scraped out the last of the pudding*).   The latter solution is always available, and is often the better.   Some writers shrink from the second *and* ("The first stanza is serious *and* straightforward, *and* sets the theme of the poem"); but in our opinion, far from being a blight, it is a touch of elegance, a welcome sign that the writer knows what he is doing.

The second most common form of unparallel series is one in which an opening word—usually an article, a preposition, or a conjunction—appears before the first element in the series and again before the last element, but is dropped before some or all of the intermediate elements.   Here are five examples of unparallel series of this sort, with the key words in italics:

> Among those present were *the* President, Secretary of State, General Abbott, and *the* English Ambassador.

> The rules state that *a* hat, coat, and *a* tie must be worn.

> Cortez was informed *that* the enemy forces numbered 2,000, they were heavily armed, and *that* their stone outworks were impregnable.

> There is no life *on* the sun, the moon, or *on* the stars.

> Inexpert writers tend to substitute the dash most commonly *for* the comma, the semicolon, and *for* parentheses.

Parallelism requires that a preposition or a conjunction be used either before every term of a series or before the first term only: that is, either *on the sun, on the moon, or on the stars* or *on the sun, the moon, or the stars.* The choice is a matter of taste. Articles are less flexible. For one thing, it is generally preferable to put the article before each term in the series rather than just the first; in the second sentence above, for example, *a hat, a coat, and a tie* is better than *a hat, coat, and tie,* which tends to make a bogus unit or ensemble out of three clearly separate items. For another, a series may contain some terms capable of taking the article and some not, as in the first and last sentences above (*the General Abbott* and *the parentheses* are impossible). In such cases, the article *must* be placed before each of the other terms— the terms capable of taking an article—to make the series parallel.

There are many other possibilities of unparallelism in series, too many to be illustrated here. The general thing to remember is that parallel construction is a principle of order, a way of telling the reader economically what elements go together or have the same weight. A sprawling sentence like *The speaker was tall, with long, shaggy hair, and wore Army fatigues* will slow a reader up unnecessarily; one does not immediately perceive its three parts as describing three roughly equal characteristics of the speaker's appearance. Either of two parallel constructions offers a clearer map of the terrain:

> The speaker was tall, shaggy-haired, and dressed in Army fatigues.

> The speaker was tall, his hair was long and shaggy, and he wore Army fatigues.

Correlatives

Parallelism in correlative pairs, like parallelism in series, requires that what is true of one element be true of the other. The four pairs in question are *either/or, neither/nor, both/and,* and *not only/but* (*also*). Errors made under this heading can often be fixed by merely switching the position of one of the correlatives, and can almost always be fixed in more than one way. The following sentences are defective, with alternative corrections indicated in parentheses:

Intransigent dates in England from about 1880; being now established, it should neither be pronounced as French nor spelled *-eant* any longer. (*be neither pronounced;* OR *nor be spelled*)

All-out war on two fronts was impossible: either we concentrated on defeating Germany or on Japan. (*or we concentrated on defeating Japan;* OR *we had to concentrate either on Germany or on Japan*)

Water pollution is a problem both in the city and the country. (*and in the country;* OR *in both the city*)

The Duke of San Lorenzo not only collected rare manuscripts, but also paintings and sculpture. (*collected not only;* OR *but also collected*)

In the first sentence, the rule says that if *neither* takes a verb phrase, *nor* should take a verb phrase; and that if *neither* takes a participle, *nor* should take a participle or some equivalent form of adjective. Similarly with the other sentences. In the second, for example, *either* is followed by a complete clause, *or* by a phrase; parallelism requires both to be followed by clauses, or both by phrases.

Correlative constructions in which both parts have not only the same subject but also the same verb may take any of three possible forms:

1. *Not only* did U Thant act quickly, *but* he acted courageously.
2. U Thant *not only* acted quickly, *but* acted courageously.
3. U Thant acted *not only* quickly *but* courageously.

1. *Either* the sketch was a genuine Picasso, *or* it was a skillful forgery.
2. The sketch *either* was a genuine Picasso *or* was a skillful forgery.
3. The sketch was *either* a genuine Picasso *or* a skillful forgery.

In sentences 1, the correlatives introduce complete clauses; in sentences 2 they introduce verbs; in sentences 3 they introduce adverbs in one case and nouns in the other.   Usually one of the possible choices sounds better than the other two: in the examples above, sentence 3 seems clearly the best choice for both. Once the various truly parallel possibilities are determined, the choice is a matter of taste.   The problem is to avoid such unparallel alternatives as *U Thant not only acted quickly but courageously* or *The sketch was either a genuine Picasso, or it was a skillful forgery.*

A surprisingly frequent error is the false pairing *neither/or*, as in *Neither the Army, the Navy, or the Marines favored American intervention.*   Whether in pairs or in series of three or more, *neither* goes with *nor* and *either* with *or.*   There are no exceptions.

MISPLACED MODIFIERS

Just as an adjective normally comes immediately before or after the noun it modifies (*a blue car, a tale too sad for words*), so an adjectival clause should be placed as close as possible to its noun.   Violations of this principle may produce the absurdities known as misplaced modifiers, of which the largest single class goes by the name of dangling participles.

Dangling Participles

A participle is the adjective form of a verb, ending either in *-ing* (present participle) or in *-ed, -en,* or *-t* (past participle); for all practical purposes, it may be treated exactly like an adjective. When a participle begins a sentence, it must modify the subject of the independent clause that follows. The following sentences are accordingly correct:

> *Ravaged* by illness and starvation, Mola's *regiment* had no choice but to surrender.

> *Shrieking* wildly, the *children* ran toward the lake.

The classic error is to place the modified noun or pronoun in some subordinate position, or to leave it to inference:

> Following the criminal's trial, past manhunts occupied Inspector Leonard's thoughts.

> After crossing the threshold, Mrs. Brooke's drawing room was the spacious apartment on the left.

The first sentence has "past manhunts" doing the following, not Inspector Leonard; the second has Mrs. Brooke's drawing room crossing the threshold. *Crossing* is technically a gerund rather than a participle (see p. 281), but the distinction makes no difference in this context.

Defective sentences of this sort can usually be corrected in either of two ways. One is to keep the participle or gerund construction but give the independent clause a suitable subject: *Following the criminal's trail, Inspector Leonard thought of past manhunts / After crossing the threshold, a visitor entered Mrs. Brooke's drawing room, the spacious apartment on the left.* The other is to leave the independent clause as it stands but abandon the participle construction: *As Inspector Leonard followed the criminal's trail, past manhunts occupied his thoughts / As one entered the front door, Mrs. Brooke's drawing room was the spacious apartment on the left.* The choice between these alternatives is a matter of taste.

The word modified by a participle must be a full noun or pronoun, not a possessive form, and must be complete in itself, not part of a compound subject or buried in a verb. The following sentences are wrong:

> Suprised at the compliment, her eyes sparkled with pleasure.

> Being the oldest, his word was law.

> Having borne him two boys, Mrs. Lincoln and her husband were hoping for a girl.

Her eyes were not surprised by the compliment; *she* was. *His word* was not the oldest; *he* was. As for Lincoln, his part in the bearing of his sons was no doubt as large as a loving husband could make it, but the equal of Mrs. Lincoln's it was not.

Other Danglers

Not only participles may be misplaced, but other adjectives and adjective phrases as well:

> Twice the size of her brother, they called her Big Bertha.
>
> While out for a stroll one morning, a thief broke into my apartment.
>
> Sad and bitter at first, Chopin's good spirits soon returned.
>
> As an orphan, Hardy has made Jude even more susceptible to the modern anxieties.

The remedy here is the same as for misplaced participles. Either convert the opening phrase to a subordinate clause, or see that the independent clause begins with a suitable noun:

> Twice the size of her brother, she was known as Big Bertha.
>
> While I was out for a stroll one morning, a thief broke into my apartment.
>
> Sad and bitter though Chopin was at first, his good spirits soon returned.
>
> As an orphan, Jude is even more susceptible to the modern anxieties.

Adverbial phrases can also be misplaced, as in the following examples, the first from a student paper, the second from the *New Republic*:

> In his fiction, Foster portrays men who wield power from a godlike height.
>
> He denounced another critic, Martin Luther King, at a 1964 news conference with women reporters as a notorious liar.

In the first sentence, *from a godlike height* makes a false sense unit with *wield power*; in the second, *as a notorious liar* is too far from *Martin Luther King* for the connection to be made without difficulty. Both sentences simply need reshuffling to bring the adverbial phrases nearer to what they modify:

> In Forster's fiction, men who wield power are portrayed from a godlike height.

> At a 1964 news conference with women reporters, he denounced another critic, Martin Luther King, as a notorious liar.

Participle Prepositions

A number of participles have acquired the status of prepositions in some uses. In these uses they are no longer subject to the rules of attachment and can be placed without concern for how they relate to the nearest noun. For example:

> *Given* Thieu's view of the chances of success, how can we blame him for seeking help?

> *Barring* acts of God, no more money was to be spent on welfare measures.

> Six more votes remained to be cast, not *counting* those of the New York delegation.

Some two dozen participles have entered this category, in the wake of such earlier participle prepositions as *according* and *concerning*; and many more will no doubt follow. Most participles, however, are untouched by this trend, and seem likely to remain so. When in doubt, attach participles carefully to suitable nouns, or avoid the participle construction altogether.

One participial phrase for which preposition status is hotly disputed is *due to*. It is correct to say *His success was due to hard work*, but can we say *Due to hard work he succeeded*? That is, can the phrase be used adverbially as well as adjectivally? *Due to* in this adverbial use is gaining ground, but is not yet generally accepted.   Our advice is to use *owing to, thanks to,* or *because of* where an adverb is needed and restrict *due to* to its undisputed adjectival use.   A rule of thumb favored by some editors is to use *due to* only where *caused by* would not sound foolish.

ANTECEDENTS

Ambiguous Antecedents

The noun to which a pronoun refers should be unmistakable. Such a farrago of pronouns as *He told him that his father had lost his shoes* is impervious to rational analysis, but a sentence with only one pronoun may be just as baffling. *During the war between China and Japan, their industrial output increased 20 percent.* Whose industrial output?   Both countries?   And if so, both equally, or is the 20 percent some kind of average? And does it make sense to quote a joint statistic like this for two countries that are fighting each other?   It is to spare the reader puzzlements of this sort that clear antecedents are desirable.

The main thing to avoid is pronouns that can refer to any of two or more possible antecedents.   In the following sentences, the ambiguous pronoun is italicized and the ambiguity is elaborated in parentheses:

Cliff asked Jack if *he* could go.   (*who?*)

The congressmen who heard the strikers' complaints described *their* experience as harrowing.   (*whose experience, the congressmen's or the strikers'?*)

Oakland is losing population to San Francisco and *its* suburbs.   (*Oakland's suburbs* or *San Francisco's?*)

They spend a lot of time drinking, and *that* is something I don't approve of.   (*drinking in general, or spending so much time drinking?*)

Omitted Antecedents

Another error is to bury the antecedent in an adjective, or to leave it to inference:

French cooking is *their* chief claim to fame.

The Dean's Office welcomes *student* inquiries about *their* draft status.

The Hawks *fumbled* five times but recovered four of *them*.

Often the best way to correct sentences of this sort is to get rid of the pronoun altogether: "French cooking is *France's* chief claim to fame." Alternatively, the pronoun should have a legitimate and unmistakable antecedent: "*students'* inquiries about *their* draft status"; "had five *fumbles* but recovered four of *them*."

Ideas and Phrases as Antecedents

Though once considered incorrect, it is now perfectly correct to use *which, this,* or *that* to refer to a general idea or statement rather than to a specific noun antecedent, provided there is no ambiguity in the reference. It is essential, however, that this condition of no ambiguity be fulfilled. The following sentences are good English:

Few blacks voted, *which* is understandable in the circumstances.

Thirty-five people were killed and two hundred wounded; *that* is all we know.

An empty icebox, dirty dishes, mud on the floor—*this* is what we get for giving Uncle Mort a key.

The following sentences, by contrast, contain ambiguities (indicated in the parenthetical questions), and are accordingly unacceptable:

The audience booed and threw fruit, *which* caused the manager to lower the curtain. (*the audience reaction in general, or the fruit in particular?*)

The commission vetoed the mayor's plan to ban weekday traffic on midtown streets; for my part, I think *this* was the right thing to do. (*what? ban traffic or veto the plan?*)

RESTRICTIVE AND NONRESTRICTIVE CONSTRUCTIONS

Apposition

Apposition, a construction in which two nouns or noun phrases, usually adjacent, refer to the same thing, may be either *restrictive* or *nonrestrictive*. To get at the complicated meaning of these terms, let us consider two examples, the first nonrestrictive, the second restrictive:

> I have a brother and a sister. My brother, *a priest,* lives in New York.

> I have two brothers. My brother *John* lives in New York.

In the first example, *my brother* is enough to tell the reader precisely who is meant, since he knows I have only one brother. My addition of *a priest* does not restrict or alter the meaning of *my brother,* but simply adds a piece of parenthetical information to a sentence that makes perfect sense without it. In the second example, *my brother* alone would not tell the reader who is meant; he knows I have two brothers, and cannot know which one I refer to until I add a name. My addition of *John* accordingly restricts the meaning of *my brother* to the particular brother I have in mind: my brother John, not my brother Elmer. Without the addition the sentence is unintelligible.

As the example indicates, the distinction between restrictive and nonrestrictive nouns in apposition is made with commas: the restrictive takes no commas, the nonrestrictive two commas (one if the noun comes at the end of the sentence). The usual error is to add commas where they are not wanted, as in the following sentences:

> Mailer's novel, *The Naked and the Dead,* shows his obsessive concern with the details of sex.

> A good place to begin is with Marx's critique of the reformist economists, Carey and Bastiat.

The commas in the first sentence imply that *The Naked and the Dead* is Mailer's only novel; the one in the second sentence implies that Carey and Bastiat alone in history, or at least in Marx's time, can properly be called "reformist economists." Neither implication conforms to the facts. Such constructions should be made either unmistakably restrictive (*Mailer's novel* The Naked and the Dead *shows / the reformist economists Carey and Bastiat*) or unmistakably nonrestrictive (*Mailer's first novel,* The Naked and the Dead, *shows / two reformist economists, Carey and Bastiat*).

Neat as this distinction is, it must sometimes be ignored. The following sentences, which ignore it, are correct:

His wife Grace was the first to volunteer.

The bond issue was floated by that notoriously corrupt and incompetent subsidiary of Amco International, the General Bionics Corporation.

Our erstwhile ally and friend in the Far East, General Pham Vong, was listed among the wounded.

Since a man has only one wife, *Grace* is clearly nonrestrictive; yet commas would place more emphasis on this name than the context warrants, and they are accordingly dropped. In the other two sentences the apposition is basically restrictive, as we can see from the simple analogous constructions *that rascal Arthur* and *my friend Flicka*; but the components are too long and complex to hold together without commas, which are accordingly added.

The exceptions, it is clear, come at the extremes of simplicity and complexity. For the 90 percent or more of all appositive constructions that fall between these extremes, the rule holds: comma or commas for the nonrestrictive, no comma for the restrictive.

Relative Clauses

The same rule holds for restrictive and nonrestrictive relative clauses (clauses introduced by *who, whom, that, which, of whom, to which,* etc.). In the first of the following examples, *who worked hard* is restrictive; in the second the same clause is nonrestrictive:

The men who worked hard received a bonus; the others were fired.

The men, who worked hard, received a bonus; the two boys were fired.

In the first example, *who worked hard* restricts the meaning of *men* to those who worked hard, whence the term "restrictive." In the second example, *who worked hard* does not restrict the meaning of *men* but simply adds to what the rest of the sentence tells us about a group of men already identified in a previous sentence. The second sentence would convey its essential meaning without *who worked hard*; the commas are in effect parentheses. In the first sentence, by contrast, *who worked hard* is essential to the message; it is not parenthetical but an integral part of what the sentence is saying.

Few distinctions are more important to good writing than this one, yet few are harder for the beginning writer to master. In our experience examples help, and we accordingly present six representative pairs of examples below. Only the first three involve relative clauses; the next two involve adverbial clauses and the last an adverbial phrase. In each case the first member of the pair is restrictive, the second nonrestrictive. Note that the distinction is always made by using a comma for the nonrestrictive (two commas if the clause is in the middle of the sentence rather than at the end), and no comma for the restrictive. All of the following sentences are correct:

R Why should I keep ice skates that are too small for me?

N I sold my old ice skates, which were too small for me.

R Senator Fulbright is one senator whose views on this subject are known.

N Senator Fulbright, whose views on this subject are known, did not vote.

R Clean government is a goal to which most officials give only lip service.

N Kavanaugh's goal was clean government, to which most officials give only lip service.

R   The headings should not be numbered as they are now.
    (*they should be numbered some other way*)

N   The headings should not be numbered, as they are now.
    (*the numbers should be eliminated*)

R   Appropriately enough, the distinguished lexicographer
    Sir William Craigie makes his home in the town where
    Dr. Johnson was born.

N   Appropriately enough, the distinguished lexicographer
    Sir William Craigie makes his home in Lichfield, where
    Dr. Johnson was born.

R   We had only one bad hurricane in 1969.   (*but we have
    had several since*)

N   We had only one bad hurricane, in 1969.   (*and none
    before or since*)

It is not always easy to determine whether a sentence should
be restrictive or nonrestrictive.   How does one choose between *I
have a lawn mower that needs sharpening* and *I have a lawn
mower, which needs sharpening*?   Between *There was a drought
one summer that dried up the lake* and *There was a drought one
summer, which dried up the lake*?   None of these alternatives is
wrong, and our advice in borderline cases of this sort is simply to
take your pick.   When in doubt, choose the restrictive.   In ordinary speech the restrictive (*that*) construction is six times as common as the nonrestrictive (*which*); the ratio in writing is much
lower, but is probably at least two to one.

That and Which

In the preceding examples we have recommended using *that*
for the restrictive and *which* for the nonrestrictive, following the
practice of most good writers and the almost universal pattern
of spoken English.   Another characteristic of spoken English is
to omit *that* altogether when it serves as the object (as opposed
to the subject) of a restrictive clause.   Here again we recommend making writing conform to speech:

Awkward

>the first books *which* Dickens wrote

Acceptable

>the first books *that* Dickens wrote

Better

>the first books Dickens wrote

We think that if you would omit *that* in speaking, you should omit it in writing. Similarly in the following:

the security which it gives	the kind of person which he was
the security that it gives	the kind of person that he was
the security it gives	the kind of person he was

Even writers who reject the highly formal *which* in such phrases sometimes retain an unnecessary and faintly irritating *that* in deference to the supposed requirements of formality. Formality has its requirements, to be sure, but this is not one of them.

SOME SYNTACTICAL BATTLEGROUNDS

A number of simple principles of syntax have been developed over the years by teachers of English in an effort to come to some sort of workable terms with the complexities of a living language. Some of these principles are sensible and to the point: the main ones have been dealt with earlier in this chapter. Others have been ill served by oversimplifiers or eroded by contrary usage; if they are still worth heeding, their claims must be convincingly restated. Still others were nonsense from the start, having nothing but their simplemindedness to recommend them.

With these last we need not concern ourselves. It was never incorrect to begin a sentence with *But* or *And*; it was never incorrect to write sentences without verbs; and if it was ever incorrect to end a sentence with a preposition, that stuffy day is long past. Our concern here is rather with practices over which tradition and usage are to some extent at war, and in particular with three members of this class: the split infinitive, the fused participle, and the use of *like* as a conjunction.

The Split Infinitive

The split infinitive can be traced back to the fourteenth century. Its chief modern forms appeared in the early seventeenth, and in the past hundred years there has been scarcely a major writer in the United States or England whose works are free of it. Is the form then completely acceptable? No, say the traditionalists; yes, say the impatient; not quite, is the advice here.

There are three possible positions for the adverb modifying an infinitive: before it (*completely to understand him*), splitting it (*to completely understand him*), and after it (*to understand him completely*). The last is recommended as natural:

In the end she decided to live *openly* with Paul.

They were too busy to look after the children *properly*.

Captain Larsen requested permission to explore the matter *further*.

The first position, before the infinitive, is less often natural, but should be preferred to splitting when it is not objectionable: "I do not want you *ever* to take such chances," "*Even* to wish for mercy would be cowardice." Only if neither outside position will do justice to the meaning should the infinitive be split:

The glare caused the men to *half* close their eyes.

He appeared to *suddenly* lose all control of the boat.

Mother had to *simply* take over the accounts.

The chief difficulty with split infinitives today is not that conservatives oppose them absolutely, but that radicals split them too freely. The battle for permission to split has long been won; the issue today is where to draw the line. Rightly or wrongly,

split infinitives make many readers uneasy. Since the last thing
you want to do is make your readers uneasy, it follows that you
should split infinitives only when any alternative arrangement
would be even less attractive.

The Fused Participle

"Fused participle" is the name given by Fowler to a very common construction midway between the pure participle or adjective form in -*ing* and the pure gerund or noun form. The three
constructions may be illustrated as follows:

Participle

I saw them dancing.

Gerund

I enjoyed their dancing.

Fused participle

I like them dancing together.

In the first example, *dancing* is an adjective modifying *them*. In
the second example, it is a noun, the direct object of *enjoyed*. In
the third example, *dancing* has the noun quality of the second
(it is the direct object of the verb), but the adjective form of the
first; it is neither a pure gerund or noun, which would necessarily
take the possessive *their,* nor a pure participle or adjective, which
could not serve as a direct object. It is a fusion of the gerund
and participle forms.

Fowler considered the fused participle a plain error, to be corrected by converting to the pure gerund form with the possessive (*I like their dancing together*), or to the pure participle form
(e.g. *I like to see them dancing together*); or by switching to a
different construction altogether (e.g. *I like watching them dance
together*). We disagree. The following sentences, all of which
contain fused participles, seem to us perfectly acceptable:

It was impossible to imagine so small a *ship being* torpedoed.

They could talk in the garden without the *servants hearing* what they said.

There was a skit about two *men* from Mars *walking* down Broadway.

The question, then, is whether all fused participles are acceptable or only some. Is it all right to say *They insisted on us paying for the tickets*? How about *John being appointed surprised everyone*? It is all right, we suppose, but most writers and all editors would say *our paying* and *John's being appointed,* and that is what we advise. In general, follow your ear. When in doubt, it is better to fuse a participle than to avoid fusing it at the cost of an awkward possessive or an unnatural wording.

Like and As

The distinction between *like* and *as* is easily made. *Like,* a preposition, compares nouns, pronouns, and noun phrases: *I am like my father / Like the women who had brought him up, Neil hated braggarts.* *As,* a conjunction, compares adverbs, adverbial phrases, and clauses: *For Johnson, as for Kennedy, there were no easy answers / Mme. de Sévigné was afraid of mice, as many women are.* *As* has other uses as well, some of which are discussed on pp. 270–271. We confine ourselves in this section to uses of *as* that bring it into conflict with *like.*

The classic error is to use *like* to introduce a clause. The following sentences illustrate this error:

Harry drives like Jack does.

These recurrent symbols clarify the poem's meaning, much like the action of a Greek drama is clarified by the chorus.

The patient sits before a screen that looks like it came from a television set.

The more vocal champions of *like* apparently consider the correct use of *as* in these sentences (*as if* in the third) affected or snobbish. However this may be, *like* is now routinely used to introduce clauses by perhaps half the English-speaking world, and bids fair in the end to drive *as* from the field.

The advice here, nonetheless, is to hold the line. The distinction between *like* and *as* is easily learned, and its proper application is regarded by discriminating people as basic to good English. If you shrink from using *as* to mean *in the way that,* for example in *Harry drives as Jack does,* use *the way* instead: *Harry drives the way Jack does.*

The following sentences illustrate the correct use of *like, as,* and *the way*:

> Alvin walks *like* an ape.
> Alvin walks *the way* apes *walk.*
>
> I have been lonely, *as* you *have been.*
> *Like* you, I have been lonely.
>
> Shakespeare, *like* Marlowe before him, wrote with actors and an audience in mind.
> Shakespeare wrote *as* Marlowe before him *had written,* with actors and an audience in mind.

The principle followed in constructing these sentences is easily summarized. When there is a verb in the phrase governed by *like/as,* use *as* (or *the way*): "the way apes *walk,*" "as you *have been,*" "as Marlowe before him *had written.*" When there is a noun only, use *like.*

What goes for *like* goes also for *unlike,* a word often misused out of desperation because there is no word *un-as* and no good equivalent. *Unlike* can only compare nouns, pronouns, or noun phrases: *Unlike Harry, I was tired / Elizabeth Taylor, unlike most people, spends $20,000 a month.* The following sentences are wrong (suggested revisions in parentheses):

> Unlike in the previous election, few charges of fraud were made. (*Unlike the previous election, this one evoked few charges of fraud.*)
>
> For Sue, unlike her sister, the experience was exhilarating (*Sue, unlike her sister, found the experience exhilarating.*)

Unlike what both sides had expected, the battle was soon over. (*Contrary to what both sides had expected, the battle was soon over.*)

Finally, there is a growing tendency, especially among college students, to write *as* erroneously for *like*; for example, *Byron, as Keats and Shelley before him, died young.* This curious construction apparently comes from an excessive fear of falling into the opposite error, that of using *like* for *as*, which, as we have seen, is by far the more common and the more loudly deplored. The new error, with its prissy, toe-in-the-water effect, seems if anything more deplorable than the old.

As this chapter has suggested, good syntax is not just a matter of rules, though rules are its necessary point of departure. It is also a matter of judging when and to what extent the rules apply, when and to what extent time and usage have passed them by, when convenience may properly be indulged at the expense of fastidiousness, and when the line should be held. The best arbiters of such matters, we think, are professional writers and editors, whose sense of the language is constantly elaborated and modified by their work. Their current practice has been the basis for our pronouncements in this chapter.

Several dozen other errors and pitfalls of syntax are discussed briefly in the Index to Current Usage, pp. 266–308.

11

ORTHOGRAPHY

Words must be not only correctly chosen (see Chapter 6) but correctly written, which is to say correctly spelled, divided, capitalized, and italicized as general usage or a specific context may require. Questions of orthography are generally less interesting than questions of diction, but they can be just as important to the writer's message. Small, even niggling, as most of them are, you cannot ignore them or answer them carelessly except at the expense of your reader's understanding.

SPELLING

For spelling, there is only one rule: if you are not absolutely sure how a word is spelled, look it up in the dictionary. If you are not allowed to use a dictionary—for example, during a test—you are on your own. English spelling is so irregular that no one should be required to memorize the spelling of more than a thousand or so of the most familiar words. A teacher who does not allow you to use a dictionary on a test will probably allow you a spelling error or two without penalty. Unless, of course, it is a spelling test.

HYPHENATION

The hyphen has four uses: to divide words at the end of a line (*Mac-/beth, syca-/more*), to divide prefixes from certain root words (*un-American, anti-imperialist*), to pull together compounds of two or more words into visual units (*brown-and-serve muffins, a get-together*), and to avoid repeating part of a word or a hyphenated compound (*pre- and postwar statistics*).

Word Division

To divide words properly simply follow your dictionary, which indicates all possible word divisions for a given word. Thus the dots in **syc · a · more** show that the word may be divided either *syc-/amore* or *syca-/more*. Proper names and words not in a dictionary should be divided between syllables; if you cannot tell for certain where a syllable ends, your best guess will probably serve. Never divide a one-syllable name or word, and never divide after the first letter or before the last.

Prefixes

The use of a hyphen with prefixes is easily learned. (1) If the root word begins with a capital letter, use a hyphen (*pre-Christian*). (2) If the prefix ends with a vowel and the root word begins with the same vowel, check your dictionary. Some such words are unhyphenated (*cooperate, preeminent*); others are hyphenated (*co-opt*); others do not appear in the dictionary, in which case use a hyphen (*co-owner, pre-educate*). (3) In all other cases do not hyphenate, save in the rare instance in which a hyphen may be used to distinguish one reading of a word from another: thus *re-cover*, "to cover again," is distinguished from *recover*.

Compounds

The third use of the hyphen—to pull together compounds of two or more words into visual units—is the most important and the most complex. The two main classes of such compounds may be illustrated as follows:

Noun compounds	Adjective compounds
a *sergeant first class*	a *life insurance* salesman
an *air-conditioner*	*hard-to-get* parts
a better *mousetrap*	a *clearheaded* woman

Observe that some members of each class are unhyphenated phrases, some are hyphenated compounds, and some are unhyphenated words. For noun compounds alone, *Webster's Third* prescribes the following bewildering variety of forms:

pocket-handkerchief	half-wit	off-season
pocket battleship	half brother	off year
pocketknife	halfback	offshoot
birthrate	makeup	vice-president
death rate	shake-up	vice admiral

How in the world, then, is one to know whether a compound should be hyphenated, run as two separate words, or made into a single word? For noun compounds the answer is easy: look up the compound in the dictionary. If you find it, use its dictionary form; if you don't find it, write it as separate words unless a hyphen seems necessary to eliminate a possible misreading.

Adjective compounds are harder to handle. Most are not listed in the dictionary at all, or are listed in their noun form only. We know, for example, that we should write *high school* thus as a noun, but should we hyphenate it or not as an adjective compound in the phrase *high school teacher*? The dictionary does not say. In effect, usage on this point is in transition, but the following broad guidelines may help.

If an adjective compound appears in your dictionary as a consolidated or hyphenated word, use the dictionary form: thus *Webster's Seventh* shows *fainthearted, hardworking, clear-sighted, hard-boiled.* If an adjective compound is not listed as such in your dictionary, either hyphenate it or write it as two (or more) words. Hyphenate number compounds (*a twenty-year period, a third-floor apartment*); participle compounds (*a card-carrying Communist*) except with adverbs ending in *-ly* (*a recently built factory*); preposition compounds (*a made-up story, an after-dinner speech*); compounds of coequal nouns (*the second Clay-Liston fight*); compounds expressing degree (*a large-scale enterprise*); and compounds of three or more words (*a door-to-door salesman, a high-silicon-content alloy*).[1] Write other adjective compounds as two words: *high school teacher, senior class party, civil rights agitation*. A hyphen would not be wrong in such expressions; but it may be a bit stilted or overformal.

Hyphenation to Avoid Repetition

Hyphens are sometimes used to avoid repeating part of a word or a hyphenated compound: *pro- and anti-Communist writing / over- and underrated movies / full- or part-time work / the food-preparing and -packaging industries*. Although Gowers calls this construction "a clumsy device that should be avoided if possible," there is often no better way to write what would naturally be said in speech. The problem is not so much to avoid the construction as to remember to add the essential hanging hyphen. Leaving it out will always produce imprecision: thus *full* for *full-* in the third example above would yield not *full-time work* but the meaningless *full work*. And it may cause deeper confusion: thus *packaging* for *-packaging* in the last example would yield not *the food-packaging industry* but *the packaging industry* in general, a very different thing.

Is usage in general moving slowly away from the hyphen? There are signs that it is. We know that British literate usage favors more hyphens than American literate usage, which in turn hyphenates more freely than American illiterate and scientific usage. At the same time, we find influential British writers like the late Winston Churchill spurning the hyphen as "a blemish

---

[1] This last construction is not attractive. At its worst, it provides horrors like this sentence, cited by Gowers: *A large-vehicle-fleet-operator mileage restriction has now been made imperative*. As Gowers remarks, such a sentence should be rewritten with prepositions: *It has now become imperative to impose a mileage restriction on the operators of fleets of large vehicles*. If it still doesn't sing, at least it has stopped croaking.

to be avoided wherever possible," and Gowers echoing this judgment to the point of recommending consolidated forms like *aftereffects* and *panicstricken* without turning a hair. The Merriam-Webster editors go even further, endorsing such extreme specimens as *radiobroadcasting* and *fluidounce*. When British grammarians and stylists agree with American illiterates, scientists, and lexicographers, who can stand against them? Our guess is that the hyphen is on its way out.

THE APOSTROPHE

In addition to forming possessives (see pp. 152–154), the apostrophe is used to form certain plurals and to form contractions.

Plurals

An apostrophe is ordinarily used to form plurals of numbers (*the 1960's, two size 9's*), letters (*two A's and three B's*), and abbreviations (*sixteen Ph.D.'s, some MP's*), and to form plurals of words used as words, book titles, and the like (*do's and don't's, and's instead of but's, a dozen* David Copperfield*'s*). Apostrophes should not be used to form other plurals. As we have seen, Mr. Jones's family is *the Joneses*, not *the Jones's*. Similarly, the plural of *New York*, for example, is not *New York's* but *New Yorks: Two New Yorks would be one too many*.

Contractions

Contractions are formed by substituting an apostrophe for some part of a word that is not pronounced in informal discourse. The words most commonly contracted are *not* (*isn't, don't*) and the various forms of *have* (*he's been, you've gone*), *will* (*I'll stay, they'd complain*), and *be* (*I'm, you're*). Although the standard contractions of *have, will,* and *be* involve pronouns, other contractions of all three are possible in dialogue: *I wouldn't've dared / The sun'll be up soon / The sky's the limit*. In writing contractions, take care to get the apostrophe in the right place (*hadn't,* not *had'nt*) and not to leave a space before or after it (*you'll,* not *you' ll* or *you 'll*).

Contractions like *'teens* (as in *girls in their 'teens*) and *'seventies* (meaning the 1970's), where the apostrophe indicates that part of a word is being used for the whole, are increasingly, and we think properly, written without the apostrophe. Some earlier travelers along this path were *'bus* for *omnibus* and *'coon* for *raccoon.*

On the status of the standard contractions in formal writing, see p. 103. Cute spellings like *ham 'n' eggs* are discussed on p. 104.

CAPITALIZATION

Capitalization is the bane of many a writer. The basic rules—to capitalize the first word in a sentence and such proper names as Henry Smith, Thursday, *War and Peace,* and the Chicago Bears—are easily learned, but once beyond the basics even the most experienced writer encounters difficulties. In this section we shall discuss some of the more persistent trouble areas.

Sentences Within Sentences

When a direct quotation makes a complete sentence within a sentence, you may either capitalize or lowercase the first word, depending on how the quotation relates to the rest of the sentence and without regard to whether or not the word is capitalized in the original. Thus, the same quotation may properly be begun with a capital letter in one context and a lowercase letter in another:

The Bible says: "Look not upon the wine when it is red."
The Bible asks that we "look not upon the wine when it is red."

In the words of Harold Wilson, "The worst is over."
Harold Wilson argues that "the worst is over."

By contrast, when a sentence within a sentence is not in quotes, do not capitalize the first word:

According to Harold Wilson, the worst was over.

The truth was plain: we had been deceived.

Art's job (he was test-flying helicopters) had been classified as hazardous.

A capital letter may follow a colon when the colon introduces a formal or weighty pronouncement, even if no quotation marks are used. For example, *He had his own version of the Golden Rule: Do unto others all you can get away with.* When in doubt, however, lowercase after a colon.

Personal Titles

Good writers capitalize personal titles when they are attached to names (*General Bert Guano, Professor Rainier*), but lowercase them when they are used alone (*Bert Guano was promoted to general / Mr. Rainier is a professor of French*). The problem comes when a title is used in place of a specific name. In a specific reference to General Guano, for example, should we write *The General called for volunteers* or *The general called for volunteers*? Both forms are common; neither is wrong. If current usage has any pattern at all, it is that the most eminent titles are the most frequently capitalized: few if any writers lowercase *the Pope, the President of the United States, the Queen of England.* For slightly less eminent titles, though lowercase is increasingly common, capitalization remains usual: *the Secretary of State, the Governor of Alaska, the Prime Minister, the Archbishop, the General.* At lower levels of eminence lowercase prevails: *the president of General Motors, the major, the professor, the judge, the coach.*

Parts Standing for the Whole

Eminent titles apart, it is usual to lowercase key words substituted for formal proper nouns. Thus, after an initial reference to the Mississippi River, we refer to it as *the river,* not *the River*; we refer to the Second World War as *the war,* to the Chinese Communist Party as *the party,* to the Chicago Public Library as *the library,* to the University of Wisconsin as *the university,* and so on. Naturally, this practice applies only when the lowercased word faithfully conveys the meaning of the full expression: a restaurant named the Old Barn cannot be referred to as *the barn,* or the Chicago Bears as *the bears.*

Points of the Compass

North, east, south, west, and their derivations cause all sorts of trouble. Should it be *Western Europe* or *western Europe?* In *the north* or *in the North?* Probably the most workable rule is to capitalize these words when they stand for a formal or semiformal political or geographic unit, and to lowercase them when they are used in a general geographical sense or merely to indicate direction. Thus *Southeast Asia* designates the area south of China and east of India and politically independent of both, whereas the geographical region *southeastern Asia* would include much of China and part of India. Similarly, *the East* refers to New England and the Central Atlantic states, or in another context to the Orient; *the east* refers to where the sun rises. A few more examples may make the distinction clearer:

Semiformal	General
West Germany	a west wind
South Korea	the south of France
North Africa	drive north to Seattle
the Far East	the east bank of the Rhine
the Southwest	southwestern Arkansas

By a semiformal name, we mean one that is sanctioned by usage (*West Germany*) or convenience (*North Africa*) rather than by formal political decree. *West Germany* is the common name for the Federal Republic of Germany, as *South Korea* is for the Republic of Korea; *North Africa, the Far East,* and *the Southwest* are convenient names for areas having no formal unity. Although not formal in the sense that *West Virginia* and *Northern Ireland* are formal, these names are in practice treated formally. The distinction between semiformal and general is more important, and is not always easy to make. When in doubt, lowercase. Adjectives derived from capitalized nouns in this class should themselves be capitalized: *Far Eastern policy, Middle Western roads, Southern hospitality.*

Historical Terms

Capitalize the names of historical eras and other historical phenomena when lowercasing would suggest a different or more diffuse meaning than the specific one you have in mind:

the Stone Age
the Reign of Terror
the Restoration
the Industrial Revolution
the May Thirtieth
    Movement

the Fourth of July
the Lost Generation
the Iron Curtain
the Great Proletarian Cultural
    Revolution

Where lowercasing would not convey a different meaning, either form is usually acceptable:

the Roman Empire/empire
the Bolshevik Revolution/
    revolution
the Pre-Raphaelite movement/
    Movement

the treaty/Treaty of
    Versailles
the French Impression-
    ists/impressionists
the Augustan Age/age

An exception is *War*, which is conventionally capitalized when the name of a war is given in full:

the Franco-Prussian War
the Sino-Japanese War of 1894–95

the Second World
    War
the War of the Roses

Book and Article Titles

In titles of books, magazine articles, songs, and other formal compositions, and in the titles and subheadings of papers that you write, capitalize the first and last words and all other words except (1) articles and (2) prepositions and conjunctions of five or fewer letters:

What Is an American?
"The Light Behind His
    Eyes"
Of Mice and Men

"When the Saints Come March-
    ing In"
Love in a Cold Climate
"What It Means to Be Ill"

ITALICS

Titles of Publications and Compositions

Italics are indicated in manuscript or typescript by underlining. Underline the names of newspapers and magazines; the titles of books, plays, and other longish pieces of writing, especially if published separately; and the names of movies, paintings, and long musical compositions:

the *Washington Post*   *Paradise Lost*
Life magazine   movies like *Easy Rider*
The Caine Mutiny   Cézanne's *View of Auvers*
The Merchant of Venice   Mozart's opera *Don Giovanni*

Do not underline the titles of newspaper or magazine articles, short stories, poems, songs, and other shortish pieces of writing, or of unpublished works. Use quotation marks:

"Chaos in Laos," editorial in the *San Francisco Chronicle*, August 1, 1971, p. 26

a senior thesis entitled "The Early English Stage"

Milton's "Lycidas"

the "Dear Abby" column

Chapter 3, "From the Long March to the Marco Polo Bridge Incident"

the short story "Epstein"

Cole Porter's "Begin the Beguine"

When in doubt, use quotation marks rather than underlining.

Foreign Terms

Underline only the most unfamiliar foreign words, not relatively common terms like ruble, fiancé, and prima donna. If a foreign expression is in quotation marks, underlining is unnecessary unless foreign and English words are mixed:

"Bonjour," said the man uncertainly.

Tolstoy's "Utro Pomeshchika" is another of his stories about peasants.

BUT: "Time to go now, *nicht wahr?*" said Charlie.

Do not underline foreign proper names:

The Comuneros and the Alumbrados joined forces in 1534.

I met her at the Piazza San Marco.

The Jeunesses Agricoles is a sort of French 4-H club.

The whole idea of underlining a foreign expression is to set it off clearly from the surrounding English. If quotation marks or capital letters accomplish this purpose, underlining is superfluous.

Emphasis

Underlining for emphasis is almost always a mistake; if you have this tendency, do your best to suppress it. Writers who underline for emphasis usually do so for one of two reasons. One is the desire to clarify a badly constructed sentence for the reader without going to the trouble of reconstructing it:

Clumsy

It was not so much the things she *had* done that made people annoyed with her as the things she had *not* done.

Rewritten

What she had done annoyed people much less than what she had not done.

The other is the desire to give writing some of the body English that intonation and gesture give to speech. Novelists sometimes use italics effectively in dialogue to convey kittenishness and other unprepossessing (or at best amusing) characteristics: "In *Ho*llywood! How *mar*velous! What's he *do*ing?" exclaims a girl in *The Catcher in the Rye,* and we know immediately what sort of girl she is.

In nonfiction, it is usually the writer that ends up sounding foolish. Here are three examples of excessive underlining from student themes:

Dogged

> I feel that punishment *can* be detrimental to a child's character or that it *could* cause damage to his psyche, but I do not think it usually *does*.

Strident

> Some people *really* have *no idea* that their parents were ever young.

Girlish

> His giggle nearly drove me *crazy*, and I thought to myself, "How am I *ever* going to survive this ghastly picnic?"

The temptation to underline can be very strong, particularly when you are exasperated at not being able to get the kind of emphasis in writing that comes so easily in speaking. But there is almost always a better way to get the reader's attention than by shouting at him. A change in wording, often a very slight one, will usually do the trick.

NUMBERS

The Twenty/21 Rule

Other things being equal, a good general rule is to spell out numbers up to twenty and use figures for 21 and over:

twelve o'clock	a sixteen-year-old	ten minutes
140 men wounded	a 21-year-old girl	45 minutes

Several exceptions to this rule are commonly made. One is that when figures for a number over 21 would suggest an exactness belied by the context, the number can be spelled out:

about a hundred years ago (*not* about 100 years ago)

sixty or eighty policemen (*not* 60 or 80 policemen)

a thousand times as good (*not* 1,000 times as good)

For numbers in four, five, or six figures this exception conventionally applies only to 1,000 and 10,000; other round numbers in this range are assumed to be approximate even if presented in figures: *an army of 80,000 men / 200,000 years ago.* For millions and billions mixed treatment is usual (*a population of over 14 million / a deficit of $163.1 billion*), with the first number often spelled out if it is one to ten (*two million beggars*) or a multiple of 100 (*seven hundred million Chinese*).

A second exception commonly made to the twenty/21 rule is to use figures invariably before *percent*: thus *1 percent, 10 percent.*

A third exception is to spell out any number that begins a sentence:

not 16 percent were Catholic *but* Sixteen percent were Catholic *or* Some 16 percent were Catholic

not 75 men showed up *but* Seventy-five men showed up *or* Only 75 men showed up

not 1865 was a memorable year indeed *but* Eighteen sixty-five was a memorable year indeed *or* The year 1865 was a memorable one indeed

This convention, which grew up because numbers do not have capital and lowercase forms like letters, no longer makes sense to many writers and editors. As the 1865 example suggests, the alternatives are particularly unsatisfactory for dates; nor is it easy to stomach something like *One thousand four hundred and eighty-one men were killed and wounded.* In the circumstances, we recommend following the convention when you can and violating it when you must.

Finally, a sequence of numbers that are essentially equal in weight or parallel in syntax should be treated the same way:

either all spelled out or all in figures. Thus in *I am 22, my sister Joan is eighteen, and my brother Dick is twelve,* either spell out *twenty-two* or run *18* and *12* in figures.

The twenty/21 rule does not apply to tabular presentation, scientific and technical writing (*carbon 14 / a factor of 2*), reference numbers (*Chapter 6 / Theorem 12*), dates (*15* B.C. / *April 3*), sports scores (*Amherst 7, Williams 6*), or any other area in which numbers are conventionally given in figures irrespective of context. It applies only where the option of spelling out is not precluded by convention, and where taking this option may solve a problem or avoid an irritation.

Other Number Conventions

Numbers linked by a hyphen to indicate a span (*pp. 326–328 / 1970–1971*) should be treated consistently: if you write *pp. 326–8* in one footnote, you should not write *pp. 205–06* in another and *pp. 171–179* in a third. The easiest way to be consistent is always to give the second number at full length, as is done in this book. If this seems a bit ponderous for dates, treat them as a separate category; the convention is *1970–71,* not *1970–1.*

A comma is conventional in four-figure numbers (as well as numbers of five and more figures) except for dates and page numbers of long books and journals. This convention applies not only to numbers like 1,234 that are read with a natural break at the comma position ("one thousand / two hundred and thirty-four") but also to numbers like 1,500, in spite of their being customarily read as "fifteen hundred" rather than "one thousand / five hundred."

Fractions are conventionally spelled out and hyphenated: *two-thirds,* not *two thirds* or *2/3* or *2/3rds.* The hyphen is standard even where the denominator can be read as a noun: *Two-thirds of my money was gone,* not *Two thirds.* Only *half* has achieved sufficient independence as a noun to drop the hyphen occasionally, as in *I took one half and gave George the other. Quarter* (the coin), *fifth* (the whiskey bottle), and other such fraction-derived nouns do not of course come under these rules for fractions.

Numbered Lists

In numbering lists, most writers use periods when each numbered item begins a new line, thus:

1. We demand that the University be closed Monday and Tuesday to honor the anniversary of the murder of Robert F. Kennedy.
2. We demand that Provost Schweinkopf resign.
3. We demand amnesty for all students accused of incendiary acts in the recent liberation of Weiss Hall.

When a numbered list is given in running text, double parentheses are usual, thus: *We demand (1) that the University be closed Monday, (2) that Provost Schweinkopf resign, and (3) that amnesty be granted to all students accused of incendiary acts in the recent liberation of Weiss Hall.* Other writers use double parentheses or single parentheses—1), 2), 3)—for both separate-line lists and lists in running text. The important thing is to be consistent: not to use (1), (2), (3) in one list and 1), 2), 3) or (*a*), (*b*), (*c*) in an analogous list several pages further on.

Prominent as the word *consistent* is in the last few paragraphs, consistency is no more important for numbers than for the other subjects covered in this chapter. Whether or not you hyphenate *junior college transfer,* or capitalize *the Senator,* or italicize a song title matters less than whether you write it the second time the same way you did the first. Four hundred years ago inconsistency was the norm; Shakespeare signed his name half a dozen different ways, and his contemporaries invented as many more. But today's writers are more orderly. A foolish consistency may be what Emerson called it, the hobgoblin of little minds; but between reasonable consistency and potential confusion there can be only one choice.

12

PUNCTUATION

Punctuation is partly a matter of rules and partly a matter of taste. Those who would make it altogether a matter of rules paint themselves into a corner: no rules can anticipate the millions of possible combinations of words that a writer may be moved to use, or his need to relate words in various ways for various effects, or his desire to slow down or quicken the reader's pace. Those who would make it altogether a matter of taste make an even more serious mistake. There are, after all, certain well-established rules or conventions for relating words, phrases, and clauses to each other, and most readers expect to see them followed, at least for the routine connections and separations.

THE PERIOD

A sentence or sentence fragment should end with a period unless it ends with a question mark or an exclamation point. A sentence occurring within another sentence must be punctuated according to the needs of the larger sentence: *She said "I am tired," but she didn't mean it / Bill spoke crossly (he was tired).* Periods are misused chiefly in making an illegitimate sentence fragment out of what is in fact properly a subordinate clause in the preceding sentence:

Wrong

He always goes fishing on August 1. Which is his birthday.

Right

He always goes fishing on August 1, which is his birthday.

Right

He always goes fishing on August 1. That is his birthday.

Another difficulty is the converse of this last, namely, making what is properly two sentences into one:

Wrong

He always goes fishing on August 1, that is his birthday.

Poor

I was hungry, I wanted some lunch.

Right

I was hungry. I wanted some lunch.

You may use a semicolon if a period seems too abrupt: *He always goes fishing on August 1; that is his birthday / I was hungry; I wanted some lunch.*

Notice that the sentence *I was hungry, I wanted some lunch* is labeled *poor,* not *wrong.* For many years this punctuation—known as the comma splice or comma fault—was anathema to teachers and editors, a sign of gross illiteracy; in some colleges it was grounds for an automatic F on a paper. But good writers persisted in using the construction, especially for certain effects of nervousness, tentativeness, and haste that no other punctuation could quite capture; and gradually it became acceptable in principle, however greatly abused in practice. The sentence fragment has come the same road, from outright rejection to qualified acceptance.   Both constructions, the comma splice and the sentence fragment, have their unique uses.   The problem is not how to avoid them altogether, but how to use them well.

A particular source of difficulty with the comma splice is the handling of direct quotations:

Wrong

"I am hungry," Marie said, "I want some lunch."

Right

"I am hungry," Marie said.   "I want some lunch."

Right

"I am hungry," Marie said, "and I want some lunch."

The writer of the first sentence has punctuated it as if it were the third; that is, he has mistaken two sentences for one.   In the second sentence, a semicolon rather than a period may be used; but a period is usual, perhaps because semicolons seem too formal for informal dialogue.

THE COMMA

The comma is the most important unit of punctuation; as befits this status, its proper use is both complex and hotly disputed. The disputants come largely from two schools of thought.   One is the old-fashioned or rhetorical school, which concerns itself with marking the natural pauses in a sentence as it might be spoken by an able speaker, and which accordingly caters to the ear.   The other is the modern or logical school, which concerns itself with clarifying the sense units of a sentence and bringing out their proper relationship to one another; this school caters primarily to the eye.   Current usage draws on the insights of both schools, with most authorities favoring the modern school in cases of out-and-out conflict.

The following discussion begins with some basics (use of the comma in appendages, series, compound sentences), moves on to more difficult matters (introductory phrases, parenthetical phrases, confluences), and ends with some general remarks on over- and underpunctuation. The basics are both the most important and the easiest to learn, but the later material is indispensable to a mastery of the comma.

Appendages

Most appendages preceded by a comma are also followed by a comma in running text:

Washington, D.C., is	June 14, 1947, was
Athens, Ohio, is	Sunday, June 14, was
The University of California, Berkeley, is	Trinity College, Oxford, is

The chief exceptions to this practice are *Jr., Inc.,* and academic degrees:

Alexander H. Jones, Jr. is	Textron, Inc. is
Robert Abrams, M.D. is	Unilever, Ltd. is

There are also, of course, appendages that take no commas at all:

John D. Rockefeller III is	8:30 A.M. is
The fifth century B.C. is	Queen Elizabeth II is

Still others take parentheses: 12:15 P.M. (EST) is.

All these last cause no problems. The thing to remember is the comma *following* appendages of the sort illustrated in the first examples above.

Series

In a list or series of three or more members, put a comma after every member but the last:

De Gaulle, Adenauer, and Churchill are mentioned most frequently.

Detectives were stationed in the drawing room, on the patio, and in the garden.

Landis was a big, fat, slovenly, but extremely agile man.

One kind of confusion caused by omitting the comma before *and* is illustrated by this sentence from the *New York Times*: "Bravo, who is justly famous for his five wives, fourteen serious gorings and love affairs with Hollywood actresses, was easily the favorite of the first-nighters."

When two adjectives precede a noun, use a comma if they modify the noun independently, that is, if their relationship is an *and* relationship. A *little, funny-looking dog* is a dog that is both little and funny-looking. If the first adjective modifies the unit composed of the second adjective and the noun, omit the comma. A *wild young man* is a young man who is wild; we read *young man* as a single unit. Most people find this distinction hard to apply, and it is accordingly breaking down, with the no-comma form increasingly favored.

Compound Sentences

In general, put a comma before the conjunction (*and, but, or, for, nor*) in a compound sentence:

I sat with Jack, and my sister sat in the balcony.

The reason was not altogether clear, but clarity was not altogether desirable.

Official invitations were sent to McNamara and Udall, and several other Cabinet members were invited informally.

In such sentences, the comma enables the reader to divide the sentence instantly into its two components. Sometimes it may eliminate false trails: for example, *Jack and my sister* in the first sentence. But even where such ambiguities are no problem, as in our second sentence, the comma offers the most economical possible clue to the sentence structure. The reader confronted with an unpunctuated sentence like *The reason was not altogether clear but clarity was not altogether desirable* must in effect hunt down the turning point for himself and put in his own mental comma, a labor the writer should have spared him.

Four exceptions may be noted. First, a compound imperative sentence does not usually take the comma:

> Shoot and be damned.

> Go down to the drugstore and get some aspirin.

Second, a short compound sentence with an introductory adverbial phrase governing both verbs is sometimes more clearly punctuated with a single comma after the opening phrase:

> In Montaigne's opinion, Medina Sidonia was right and Sir Francis Drake was wrong.

> As my grandfather used to say, most people are fools and the rest are swine.

Third, the comma can be omitted in a very short sentence (except before *for*):

> Anne forgot and so did Mary.

> He went but she stayed home.

Fourth, in a very long compound sentence, or one with internal punctuation in one or both of its clauses, a semicolon is usually better than a comma. A semicolon is of course obligatory if there is no coordinating conjunction, save where the comma splice is deliberately used for a special effect (see pp. 195–196).

Opening Phrases

Many writers put a comma after an opening phrase or clause only if it is seven words long or longer:

> In the Sudan there are very few large cities.

> Among the Wolagusi warriors of the northern Sudan, property squabbles are frequent.

>When Aunt Laura arrived the fun began.
>
>When Aunt Laura and Uncle Harry arrived, the fun began.

Other writers put a comma after all introductory phrases, regardless of length:

>In 1917, the Bolshevik Revolution occurred.
>
>When Lincoln died, the nation mourned.

These practices are equally acceptable; our advice is to choose one or the other and stick with it. In borderline cases let your ear be your guide. Single words like *however* and *incidentally*, short phrases like *for example* and *in other words*, are commonly followed by a pause in speech, and hence by a comma in writing. Other single words like *thus* and *therefore*, other short phrases like *in some ways* and *at one time*, are commonly followed by little or no pause in speech, and normally by no comma in writing. If you simply cannot decide, add the comma.

When an opening phrase or clause ends with a preposition, always add a comma to keep the preposition from being read as part of what follows it:

>To begin with, the overture is weak.
>
>From late June on, the beach is crowded.
>
>Whatever condition he is in, the office is no place for him.

Parenthetical Phrases

Place commas before and after a phrase or clause in a sentence that would be complete and coherent without that phrase or clause:

>Mother was amused, oddly enough, and so was Dad.
>
>"You are a traitor," she said quietly, "and a coward."
>
>Only San Salvi, the home of Andrea del Sarto's *Last Supper*, was spared.

If such a phrase ends the sentence, a comma should precede it: *Oveta Culp Hobby was the first WAC colonel, if I am not mistaken.*

This convention applies only to truly parenthetical or nonrestrictive phrases, phrases that might as readily have been put between parentheses as between commas: *Mother was amused (oddly enough), and so was Dad / The total amount was under ten dollars (I think).* The convention does not apply to defining or restrictive phrases, phrases that could not be placed in parentheses without distorting the intended meaning. (For a fuller discussion of restrictive and nonrestrictive constructions, see pp. 169–173.) In the following sentences, a comma at any of the points indicated by brackets would be wrong:

He was a friend of the poet [ ] Matthew Prior.

Stores [ ] with high reputations [ ] often overcharge.

A man [ ] who would do that [ ] would do anything.

Here the phrases following the opening brackets do not merely comment parenthetically on the preceding words but complete them. *Stores (with high reputations) often overcharge,* for example, would be nonsense; not all stores are in question, only *stores with high reputations.*

In some sentences, notably those in which a conjunction is followed by a longish introductory phrase or clause, the distinction between parenthetical and nonparenthetical expressions is hard to apply, largely because the ear and eye approaches to punctuation clash. The following sentences, with brackets where commas are possible, illustrate the problem:

The repairman said that [ ] for all practical purposes [ ] the heating system could be regarded as adequate.

Cromwell had made his preparations, and [ ] if the worst happened [ ] he was ready.

The logical school would plump for two commas in each case, to telegraph the construction of the sentence clearly. The rhetorical school would omit the opening commas, on the ground that since there would be no pause in speech after *that* and after *and,* a comma after either would be irritating.

We incline to the rhetorical school. If the phrase is too long to leave without commas, put a comma at the end but do not slavishly add one at the beginning. Follow your ear. In the following sentences one comma seems adequate:

> He said that *whatever the judge's decision might be,* he would accept it.

> Abbott was at first inclined to sue, but *when he remembered the promise he had made,* he changed his mind.

Confluences

"Confluence" is Fowler's term for a construction in which two syntactically parallel elements, one following the other, flow simultaneously into the sentence somewhere short of its end:

> Some, if not all [,] of the teachers were on strike.

> His approach was more delicate, more ingenious [,] than mine.

> Ney's courage was his foremost, perhaps his only [,] virtue.

> Many people are opposed to, or at least annoyed about [,] the new zoning regulations.

The question is whether the comma shown in brackets should be added or not. We think it should be, so as to connect the first element of the sequence more securely with the words that follow the second. Without the comma, the construction is not immediately clear.

Clarity

Consider the following sentence:

> The headmaster of the academy would on ceremonial occasions refer to the school as a patriotic institution [,] and to

the boys and the recent alumni as their nation's best hope for a glorious future.

Although this is not a compound sentence, to add the comma shown in brackets is a service to the reader. It converts an unwieldy mass of 34 words into two more manageable units of 17 words each; and it adds weight to the *and* immediately following it, which might otherwise appear to be coequal with the lesser *and* four words farther on. In the following sentences, the commas help to separate units of thought that might otherwise be muddled by the proliferation of *and*'s:

> There are two kinds of great men: men of wit and wisdom [,] and men of power.

> He distrusted the Americans [,] and the Canadians and the English as well.

> They disallowed my vote for Ralph Nader and John Lindsay [,] and Oliver's vote for Bill Cosby and Shirley Chisholm.

Commas must not, of course, be added indiscriminately simply to break up a long sentence for the eye, or to distinguish one weight of *and* from another. In the following sentences it would be wrong to add commas at the bracketed points:

> Whether it is right or wrong to imprison for life a man [ ] who has committed four or more relatively trivial offenses [ ] has been for years a subject of debate in the law schools.

> Given the situation in Eastern Europe and Germany [ ] and Hitler's megalomania, war was inevitable.

Although the first sentence is long and some division of it for the eye would be welcome, none is possible; commas at the indicated places, by making the *who* clause parenthetical rather than defining, would make the sentence unintelligible. In the second sentence, the later *and* marks a bigger division than the earlier, but a comma would make the sentence lame. Neither sentence can be improved by adding commas; both must be left as they are or rewritten.

Over- and Underpunctuation

In the end, there remains a great region of discretion, in which writers may use commas or not as strikes their fancy. Within this region of discretion, some like their punctuation heavy, some medium, some light. We like ours medium.

A distinguished exponent of heavy punctuation is the *New Yorker*, from which the following extract is taken:

> During the morning, more or less as Toperih-peri had predicted, the Turkana, avoiding the pass, which, as Toperih-peri could have told them, was sure to be guarded, had entered the district between Morukore and Kalapata and, turning north instead of south, raided a neighborhood on the plain.

Here we agree with Fowler: "Any one who finds himself putting down several commas close to one another should reflect that he is making himself disagreeable, and question . . . whether it is necessary."

As an example of light punctuation, here is James Joyce's *Portrait of the Artist as a Young Man*:

> His heart trembled; his breath came faster and a wild spirit passed over his limbs as though he was soaring sunward. His heart trembled in an ecstasy of fear and his soul was in flight. His soul was soaring in an air beyond the world and the body he knew was purified in a breath and delivered of incertitude and made radiant and commingled with the element of the spirit.

Underpunctuation of this sort causes the very trouble, especially with *and*, that we have mentioned earlier as a reason for adding commas; many of Joyce's sentences have to be read a second time to be read properly. Where a Joyce leads we gladly follow, but few would be so quick to indulge a lesser writer.

In short, the extremes of heavy and light punctuation seem to us excessively hard on the reader: the first belabors him to no purpose; the second ignores his need for signposts. We accord-

ingly recommend medium punctuation.   We close this section
with a brief passage from the *New Yorker,* first as that magazine
printed it, next as Joyce might have punctuated it, and finally as
we would punctuate it:

Heavy punctuation

> But the people had delayed, and, seemingly by accident, had
> speared the ox just as the Turkana were coming in.   More-
> over, the ox, of its own volition, had run in a circle for
> almost a mile.

Light punctuation

> But the people had delayed and seemingly by accident had
> speared the ox just as the Turkana were coming in.   More-
> over the ox of its own volition had run in a circle for almost
> a mile.

Medium punctuation

> But the people had delayed, and seemingly by accident had
> speared the ox just as the Turkana were coming in.   More-
> over, the ox of its own volition had run in a circle for al-
> most a mile.

THE SEMICOLON

The semicolon weighs about twice as much as a comma and
half as much as a period.   From its weight we may infer its two
main uses: as a strong comma, and as a weak period.   As a strong
comma, it is used chiefly between phrases with internal commas:

> Those missing were R. A. Abramovitz, the director of the
> bank; Elma Snyder, the chief cashier; and two tellers, Joseph
> J. Petrullo and Louise Kreps.

> Despite the news from the northern front, the invasion was
> not canceled; but weekend passes were given out, at least
> to some of us.

As a weak period, it connects independent clauses that are too closely linked to be separated by a period, or too short and undramatic to stand by themselves:

> Such sentiments are not rare; on the contrary, they are very common, especially among policemen.

> *Probe* is a good word for headlines; it takes less space than *investigate*.

An excess of semicolons gives writing a stuffy and pompous air. They are particularly inappropriate in dialogue, and should be used sparingly in informal or colloquial writing. In standard expository writing, however, the semicolon is indispensable. Its chief virtues are two. As a strong comma, it makes possible the clear and orderly grouping of complex units, especially in series. As a weak period, it helps make possible the pleasing variation of pace and rhythm that is essential to good writing.

THE COLON

The colon was initially, many centuries ago, nothing more than a strong semicolon, halfway in weight between a semicolon and a period. Today, its use is very different. In Fowler's phrase, the colon "has acquired a special function: that of delivering the goods that have been invoiced in the preceding words." The colon in its modern use is the equivalent of *namely* or *that is*:

> I have seen every National League team but three: the Giants, the Braves, and the Mets.

> The message was clear: our views were not welcome.

> I remember her words: "May God forgive these men!"

As remarked in Chapter 11, a normally lowercase word following a colon should not be capitalized even when it begins a complete sentence, unless the sentence is either in quotation marks or especially formal or weighty.

There are three restrictions on the use of the colon. First, do not subordinate a colon to a lesser piece of punctuation. A colon yields only to a period: the goods it delivers must accordingly consist of all the words from the colon to the end of the sentence. Not some; all. The following sentences improperly subordinate colons to a comma and a semicolon, respectively:

If he said: "I am innocent," he was lying.

There were three men: Taylor, Adams, and Szyszniewski; and two women.

The first sentence can be fixed by simply deleting the colon, the second by changing the colon and the semicolon to parentheses or dashes. Alternatively, *There were two women and three men: Taylor, Adams, and Szyszniewski.*

Second, do not subordinate a colon to another colon; in other words, never use more than one colon in a sentence. The following sentences violate this restriction:

The American delegation was distinguished: Nixon, Agnew, and two Cabinet members: Rogers and Mitchell.

The vote was as follows: California: aye, 85; nay, 15; Oregon: aye, 60; nay, 7.

The colons in sentences like this are visually equal but syntactically of different weight. The writer knows how they dovetail, but the reader is left the work of sorting things out for himself.

Third, a period should not be subordinated to a colon. Consider the following examples:

We hesitated to rent the house for several reasons: the garage had no roof. The bathroom had no fixtures. And the yard was piled high with junk.

Remember two things: first, the dependent countries will be hard hit; their coal supply may be cut in half. Second, the rich industrial countries will benefit most.

In each example, the first period, which the reader expects will mark the end of what the colon has promised to deliver, marks instead a mere halfway point. The first example above can be fixed simply by changing the periods to commas. In the second, since there is no apparent way of delivering the invoiced goods without an internal period, we recommend making "Remember two things" a separate sentence.

THE DASH

The overuse of dashes gives writing a breathlessness that is rarely appropriate, and in some cases a bogus dramatic quality. Dashes may legitimately be used for emphasis (for example, to bring out a paradox), or in pairs for long or complicated parenthetical insertions. They should not be used where commas would serve as well.

There are two dash constructions: the double dash (*Johnny ran away again—he does every Sunday—and was brought home by Chalmers Johnson*) and the single dash (*We were broke—not a penny left*). In a given sentence neither of these constructions may be used more than once, nor may the two be used together. The following sentences are all unacceptable:

Two double dashes

> For Austria—Hitler's fatherland—not a penny; for Hungary—the cradle of freedom—all possible aid.

Double dash plus single dash

> He loved his work—he lived for nothing else—but he was fired—no one ever knew why.

Two single dashes

> Napoleon was his idol—the greatest man of the age; but Guizot was his master—the man of the moment.

The single dash, like a colon, governs everything from itself to the end of the sentence; the first of two dashes governs everything up to the second. If dashes are used with a semicolon, the semicolon should be subordinate, as in this sentence from the *New Yorker*: "I found myself getting annoyed with Gould, not because of his gloating over the settling of old scores—that was all right with me; I believe in revenge—but because of his general air of self-satisfaction." Compare this correct sentence with the incorrect Napoleon sentence above, in which the sequence of punctuation is identical.

PARENTHESES

In the nineteenth century and earlier, commas and semicolons were used in immediate conjunction with dashes, but in modern usage no punctuation may immediately precede or follow a dash. Parentheses, which do not suffer from this restriction, can sometimes clear away ambiguities that pairs of dashes or commas cannot handle. In the following ambiguous sentences parentheses are the obvious remedy:

> The card featured Peterson, Gilroy—known as the "Terre Haute Tiger"—Morse, and Martin.

> Three vegetables—carrots, beans, and brussels sprouts—and two fruits—avocados and raspberries—were particularly vulnerable to "smog fallout."

> The chief culprits were Mr. Ward, the sales manager, and Mr. Tyler.

In the first sentence, parentheses would rule out the possibility that we are talking about somebody named Gilroy Morse: *The card featured Peterson, Gilroy (known as the "Terre Haute Tiger"), Morse, and Martin.* In the second, parentheses would bring order to a badly fragmented sentence: *Three vegetables (carrots, beans, and brussels sprouts) and two fruits (avocados and raspberries) were particularly vulnerable.* In the third, parentheses would show us that two men were involved, not three: *Mr. Ward (the sales manager) and Mr. Tyler.*

Beginning writers make two errors in using parentheses. One is overusing them: their residual connotation of a whispered aside, or a trivial qualification, makes them irritating in large quantities. The other is making them enclose too long a parenthetical passage, especially one so long that the reader loses his bearings before he gets to the end of it. Make your passages in parentheses few, and make them short.

A sentence with parentheses in it is punctuated exactly as it would have been if the words in parentheses had been omitted. The punctuation follows the closing parenthesis except when the passage consists of a whole sentence or several sentences, in which case the final period is placed inside the closing parenthesis. Thus:

There were only two of us (me and my sister).

(There were only two of us, me and my sister.)

QUOTATION MARKS

Quotation marks have two main uses: to set off passages attributable to speakers or writers other than the present writer at the time of writing, and to alert the reader to words or phrases that are being used in some unfamiliar or unusual sense.

Punctuation and Capitalization with Quotation Marks

Always put a comma or a period inside the closing quotation mark, a semicolon or a colon outside. This is one of the very few rules of writing that have no exceptions, and at the same time one of the rules most frequently violated in student writing.[1] For other punctuation, use your common sense: a question mark or an exclamation point, for example, goes inside the quotation marks if it is part of the quotation, otherwise outside. If a quotation runs to more than one paragraph, all paragraphs should begin with quotation marks, but only the last should end with one. With this exception, all quotation marks come in pairs.

Quotation marks following *said* and equivalent words may be preceded either by no punctuation, or by a comma, or by a colon, depending on the context and the writer's taste. The following sentences are all acceptably punctuated:

[1] Perhaps students are led astray by older books and books printed in England, many of which follow a different system for commas and periods. The system recommended here is all but universal in current American publishing.

She said "I dare you!"

He replied, "I'll do my best, but I can't promise anything."

The ad read: "Experienced waitress wanted; age 21–45; short hours; no Sundays."

Single quotation marks are used exclusively for quotations within quotations: *"That's unfair," said his wife. "All I said was 'You're wrong.'"* Note that the closing quotation marks both go outside the period.

If words in quotation marks make a full sentence, or a sentence fragment or exclamation used as a sentence, the first word quoted should be capitalized. Otherwise a normally lowercase word should be left lowercase:

According to Schlesinger, Kennedy replied "Never again."

When he said "Where's the food?" everyone laughed.

Red Smith calls the 1927 Yankees "the greatest baseball team of all time."

Superfluous Quotation Marks

Quotation marks should be used sparingly to set off words and short phrases from their context. If you use a word in an unusual sense, or if you coin a new word for some special use, explain matters clearly the first time you use the word and thereafter write it without quotation marks. If you use slang, use it boldly; quotation marks make slang look defensive and self-conscious. In general, if quotation marks do not make any distinction worth making, drop them. In the following sentences, all the quotation marks should be eliminated:

When I was little, my family called me "Bobo."

"Communism" has a different definition in every country.

I was feeling "blue."

In the summer Mario offers "guided tours" to visitors.

As the last example suggests, quotation marks may be worse than superfluous; carrying as they do the connotation of something-fishy-here, they may actually suggest the opposite of what the writer intends.   Thanks to the quotation marks, we get the feeling that whatever Mario is up to, it is something sufficiently sinister to make a wise visitor look elsewhere for a guide.

PART **4**
THE RESEARCH PAPER

13

RESEARCH AND NOTE-TAKING

Every educated person should be able to investigate a subject, evaluate the facts and opinions he encounters, and present his findings in a readable and orderly way. Training in how to do this is what the research paper is all about. It is a practical as well as an academic exercise. As our society grows more complex, it places increasing demands on its educated citizens to sift out from the glut of available information the information relevant to a particular need and to report that information reliably to others. The day when an engineer or a business executive could make it through life without ever reading or writing a word is over. Professional men and women in particular are frequently called on to write papers and deliver them at professional meetings. Rotarians, revolutionists, PTA activists, even mere writers of letters to the editor, need training of the sort the research paper provides.

Some English courses require a so-called critical paper rather than the traditional research paper. The critical paper is based on a relatively circumscribed body of information, usually literary or historical. This information is sometimes conveniently supplied in the form of "sourcebooks" or "casebooks" like David Levin's *What Happened in Salem?*, a gathering of testimony from five Salem witchcraft trials in 1692, or Milton P. Foster's *Gulliver Among the Houyhnhnms,* which consists of the Houyhnhnm section of *Gulliver's Travels* followed by critical articles on that famous section. There are literally dozens of books like these—on novels and poems, on comedy and tragedy, on literary, scientific, and historical figures. With their help, both the teacher and the student can master a fairly complex body of knowledge with minimum inconvenience, making it possible to emphasize discussion, thinking, and writing rather than legwork, often futile, in the understocked college library.

For all its conveniences, however, this approach has its shortcomings. The library is your prime educational resource; you should discover its pleasures and treasures early and not get detoured around them. Even if a sourcebook or casebook is assigned, you would do well to go beyond it and look at some of the library's books and articles on your subject. It is better that you explore the library as a freshman than as a junior—or as an aging graduate lost in a labyrinth that should long ago have become familiar.

CHOOSING A SUBJECT

Even if you are using a sourcebook, you will be asked to choose a subject. Your teacher's first advice will undoubtedly be to limit your subject to something you can handle in reasonably short compass (usually from a thousand to five thousand words). With a book like *What Happened in Salem?* you might choose to compare one of the witchcraft trials with Arthur Miller's play *The Crucible,* or the Salem trials with the political "witch-hunting" of the early 1950's or the racist persecutions of the 1970's. Above all, the subject should be one that interests you, one that you would be happy to know more about. This does not mean you should stick to what you know, or what you know you like; investigating new worlds of intellectual interest is, after all, one of the joys of education and one of the rewards of the research paper. But there should be a point of intersection with *you*. The trouble with the old-fashioned kind of research paper was precisely here: it tended to encourage topics like "The History of Water-Skiing" or "The Introduction of the Camel into America"—topics of little interest to the student himself and chosen out of desperation or the *Reader's Digest*.

How do you know what you are interested in before you have investigated it? Often you don't; you must play some hunches. Let us assume your teacher has assigned a conventional research paper and suggested that you write on one of the following general topics:

> "Doing Your Thing" as an ethical concept
> Violence, official and unofficial
> Pollution: in literature and in lakes
> The population explosion and the race question
> The grossness of the gross national product
> Marijuana and the generation gap

Let us say you decide on the last topic. Perhaps you have had direct experience with marijuana; perhaps you have been in arguments about it and wished you had more evidence to support your claims; perhaps you simply welcome the opportunity to find out what all the fuss is about. Or maybe you find the other topics a bore. At any rate, you settle on "Marijuana and the generation gap." The main question here, it seems to you, is why there are strict laws against marijuana when other drugs like tobacco and alcohol are perfectly legal. Is it strictly because of the generation gap—because tobacco and alcohol are the vices of the old and marijuana is the vice of the young? Or are there solid scientific reasons for outlawing marijuana?

RESEARCH: BOOKS

Your first step is to consult the card catalog in your college or university library. You look up "Marijuana" there and find only one entry, a book by Will Oursler; but a cross-reference card leads you to "Marihuana," where you find eight books listed, all but two published since 1968—an indication of how interest in the subject has recently mushroomed. You cannot see why the titles of most of the entries under "Marihuana" use the spelling

"Marijuana"; obviously either spelling is acceptable, so you leave that particular mystery unresolved.   Here are the nine entries:

Goode, Erich. *Marijuana.* New York: Atherton Press, 1969.

Kaplan, John. *Marijuana—The New Prohibition.* New York: World Publishing Co., 1970.

Moore, Laurence A. *Marijuana (Cannabis) Bibliography, 1960–1968.* Los Angeles, Calif.: Bruin Humanist Forum, 1969.

Oursler, Will. *Marijuana: The Facts, the Truth.* New York: Paul S. Eriksson, Inc., 1968.

Rowell, Earle Albert, and Rowell, Robert. *On the Trail of Marijuana, the Weed of Madness.* Mountain View, Calif.: Pacific Press, 1939.

Saltman, Jules. *What About Marijuana?* New York Public Affairs Pamphlet No. 436, Public Affairs Committee, July 1969.

Simmons, J. L., ed. *Marihuana: Myths and Realities.* North Hollywood, Calif.: Brandon House, 1967.

Smith, David E., ed. *The New Social Drug: Cultural, Medical, and Legal Perspectives on Marijuana.* Englewood Cliffs, N.J.: Prentice-Hall, Inc., 1970.

Steinbeck, John. *In Touch.* New York: Alfred A. Knopf, Inc., 1969.

Of these books the Kaplan and Goode are out on loan to students, the Simmons is at the Law Library, the Steinbeck is lost, and the Rowell is inexplicably charged out to the Women's Gym, half a mile away.   You put in recall requests and begin to be glad you started your research early.   The Oursler, Saltman, and Smith volumes are in, and you take them out.   You decide to ignore the Moore *Bibliography* for now, since you have only five weeks and know you will be lucky to get through even one book thoroughly.   You are disappointed not to get the Kaplan book, which is the only one you have heard about; but luckily you are able to borrow it from a friend.   The Simmons, you discover, has been brought out in a low-priced paperback edition, which you buy at the campus bookstore. While there you pick up another paperback that looks helpful: *The Marihuana Papers,* edited by David Solomon.

So you start out with three books from the library and three others that you have bought or borrowed. You soon decide to concentrate on the Kaplan book, since it is relatively recent and directly on your subject, and to spend some time on the Smith and Solomon collections, since they both contain a wide-ranging selection of opinion. The Saltman pamphlet is a perfunctory *Reader's Digest* treatment of the subject; you put it aside. You do the same with the Oursler book, which reads too much like a novel to serve your purposes. At first glance, the Simmons book also seems to offer more entertainment than edification; but since you own the book and since it has a useful glossary, you plan to look further into it.

Figure 1 shows the Library of Congress catalog card for the Kaplan book as it appears in a library card catalog. Some of the items are of interest mainly to librarians; others are of more general interest. For whatever books you intend to use, you should in due course make out your own bibliography card (see p. 228).

Besides the card catalog, you may have occasion to use one or more reference guides. One of the best is the *Bulletin of Bibliography,* a periodical that presents bibliographies on selected

Figure 1

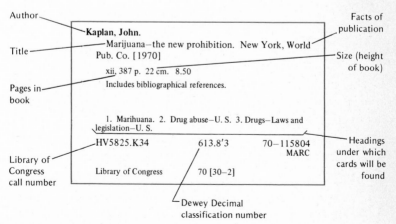

subjects and reviews books containing bibliographies—often very amusingly. You find that the October-December 1969 issue of the *Bulletin* has a bibliography entitled "Drugs—A Selective Bibliography for Educators on the Secondary and College Level" compiled by Jean B. Condito, a high school librarian. Most of this bibliography deals with the so-called hard drugs, notably amphetamines, barbiturates, and heroin; but there are also sections dealing with the hallucinogens in general (a family of non-addictive drugs including LSD and mescaline) and with LSD and marijuana in particular. The section on marijuana offers a long and useful list of books, pamphlets, and magazine articles on the subject; most of the books you know of already, but you make notes on some of the articles. A film on marijuana entitled *Assassin of Youth* is also listed; this sounds like a blast from across the generation gap, and you wish somebody would risk the hoots of your friends and show it on campus.

Another book to check is the annual *Bibliographic Index*, which lists recent bibliographies by subject for a great many subjects. You check from 1966 until April 1971 (the latest Supplement) and find only the book by Erich Goode listed.

Still another reference guide that can save you time is the *Book Review Digest*. Here, for example, are some entries for the Solomon book as listed in the BRD for 1969:

> "[The book] is the basic reference work on marihuana. . . . Although the nonprofessional will find that some chapters . . . are too technical or jargon-laden for comfort, most chapters are in fairly straightforward prose; and some of the literary selections included are quite entertaining. . . . A good part of this anthology could of course be titled 'The Case Against the Federal Narcotics Bureau.' . . . [The] book convinces one that the Bureau's favorite myths about marihuana . . . are indubitably myths. But [Mr. Solomon] doesn't make the case as airtight as it could be made. . . . All my objections to Mr. Solomon's book are ultimately quibbles. The important fact is that it is by far the best guide to its subject."
>
> Ned Polsky
>
> Book Week p5   Ja 15 '67   1400w

"The compiler of [this anthology] quotes out of context and changes the emphasis in some of the sources he uses. . . . [His] book is frequently repetitious and contains contradictory statements. The general philosophy seems to be that since alcohol is so much more dangerous than marihuana, marihuana should be made legal. . . . Since there is considerable doubt among the authorities about the active principles and potential dangers of marihuana, since inaccuracies and misplaced emphases abound, and since most of this material is already available, this book should be bought by only the most comprehensive collections."

W. K. Beatty
Library J   92:130   Ja 1 '67   400w

"[This] book was put together by David Solomon, whose qualifications are limited to the fact that he is a former editor at *Esquire, Playboy,* and *Metronome,* and his bias is plainly evident. . . . Bolstering [his] familiar argument are 400-plus pages of statements, essays, papers, adulatory fiction, and documentary evidence, some of which are impressive, some simply a drag. . . . The most comprehensive defense argument comes from the famed 1944 LaGuardia Report, written by responsible scientists and sociologists (though heavily attacked by the A.M.A. at the time)."
Time   89:84   Ja 27 '67   550w

Clearly these reviewers see the volume from their different points of view, the first as a liberal, the second as a librarian, the third as a popular journalist. Of the three, the second impresses you as the most level-headed; the first seems too extravagant in his praise, the third too given to *ad hominem* denunciation. You think Beatty's review might come in useful, so you make out a tentative bibliography card for the *Library Journal,* Volume 92, page 130, for January 1, 1967; "400w" means 400 words.

Suppose now that you are trying to decide whether the Solomon book or Oursler's *Marijuana: The Facts, the Truth* is better for your purposes. You find these two reviews of the Oursler book in the BRD for 1969:

"Oursler brings to [his] task a wide experience as a writer of varied interests and an earned competence as an acute observer of the American scene. Although the arrangement of the chapters . . . lends itself to a certain amount of repetition, the research is thorough and sufficiently broad in scope to encompass the many facets of the problem. . . . In his quest for objectivity . . . Mr. Oursler does tend to give equal weight, along with more scientific findings, to the testimonies of admitted users of the drug, despite their recognized bias. This tendency is assuredly offset by his explicit recognition of self-contradiction, however unconscious, in many of these testimonies."

A. L. Fleming
Best Sell   28:389   D 15 '68   450w

"[The author] once wrote a book with Harry Anslinger, *The Murderers* [BRD 1962], so he is automatically 'out of it' as far as the 'liberal' attitude toward drugs and users is concerned. . . . The points Mr. Oursler wants to make could have been made more forcefully if the text had been pruned to half the size. . . . [His book] will be needed in exhaustive collections on the subject."

W. K. Beatty
Library J   94:59   Ja 1 '69   160w

You have an interesting difference of opinion here. To the bookseller, Mr. Oursler is exceptionally objective; to the librarian he is obviously biased. Which can you believe? You have already met Mr. Beatty and incline to trust him, but neither critic seems to have any special credentials on the subject of marijuana. At this point, the striking difference of opinion is what impresses you most; since you may want to make something of that difference, you make out two more bibliography cards.

Finally, in an idle moment you look up the lost Steinbeck book just to see what it was about. You find to your surprise that you want to read the book if you can, since the use of marijuana by American soldiers in Vietnam interests you quite apart from the demands of your research paper. Here is the entry that convinced you:

"The son of the famous John Steinbeck III allowed himself, at twenty-one, to be drafted and sent to Southeast Asia. He was eager for 'a paradise of potential crystallized experience.' He took a good look, fell in love with the people of Vietnam [and] turned dovish. . . . The most extraordinary part of the book he has written concerns his experiences with and observations on the extensive use of marijuana by American troops in Vietnam. . . . The young Steinbeck displays an extraordinary talent for storytelling, a keen sense of issues, and a granite ability to keep his disenchantment cool. He emerges from his first book as a kind of literary Sidney Poitier. If Stanley Kramer made a movie about a hippie, he would undoubtedly be someone like Steinbeck."

Lee Israel

Book World   p5   F 9 '69   550w

Later you discover that John Steinbeck IV was arrested on a marijuana charge in October 1967, and you record this information on a card. It may be useful later, or again it may not. Every good job of research yields superfluous notes, yet the experienced researcher would rather have too many notes than too few, and will even take notes on points seemingly tangential to his central topic. For example, here is a statement by Dwight Macdonald about the glut of writing today that you may have stumbled across in the library or learned about from a friend. It has nothing to do with marijuana, but it may well be relevant to the way you feel at this point about your paper. Having it among your note cards may even make you feel better about the hard work ahead of you.

The problem is as acute in the groves of Academe as in the profane world of journalism—one has only to consider the appalling mass of words available in any large college library on any topic of scholarly interest (that is, now that the "social sciences" have so proliferated, on any topic). The amount of verbal pomposity, elaboration of the obvious, repetition, trivia, low-grade statistics, tedious factifications, drudging recapitulations of the half comprehended, and generally inane and laborious junk that one encounters suggests that the thinkers of earlier ages had one decisive advantage over those of today: they could draw on very little research.

Although you cannot avoid adding to that appalling mass of words, you resolve that you will not add to the verbal pomposity if you can help it.

RESEARCH: PERIODICALS

You have learned by now that widespread interest in marijuana dates from about 1965. You decide, therefore, to concentrate mainly on newspaper and magazine articles published since that year. There are three main periodical indexes, the first of which is not usable in your present research:[1]

Poole's Index to Periodical Literature (indexing many nineteenth-century periodicals)

Reader's Guide to Periodical Literature (covering popular magazines from 1900 to the present)

Social Sciences and Humanities Index, known until April 1965 as *International Index to Periodical Literature* (listing articles in a wide range of scholarly journals)

Remember that the *Reader's Guide* covers only popular magazines. You must consult the *Social Sciences and Humanities Index* for more scholarly articles.

Consulting the *Reader's Guide,* you find five articles listed under "Marijuana" in the four years from March 1963 until February 1967. In the next four years, from March 1967 until February 1971, you find 149 articles listed, 50 of them appearing in 1970–71 alone. Several of them sound sufficiently interesting for your purposes to be worth looking up:

[1] There are vast numbers of other indexes and reference books as well. A good list of such books appears in Constance M. Winchell, *Guide to Reference Books,* 7th ed. (1951). And nearly every medium-sized and large college library has a reference librarian who specializes in helping people find information.

Great marijuana hoax   A. Ginsberg   Atlantic   218:104+   N '66

America's social frontiers: Why not smoke pot?   Cur   95:39–41
   My '68

Marijuana or alcohol, which harms most?   U S News   64:15
   F 5 '68

Politics of pot   J. Sterba   Esquire   70:58–61+   Ag '68

Crackdown   Nation   208:293–4   Mr 10 '69

Nixon drug law   Life   67:32   S 5 '69

Grass and the brass   D. Sanford   New Rep   162:11–12
   Ap 25 '70

In these abbreviations the first item is the title, the second the author (omitted for anonymous articles), the third the periodical title, the fourth the volume or issue number followed by the page or pages, the fifth the date. Journal abbreviations are spelled out in a separate section of the *Guide*.

In the *Social Science and Humanities Index* you find only five articles listed under "Marihuana" in the five years between April 1965 and March 1970, but two of them strike you as probably worth reading.[2] The entries read:

Beyond the pleasure principle   R. Coles   Part R   34:415–20
   Sum '67

Multiple drug use among marijuana smokers   E. Goode
   Soc Prob   17:48–64   Sum '69

You then ask the reference librarian what other indexes might be useful. She suggests *Psychological Abstracts,* an annual collection of résumés of new books and articles in various psycho-

---

[2] It is well to check both guides. The *Reader's Guide* has more on some subjects, the *Social Science and Humanities Index* more on others. For example, on "Imagery," listed in both indexes, the *Reader's Guide* for 1966–67 refers you to "Figures of Speech," where only one entry is listed; the *Social Science and Humanities Index* for the same period has 24 entries under "Imagery," plus cross-references under "Figures of Speech" to "Metaphor," "Synecdoche," "Clichés," and "Shakespeare."

logical categories. Checking the indexes, you find no mention of marijuana until 1969. The index entries read as follows:

Avoidance and visual discrimination, monkey, 2280

Marijuana psychosis, case report, 16127

Marijuana use and legalization, political controversy, 14269

Since the effect of marijuana on monkeys seems rather specialized for your purposes, you decide to ignore the first abstract. You are curious about the second, which summarizes an article in the *Canadian Psychiatric Association Journal,* 1969, Vol. 14, No. 1, pp. 77–79, about a "30 yr. old white male's acute psychotic reaction to 1 year daily use of marijuana." This seems odd, since you have always heard that marijuana was relatively harmless; later you discover to your own satisfaction that psychotic reactions to marijuana are in fact very rare. The third reference deals with an article by Erich Goode in the *Journal of Health and Social Behavior,* 1969, Vol. 10, No. 2, pp. 83–94, entitled "Marijuana and the Politics of Reality." This strikes you as worth investigating, but you find that Vol. 10 of *JHSB* is at the bindery and inaccessible. Later you discover with pleasure that the article is reprinted in the Smith book.

Now you remember the articles you listed for future reference from Jean Condito's bibliography in the *Bulletin of Bibliography.* Some of the same articles are listed in the *Reader's Guide,* but others are from educational journals that you have not yet run across. Two that interest you are listed in the *Bulletin* as follows:

Brill, H. "Case Against Marijuana," *Journal of School Health,* 522–3, Oct. 1968

Der Marderosian, A. H. "Marijuana Madness," *Journal of Secondary Education,* 43:200–5, May 1968

These references make you wonder whether you should not consult some reference guide to educational articles. The reference librarian refers you to the *Education Index,* and further suggests that you consult the current list of international medical literature in the *Index Medicus,* paying particular attention to British articles, since the British, she thinks, are less convinced than the Americans that the drug is harmless. Though you did not initially intend to investigate the medical side of the subject, you are becoming convinced that you cannot ignore it. You find nothing new in the *Education Index,* but the *Index Medicus* lists a number of promising titles:

A case for Cannabis? Tylden E. et al. Brit Med J 3:556
    26 Aug 67

Potted Dreams. Brit Med J 1:133–4 18 Jan 69

Is it all right to smoke Pot? Glatt MM. Brit J Addict
    64:109–14 May 69

Cannabis: a short review of its effects and the possible dangers
    of its use. Leonard BE. Brit J Addict 64:121–30
    May 69

Runaways, hippies, and marihuana. Kaufman J. et al.
    Amer J Psychiat 126:717–20 Nov 69

What are you going to do with all this material? First of all, note that it is not as much reading as it may seem to be. Your eighteen selections from the *Reader's Guide,* the *Social Sciences and Humanities Index, Psychological Abstracts,* the *Bulletin of Bibliography,* and the *Index Medicus* come to less than a hundred pages all told. Add fifty pages for another half-dozen articles to which you will be led by your reading of these eighteen —or such of them as you are able to locate, which may be only ten or twelve—and you will still almost certainly be spending less time reading and pondering periodical articles than you did discovering which ones you want to read and making notes on their whereabouts.[3]

Another thing that lightens your burden is an increasingly sure sense of priorities and possibilities, of what you want to concen-

[3] You will run across still other articles in your reading of daily newspapers and magazines, or as the result of conversations. Several quotations from such sources appear in the sample research paper below, pp. 240–253, and the sources appear in the paper's bibliography.

trate on and what you want to stay away from. After your initial period of floundering about, things are beginning to fall into place. You tentatively decide, so far as possible, to get your objective data on marijuana from the Kaplan book, and to get arguments and expressions of opinion from periodical articles and other short papers. From now on, this will be your general working strategy, though you remain ready to pick up diamonds where you find them.

BIBLIOGRAPHY CARDS

As you gather lists of the books and articles you intend to read or consult (or better still, while you are consulting them), you should make out a set of cards to be used in preparing the bibliography for your paper. A card for the Solomon book will read as shown in Figure 2. The entry for this book that ultimately appears in your bibliography will read as follows:

Solomon, David, ed. *The Marihuana Papers*. New York: New American Library, 1968.

Figure 3 shows a sample bibliography card for a periodical article. Volume numbers may be given in roman numerals rather than arabic numbers, but arabic is now usual. One handy style is

Figure 2

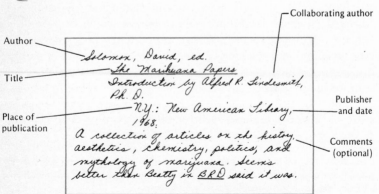

Author —

Title —

Place of publication

Collaborating author

Publisher and date

Comments (optional)

Figure 3

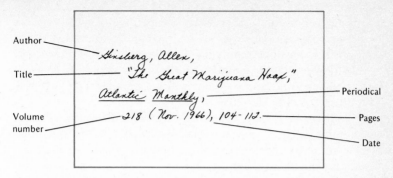

"164:18 (Apr. 22, 1972)," meaning that the article begins on page 18 of the April 22, 1972, issue of the periodical, which issue will be found in Volume 164 of the bound series in the library. The same style can be used for footnotes, in which case the second number is the page cited. Note that whenever the volume number of a periodical is given, "p." or "pp." is omitted before the page citation that follows.

The bibliography for this paper, in final typed form, appears on pp. 252–253. Footnote citations, which differ in form from bibliography entries, are illustrated on pp. 240–251.

NOTE-TAKING

Although there are many ways of taking notes, the beginning researcher does well to keep his notes on cards.[4] You will probably take four kinds of notes: (1) quotations from your reading, (2) paraphrases of passages from your reading, (3) statements of fact, and (4) original ideas inspired by your reading—i.e., your own questions about or critical comments on what you read.

In quoting material, make sure you quote exactly and indicate by ellipsis (. . .) any material you omit. Suppose you want to quote a statement from the Ginsberg essay mentioned above. You are not sure you will use it, but it seems promising enough

---

[4] Some teachers recommend using 3 x 5 cards for bibliography entries and larger cards for notes. This system has the virtue of keeping the two kinds of information clearly distinguishable.

to save for future reference.   Your card is shown in Figure 4.
Figure 5 shows a card paraphrasing a comment that did not seem
worth quoting in full.   Here Goode's words "who are comfortable
with an unconventional view of sex" are put in quotation marks
to keep them distinct from your paraphrase.   This is important;
to take down without quotation marks words or phrases that are
in any way unique to the author you are paraphrasing is to risk
plagiarism (see pp. 260–265).

In your paper it may strike you as awkward to put "who are
comfortable with an unconventional view of sex" in quotation
marks, since the phrase is not particularly eloquent; still, the
words appear to be carefully chosen, and if you use them you
must quote them.   An alternative possibility is to paraphrase if a
suitable paraphrase can be found.   At all events, you should deal
with this problem when you get to it, not anticipate it in your
note-taking.   Since you will ultimately have to give credit in your
text or footnotes not only for material quoted verbatim but for
paraphrased material as well, and since the credit you give will
depend heavily for accuracy and completeness on what you have

Figure 4

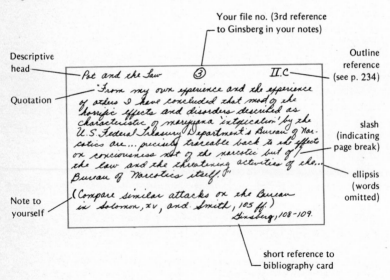

Figure 5

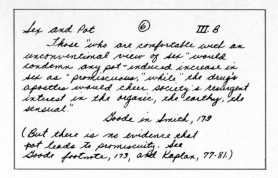

> Sex and Pot   ⑥   III. 8
>   Those "who are comfortable with an
> unconventional view of sex" would
> condemn any pot-induced increase in
> sex as "promiscuous," while "the drug's
> apostles would cheer society's resurgent
> interest in the organic, the earthy, the
> sensual."
>   Goode in Smith, 179
>
> (But there is no evidence that
> pot leads to promiscuity. See
> Goode footnote, 173, and Kaplan, 77-81.)

written on your cards, it only makes sense to bend over back-
wards to keep things straight in the note-taking stage.

Figure 6 shows a card containing a statement of fact. Since
botanical information about marijuana can be found in encyclo-
pedias and in nearly all books on the subject, it requires no
special acknowledgment in your paper. You see no immediate
use for this information in your outline, but it is so fundamental
that you decide to record it anyway for possible use early in your
paper.

The fourth kind of card records ideas that come to you as your
reading progresses. Maybe you want to argue with something
you are reading; maybe you are annoyed by what seem to you
contradictions or irresponsible statements; maybe your imagina-

Figure 6

> Fact   I(?)
>   Marijuana consists of the flowering tops
> and leaves of the female Indian hemp plant,
> Cannabis sativa. The sticky resin in the
> tops is the intoxicating element. The resin
> itself when prepared for smoking or eat-
> ing is called hashish, or "hash." There
> are many varieties of American marijuana,
> nearly all much less strong than Asian
> or European Cannabis. The active element-
> trans-tetrahydrocannabinol- has been
> synthesized (THC).
>   Solomon, xiii ff.
>   Weil, 1234-36.

Figure 7

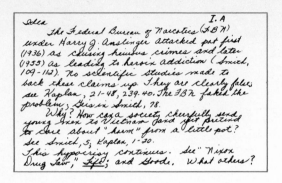

tion is fired by a moving argument or appeal. Catch such birds on the wing or they will fly away. Make sure, however, that you also record what you are reacting *to*. In your paper you will need evidence to back up what you say, and this evidence will usually be found in the printed passage to which your remarks are a response. Figure 7 shows this sort of card.

Getting your information on these cards straight and complete from the outset will save you at the very least one thankless trip to the library to fill in what you left out and clear up what you got wrong. And it may well spare you more: the confusion of writing weeks later from notes too sketchy to make sense of, or the boredom of hunting in vain for something you remember having seen but did not think to record. Never count on your memory. When you see something you think you may use, write it down and write down where to find it.

PHOTODUPLICATION

Most libraries these days have Xerox or other duplicating machines that students can use for a few cents a page. Though a duplicated page is no substitute for a note card, it relieves you of the worry of accuracy and permits you to write shorter notes. Figure 8 shows a sample Xeroxed page, Figure 9 a sample note card referring to that page.

Figure 8

counter-culture, which, while not explicitly opposed to academic pursuits, complements them with a focus on the present, on 'existential' values, on personal experimentation, and on deliberate self-transformation as a way of creating meaning. Participation in this counter-culture provides a powerful support for efforts to explore oneself, to intensify relationships with other people, to change the quality and content of consciousness. It provides a sanctioning context for drug use as one of the pathways of changing the self so as to create meaning in the world.

DRUGS AS A COMMENTARY ON SOCIETY

"It is widely feared that student drug use is a commentary upon American society; words like degeneracy, addiction, thrill-seeking and irresponsibility are eventually introduced into most popular discussions of student drug use. So, too, student drug use is said to be related to the excessive permissiveness of parents, to the laxness of adult standards, to breaches in law enforcement, to disrespect for law and order, and to an impending breakdown of our social fabric.

"Although these particular interpretations of the social implications of drug use are incorrect, drug use *is* importantly influenced by social, political and historical factors. Those students who lust after significance or reject the prevalent values of American society are in fact reacting to and within a societal context. The sense of being locked-off and enclosed in an impermeable shell is related not only to individual psychological states like depression, but to broader cultural phenomena. And the fact that a considerable number of the most able students have become convinced that significance and relevant experience are largely to be found within their own skulls is indirectly related to their perception of the other possibilities for fulfillment in the social and political world. In a variety of ways, then, student drug use is a commentary on American society, although a different kind of commentary than most discussions of youthful 'thrill-seeking' would lead us to believe.

"To single out a small number of social changes as especially relevant to understanding student drug use is to make a highly arbitrary decision. A variety of factors, including rapid social change, the unprecedented possibilities for total destruction in the modern world, the prevalence of violence both domestic and international, the high degree of specialization and bureaucratization of American life, and a host of others are relevant to creating the context of values and expectations within which drug use has become increasingly legitimate.

"But of all the factors that could be discussed, three seem particularly relevant: first, the effect of modern communications and transportation in producing an overwhelming inundation of experience, which I will term *stimulus flooding;* second, the effect of *automatic affluence* in changing the values and outlooks of the young; third, the importance of recent social and historical events in producing a kind of *social and political disenchantment* that leads many students to seek salvation through withdrawal and inner life rather than through engagement and societal involvement.

"Every society subjects its members to pressures and demands that

Figure 9

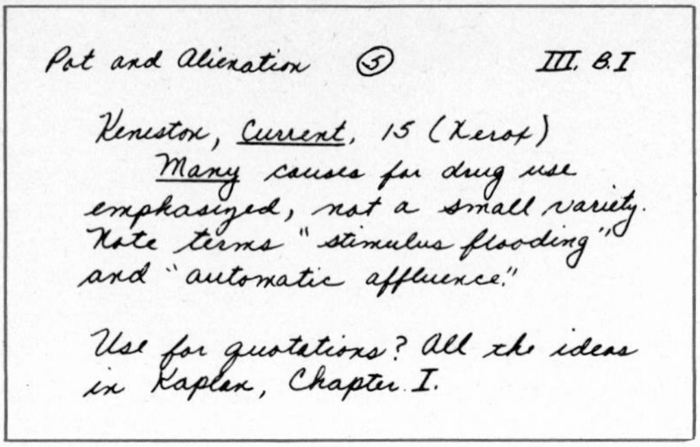

> Pot and alienation ⑤   III. B.1
>
> Keniston, *Current*, 15 (Xerox)
>   __Many__ causes for drug use
> emphasized, not a small variety.
> Note terms " stimulus flooding "
> and " automatic affluence."
>
> Use for quotations? All the ideas
> in Kaplan, Chapter I.

THE OUTLINE

All the note cards shown in Figures 4 to 9 carry outline references: numbers tentatively keyed to your emerging idea of the possible structure of your paper, or more often added later when you have a reasonably firm working outline. Early in your reading you sense the main issues with which you will deal and   t to chart your course. You conclude that the marijuana controversy has three critical aspects—the legal, the physical/psychological, and the social/political—and you decide that all three aspects, broad as they are, are relevant to any paper on marijuana and the generation gap. Since these three categories cover a lot of ground, your paper will unquestionably have to be far less ambitious than your outline. That is normal; outlines are made to be trimmed. Think of your outline as a frame of reference for your notes, a way of keeping them in order; and as a way of limiting and focusing your project from the start. So, early on, playing on hunches and sparse knowledge, you jot down the following tentative outline plan:

"*Thesis*: American anti-marijuana crusaders have historically offered three main arguments: (1) that pot causes insanity, (2) that it leads to crime, and (3) that it leads to the use of addictive drugs like heroin. The first argument was characteristic of the 1920's, the second of the 1930's; the last is the one we hear most today. According to most legal and medical experts, all three arguments are false. Then why make them? Maybe because there is some need to identify pot with evil—some irrational need based on prejudice and unconscious hostilities. How to describe this need? What to do about it?"

From this plan you work out a possible outline for your paper, entering references to your reading at the appropriate places.

Working Outline

I. The laws against manufacturing, selling, or possessing pot have been made steadily tougher since the 1930's on three main grounds:

  A. Pot causes insanity and related mental/moral decay
    1. Rowell's claims in *On the Trail of Marijuana* (Smith, 106–107)
    2. The idea of the "dope fiend" (Ginsberg, 107)
    3. Anslinger's letter to the A.M.A. in 1943 (Solomon, xxvii)

  B. Pot causes crime
    1. Anslinger's campaign to spread this idea (Smith, 109; Kaplan, 88–98)
      a. Connection between "hashish" and Persian sect of "assassins" (Smith, 109; Solomon, 32–33)
      b. Marijuana Tax Act of 1937 (Solomon, xiv–xv; McGlothlin in Simmons, 182–187; Smith, 106)
    2. Testimony before the House Ways and Means Committee, 1937 (Solomon, xxv; Kaplan, 233–234)
      a. The horror stories (Smith, 110)
      b. Anslinger's denial that pot leads to heroin (Kaplan, 234)

  C. Smoking pot leads to shooting heroin
    1. Anslinger's later statement (1951) that pot does lead to addictive drugs (Kaplan, 234; Smith, 112; Solomon, 55)
    2. Testimony of Henry L. Giordano in 1968 (Kaplan, 232; Ginsberg in Solomon, 239; Oteri and Silverglate in Simmons, 156–162)

3. The "stepping-stone theory"—tobacco to alcohol to drugs (Kaplan, 233, 245; Shick et al. in Smith, 60; Sanford, *N. Rep.*, Feb. 28, 1970, 19)

II. Is pot really dangerous enough to warrant such tough laws?
  A. There is no significant evidence to that effect
    1. No evidence that marijuana leads to insanity
      a. Psychotic reactions very rare except in already unstable persons (*Psych. Abstr.*, 16127; McGlothlin in Simmons, 179; Allentuck et al. in Solomon, 413; Keniston, *Current*, 8; but see Tylden, *Br. Med. J.*, Aug. 26, '67)
      b. Mental and psychomotor impairment greater with marijuana-naïve persons on tests than with regular users (Weil et al., 1242)
      c. No long-term mental or physical effects (Arnold in Simmons, 120–121; Stockings in Solomon, 424)
    2. No established connection between marijuana and crime
      a. FBN's methodology and "evidence" worthless (Kaplan, 135)
      b. No established connection between hashish and "assassins" (Kaplan, 135; Smith, 109–110)
      c. LaGuardia Report's claim that "marijuana use is trivial as a cause of crime"—and A.M.A. rebuttal (Solomon, xxvii, 277–410; Lindesmith in Solomon, 57–58; Kaplan, 73; Goode in Smith, 174–175)
      d. Studies showing no relation between marijuana use and aggression (Kaplan, 135–136; Smith, 109–110; McGlothlin in Solomon, 467–468; McGlothlin & West, *Am. J. Psychiat.*, Sept. '68, 372–373; but see Etzioni, 39)
    3. No proof that pot leads to heroin (conclusive argument in Kaplan, 232–262; also Lindesmith in Solomon, 57–58; Oursler, 57; Etzioni, 39)
  B. There is evidence to show that marijuana is non-addictive and probably less physically dangerous than alcohol and cigarettes

1. Goddard's statement (*Time,* Apr. 19, '68, 52, 53; *USN&WR,* Feb. 5, '68, 15; Etzioni, 38–39)
2. Other statements and views (Oursler, xii; Nowlis, 7; Solomon [various writers], xxvii–xxviii, 41, 49, 91–92, 119, 123; Kaplan, 12, 13, 35, 37, 190, 211, 213, 228, 236–306 [esp. 304])
3. The immeasurability of the problem in exact terms (Kaplan, 59–61; and above refs)

C. Many claim that the damaging thing about marijuana is its illegality—i.e. the trouble lies in the law itself (Kaplan, 30–36; Laqueur in Oursler, xiii; "Nixon Drug Law," *Life,* Sept. 5, '69, 32; Stokes, *Current,* 113; McGlothlin & West, 370; Ginsberg in Solomon, 241)

III. Why, then, do we have such tough laws on pot?

A. Struggle for power and authority (Kaplan, 8–12; Smith, 2; Goode in Smith, 183; Leary in Solomon, 125)
B. Conflict over life styles (Kaplan, 4–19; Etzioni, 30; Keniston, *Current,* 5–19; Carey in Smith, esp. 96)
C. Differences in moral values (often same as B) (Kaplan, 17, 33, 89; Solomon, xxvii; Becker in Solomon, 90–94; Town in Smith, 130; McGlothlin & West, 378; Kerr in *N.Y. Times,* Jan. 12, '70)

IV. Conclusion: What should be done?

This is a working outline, not a final one. It shows that you have far more material than you can use if your paper is to be kept to three or four thousand words. It also tells you how little you know and how much there is yet to learn: What is to be said, for example, under heading IV? Still, you have cut a path through a forest of material, and your paper will now be much easier to write. Your theme and the main direction of your argument have been defined; there will be changes and unexpected difficulties, but your general course is charted.

The outline shown here is neither a pure topic outline nor a pure sentence outline, but a mixture of the two; the sentences tend to become topics at the lowest level because you do not want to make firm commitments yet. Note that all subdivided topics have at least two subtopics. Why? Because if you divide something, you get at least two parts; a topic divided into one subtopic is an absurdity. Note, too, that the outline includes possible references to be cited under each heading. Now is the time to decide what materials you will be using in what sequence —not later, when you will be concentrating on other matters.

Now, with your research done (or at least abandoned) and your tentative outline complete, you are ready at last to begin writing.

14

WRITING THE
RESEARCH PAPER

The outline that ends the previous chapter is not the sort of thing a person can strike off after an hour's thought, or even after a weekend's reading. It has taken shape in the course of three weeks or more of reading and thought, and perhaps after one or more false starts. It is a distillation of what you know and what you think you know at the time you have stopped reading and are ready to start writing.

Your working outline is not necessarily the ideal one for your purposes. Indeed, if your research has been thorough, your outline may well cover too much ground for the short or medium-length paper that you have been assigned. That is exactly what has happened here; something has to go. But you have been more and more drawn to one aspect of the question anyway: why American lawmakers have reacted so strongly against marijuana. You still intend to end up saying something about the generation gap, but in the body of the paper you will confine yourself so far as possible to the history of the marijuana laws and their enforcement. You may wish to make a second working outline to reflect this new and narrower focus.

In the following pages we give the paper that may have emerged from the process just described.

MARIJUANA AND THE GENERATION GAP

For the crime of possessing less than half an ounce of marijuana, Dr. Timothy Leary in 1966 was fined $30,000 and sentenced to thirty years in prison.[1] Although the Supreme Court overturned Leary's sentence on appeal, thus rendering the federal law on marijuana "constitutionally unenforceable,"[2] most states, having copied the federal statutes, have equally severe laws. California, for example, allows a sentence of up to ten years' imprisonment for a first offense of marijuana possession.[3] Moreover, despite clear evidence that "marijuana penalties neither deter amateurs nor root out professionals,"[4] some government agencies want to make the federal statutes still more severe. Can we explain this paradox?

The recent history of drug enforcement shows the futility of such measures. "Since the penalties were raised in 1956, juvenile drug arrests have risen more than 800%, and hardly a dent has been made in the volume of professional narcotics traffic."[5] Clearly harsher penalties are no rational response to this statistic, but reflect some deeper unease among legislators and their older constituents. Leary claimed that the real charge against him was "heresy," that he was in effect the victim of a witch-hunt. [6]

---

[1] Timothy Leary, "The Politics, Ethics, and Meaning of Marijuana," in David Solomon, ed., The Marihuana Papers (New York, 1968), p. 122.

[2] John Kaplan, Marijuana—The New Prohibition (New York, 1970), p. 32.

[3] Ibid., pp. 31–32.

[4] "The Nixon Drug Law," Life, 67:32 (Sept. 5, 1969).

[5] Ibid.

[6] Leary, p. 122.

Leary's case is scarcely unique. Senator Thomas Dodd, who appealed in
vain in 1962 for a reduction of the minimum mandatory federal sentence,
cites an even more striking case. He quotes from a U.S. District Judge:

> The mandatory sentence can work extreme injustice. I was compelled to im-
> pose a five-year sentence on a Marine veteran of the Korean campaign who
> was found with three or four marijuana cigarettes. He had been drinking in
> Tijuana and was arrested at the border. Obviously three or four cigarettes
> did not make him a peddler and these were not commercial amounts. He had
> a spotless civilian record and an excellent military career. He had received a
> Purple Heart and had been wounded in action and had a wife and children.
> I held up sentencing 60 days with the defendant's consent, to attempt to get
> the U.S. attorney to file a tax consent on a smuggling charge which would
> not have carried at least a five-year sentence. I was unsuccessful. I sentenced
> the man to five years in the penitentiary without parole.[7]

Such flagrant miscarriages of justice are perhaps no longer likely since
the passage of the Nixon Administration's Drug Control Bill in October
1970, which changed mere possession of marijuana from a felony to a mis-
demeanor and gave judges the power to dismiss charges or grant parole or
probation to first offenders. Yet the general emphasis of that bill on sterner
enforcement of the drug laws was perfectly in keeping with the steady increase in the severity of marijuana legislation since the 1920's.[8] Until about
1923, according to Roger C. Smith, narcotics addiction tended to be regarded as "an unfortunate occurrence, but not really the fault of the individual."[9] After that date—owing largely to hysteria generated by a press cam-

---

[7] Quoted from Proceedings of the White House Conference on Narcotics
and Drug Abuse, Washington, D.C., September 27–28, 1963, in David E.
Smith, ed., The New Social Drug: Cultural, Medical, and Legal Perspectives
on Marijuana (Englewood Cliffs, N.J., 1970), p. 114.

[8] For a full account of the Drug Control Bill of 1970, see New York
Times, October 28, 1970, p. 1. A good brief account of marijuana legislation
in the United States is Roger C. Smith, "U.S. Marijuana Legislation and the
Creation of a Social Problem," in David E. Smith, ed., The New Social Drug,
pp. 105–117.

[9] Ibid., p. 108.

paign—drug clinics were closed and the addict was generally considered "no longer a victim, but a threat."[10] The Federal Bureau of Narcotics, formed in 1930 and staffed largely by former Prohibition agents, went along with this new approach. During its first years it concentrated on hard drugs and paid little attention to marijuana. By the late 1930's, however, the popular press had alerted public opinion to the "marijuana menace," and the FBN soon raised the same cry.[11] How was that "menace" defined?

A typical anti-marijuana crusader of the 1930's was Earle Albert Rowell. In his book On the Trail of Marijuana, the Weed of Madness, he made the extravagant claim that the drug destroyed willpower, eliminated the line between right and wrong, led to rape and murder, and ultimately caused insanity. His greatest concern was to expose a plot by the tobacco industry to introduce marijuana into cigarettes and cigars, thus achieving "the destruction of the morals and the health of the nation."[12] Essentially the same harmful effects had been claimed for marijuana by some New Orleans newspapers as early as 1926, exposing what they called the "Muggles" trade.[13]

When the FBN got into the act it made similar assertions, none of them backed by scientific research. In 1937, just before the passage of the Marijuana Tax Act (the first federal legislation prohibiting the use of marijuana), FBN Commissioner Harry J. Anslinger wrote: "How many murders, suicides, robberies, criminal assaults, holdups, burglaries, and deeds of maniacal insanity it causes each year, especially among the young, can only be conjectured."[14] Twelve years later, in a foreword to a pamphlet on the threat of

---

[10]Ibid.

[11]Ibid., p. 107.

[12]Ibid., pp. 106–107.

[13]Kaplan, p. 88.

[14]Harry J. Anslinger, with Courtney Cooper, "Assassin of Youth," American Magazine, 124:18 (July 1937), quoted in Kaplan, p. 89.

marijuana in Latin America, Commissioner Anslinger praised the author for being "completely impartial, which is the basic requirement of all scientific investigation."[15] Here is part of the pamphlet's closing paragraph: "With every reason, marijuana, a drug of the Old as of the New World, has been closely associated since the most remote times with insanity, with crime, with violence, with brutality."[16]

Before the passage of the Marijuana Tax Act, Commissioner Anslinger and his associates publicized a number of highly doubtful horror stories connecting marijuana smoking with insanity and violence. John Kaplan, in his definitive study of marijuana and the law, has collected pages of this FBN "evidence," a shocking record of propagandizing on the part of a man and a Bureau charged with high public responsibility. One of Anslinger's arguments was particularly fanciful:

In the year 1090, there was founded in Persia the religious and military order of the Assassins, whose history is one of cruelty, barbarity, and murder, and for good reason. The members were confirmed users of hashish, or marijuana, and it is from the Arabic "hashshashin" that we have the English word "assassin."[17]

Any proof that hashish made the assassins cruel or barbaric? None whatever. Such an argument, as Kaplan clearly shows, is simply not admissible as evidence.

Arguments like this, preceded by years of yellow journalism that had primed the public to think of marijuana as a "killer-drug," made the passage

---

[15]Foreword to Pablo Osvaldo Wolff, Marijuana in Latin America: The Threat It Constitutes (Washington, D.C., 1949), quoted in Kaplan, p. 102.

[16]Wolff, p. 52, quoted in Kaplan, p. 103.

[17]"Assassin of Youth," p. 18, quoted in Kaplan, p. 112. Commissioner Anslinger's equating of marijuana with hashish (a much stronger form of the drug) is a common error.

of the Tax Act predictable:[18]

Accepting uncritically the testimony and recommendations of the Federal Bureau of Narcotics, Congress equipped the Marijuana Tax Act with sharp teeth: five years' imprisonment, a $2,000 fine, or both, were the penalties provided for [possessing] even a minute quantity of the herb.[19]

One bit of testimony given by Commissioner Anslinger before the congressional committee considering the Act is particularly interesting. Congressman Dingell of Michigan asked Anslinger: "I was just wondering whether the marijuana addict graduates into a heroin . . . user?" Anslinger replied, "No, sir; I have not heard of a case of that kind. I think it is an entirely different class. The marijuana addict does not go in that direction."[20] By 1951 Anslinger was not so sure,[21] and by 1955 he was singing an altogether different tune. To a Senate subcommittee investigating drug abuse he remarked, "Our great concern about the use of marijuana . . . [is] that eventually, if used over a long period, it does lead to heroin addiction."[22]

This is now the leading argument of the FBN, and Anslinger has repeated it many times. In 1960 he told another subcommittee: "Yes, sir. That is the beginning, especially in the New York and Los Angeles areas. They start on marijuana and get sort of a jaded appetite and want to get to something real.

---

[18]David Solomon, "The Marihuana Myths," Editor's Foreword to The Marihuana Papers, p. xv. The LaGuardia Report of 1938, based on a study conducted by the New York Academy of Medicine, concluded, in part, that "In most instances, the behavior of the [marijuana] smoker is of a friendly, sociable character. Aggressiveness and belligerency are not commonly seen." Quoted in Solomon, p. xvii.

[19]Solomon, p. xv.

[20]Hearings on H.R. 6385 (Taxation of Marijuana) Before the House Committee on Ways and Means, 75th Congress (1937), quoted in Kaplan, pp. 233–234.

[21]See interview in U.S. News & World Report, quoted in Kaplan, p. 234.

[22]Quoted by Roger C. Smith in D. E. Smith, p. 112.

Well, they switch to heroin, and that is when the trouble starts."[23] He was less definite on the connection between marijuana and crimes of violence: "It does not follow that all crime can be traced to marijuana. There have been many brutal crimes traced to marijuana, but I would not say it is a controlling factor in the commission of crimes."[24] But in his book The Murderers, published two years later, Anslinger wrote:

Much of the most irrational juvenile violence and killing that has written a new chapter of shame and tragedy is traceable directly to this hemp intoxication. . . . A sixteen-year-old kills his entire family of five in Florida [etc., etc.] . . . Every one of these crimes had been preceded by the smoking of one or more marijuana "reefers."[25]

Inconsistent as Anslinger's arguments are with the truth and each other, they have one consistent purpose: to keep penalties high. According to Roger Smith, "The FBN is dedicated to the notion that increasing penalties is the only way to limit the traffic in narcotics."[26] And Congress has agreed. The Narcotic Control Act of 1956, for example, authorizes minimum mandatory sentences for selling narcotics, with no chance for probation, suspended sentence, or parole, plus an optional fine of up to $20,000.[27] Marijuana is specifically included in the term "narcotics," though it is not pharmacologically in the same class with heroin and other hard drugs.[28]

---

[23]Ibid., p. 113.

[24]Ibid., p. 112. Smith refers the reader to Alfred R. Lindesmith, The Addict and the Law, p. 230, for a detailed description of Anslinger's testimony.

[25]Harry J. Anslinger and Will Oursler, The Murderers (New York, 1962), p. 24, quoted in Kaplan, p. 97. Oursler subsequently published his own tract entitled Marijuana: The Facts, the Truth (New York, 1968).

[26]Roger C. Smith in D. E. Smith, p. 113.

[27]Ibid.

[28]William H. McGlothlin and Louis Jolyon West, "The Marihuana Problem: An Overview," American Journal of Psychiatry, 125:270–278. (Sept. 1968).

What can we say about the arguments of the FBN and the repressive legal measures they have produced? The first thing to say is that most of the arguments are simply not true. There is no serious evidence that marijuana leads to insanity or psychosis;[29] there is even less establishing that marijuana leads to acts of violence;[30] and there is seemingly "no causal relationship between marijuana use and that of heroin."[31] Much of what scientific evidence there is about marijuana is of recent origin, but some has been around for a long time.[32] In any event, the FBN does not seem much interested in scientific evidence. Of the "Marijuana Crimes" cited by the Bureau in 1936, "in not a single case was there a serious attempt to establish that marijuana was in fact the cause of the crime."[33] In 1966, the newly appointed Commissioner

[29] Few deleterious long-term effects from smoking marijuana have been reported. See Andrew T. Weil, Norman E. Zinberg, and Judith M. Nelson, "Clinical and Psychological Effects of Marihuana in Man," Science, 162: 1234-1242 (Dec. 13, 1968); Samuel Allentuck and Karl Bowman, "Psychiatric Aspects of Marihuana Intoxication," in Solomon, pp. 411-416; and Kaplan, pp. 52-87, 141-198. But see also some negative views in "Potted Dreams," British Medical Journal, 1:133-134 (Jan. 18, 1969), and Elizabeth Tylden et al., "A Case for Cannabis?," British Medical Journal, 3:556 (Aug. 26, 1967).

[30] See Kaplan, pp. 73, 88–140; Alfred R. Lindesmith, "The Marihuana Problem: Myth or Reality?," in Solomon, pp. 57–58; and Erich Goode, "Marijuana and the Politics of Reality," in Smith, pp. 174–175.

[31] Kaplan, p. 259. Yet as late as August 1970 two leading insurance companies, Occidental Life of California and Metropolitan Life, refused to insure marijuana smokers. Here was the reason given by Paul Nichols, an Occidental official: "We find that marijuana can constitute a hazard to life directly as a result of its usage and in addition, indirectly through progression to deadly drugs, such as heroin." (San Jose Mercury, Aug. 28, 1970.) One wonders what medical opinion the company consulted.

[32] For example, the LaGuardia Report of 1944. The Journal of the American Medical Association editorially criticized the report, but, writes Dr. Alfred R. Lindesmith, "the conclusions of the report enjoy considerable status and are undoubtedly far closer to the realities of the situation than is the view represented by the A.M.A. editorial." Lindesmith in Solomon, p. 60.

[33] Kaplan, p. 93.

of Narcotics, Henry L. Giordano, introduced into evidence at a Senate hearing a pamphlet entitled What Is So Bad About Marijuana? whose unnamed author blamed "aggressive adolescents at odds with the conventional norms of our society" for popularizing a drug that has "a worse effect than heroin," that is "more intoxicating than alcohol," and whose abuse is "likely to lead to insanity . . . and . . . responsible for numerous and varied major crimes."[34] Not much had changed in thirty years!

In criticizing the FBN's arguments, I am not saying that marijuana is harmless; evidence on its long-term effects is still too inconclusive to say much one way or the other.[35] My concern is with another question, namely why, since there is so little evidence that marijuana is harmful, our society has elected to penalize its users so severely. Why are there no comparable penalties on the use of cigarettes and alcohol?

A large body of highly credible evidence lends force to this comparison. For example, a study conducted in 1925 by authorities in the Panama Canal Zone of the use of marijuana by soldiers stationed there concluded, in the words of the editor of the Military Surgeon, that "the smoking of leaves, flowers, and seeds of Cannabis sativa is no more harmful than the smoking of tobacco or mullein or sumac leaves."[36] Dr. Alfred R. Lindesmith, author

---

[34]Hearings Before a Special Subcommittee of the Senate Committee on the Judiciary, 89th Congress (1966), p. 459, quoted in Joseph S. Oteri and Harvey A. Silverglate, "In the Marketplace of Free Ideas: A Look at the Passage of the Marihuana Tax Act," in J. L. Simmons, ed., Marihuana: Myths and Realities (North Hollywood, Calif., 1967), p. 157.

[35]Careful investigators tend to advise people to "stay off it" until more is known. See M. M. Glatt, "Is It All Right to Smoke Pot?," British Journal of Addiction, 64:113 (May 1969), and B. E. Leonard, "Cannabis: A Short Review of Its Effects and the Possible Dangers of Its Use," ibid., pp. 121-130.

[36]Quoted in Norman Taylor, "The Pleasant Assassin," in Solomon, p. 41. Cannabis sativa is the scientific name of the most common kind of marijuana plant. For other references to this report, see Allen Ginsberg, "First Manifesto to End the Bringdown," in Solomon, p. 240, and Mayor F. H. LaGuardia, Foreword to "The Marihuana Problem in the City of New York," in Solomon, p. 280.

of The Addict and the Law, writes: "Intrinsically . . . marihuana is less dangerous and less harmful to the human body than is alcohol."[37] Kaplan, after a most careful appraisal, writes that "marijuana is no more harmful to the individual or to society than is alcohol, and indeed, it is quite likely that marijuana is less so."[38] Finally, Dr. James L. Goddard, former head of the Food and Drug Administration, declared in 1967: "Whether or not marijuana is a more dangerous drug than alcohol is debatable—I don't happen to think it is."[39] This statement, which flew in the face of establishment opinion in Washington, led to demands for his resignation, which he tendered some months later.

In short, there are good reasons to believe that marijuana is both physically and psychologically as benign a drug as alcohol and tobacco, yet our official society has reacted in savage opposition to it. Why? The question is not an idle one, given the fact that some ten million Americans are legally criminals as a result of smoking marijuana.[40] Perhaps half to three-quarters of all college undergraduates have smoked at least one joint;[41] they too are criminals. Such figures stir disrespect for the law itself, and indeed many critics argue that the most dangerous thing about marijuana is its illegality. Kaplan observes:

---

[37]"The Marihuana Problem," in Solomon, p. 49.

[38]Kaplan, p. 305.

[39]Quoted in Amitai Etzioni, "America's Social Frontiers: Why Not Smoke Pot?," Current, 95:38 (May 1968).

[40]Ten million is the estimate of Dr. Stanley Yolles, quoted in Gertrude Samuels, "Pot, Hard Drugs, and the Law," New York Times Magazine, Feb. 15, 1970, p. 4.

[41]The figure for one leading university in 1968 was 69 per cent, according to a study by Richard H. Blum and associates cited in Kaplan, p. 23. John Steinbeck IV estimated that "about sixty per cent of American soldiers between the ages of nineteen and twenty-seven smoke marijuana." In Touch (New York, 1969), p. 197.

In part because marijuana users—unlike cheaters—do not rationalize their use of the drug as an aberrant event unrelated to their total personality, it becomes especially unhealthy for their society to declare them serious criminals. It is obvious that when any society criminalizes such a large percentage of its young people, it raises very serious social problems. . . . It is hard to see . . . how a realization that one has committed what is officially a very serious crime can fail to engender at least a somewhat more generalized lack of respect for the law and the society that has so defined one's action.[42]

Moreover, it is clear that the marijuana laws, unlike certain archaic state laws on fornication and sexual deviation, have society's general approval. That is why the law is enforced so sternly, and why, for example, the U.S. attorney could stand firm against Senator Dodd's District Judge. The marijuana smoker cannot stop with a "generalized lack of respect for law and society"; he must live in fear of the police and the courts. He is not only technically a criminal, but psychologically an alienated man.

His alienation may take any of a number of forms. Kenneth Keniston draws an illuminating distinction in this regard between "seekers" and "heads." Seekers are anti-war, anti-pollution, and anti-poverty idealists who are not "in any systematic way 'alienated' from American society" but who "have not really made up their minds whether it is worth joining, either." Heads are thoroughly disenchanted with the career-oriented goals of middle-class America. They are convinced, in Keniston's words, that

American society is trashy, cheap, and commercial; it "dehumanizes" its members; its values of success, materialism, monetary accomplishment undercut more important spiritual values. . . . For heads, the goal is to find a way out of the "air-conditioned nightmare" of American society. What matters is the interior world, and, in the exploration of that world, drugs play a major role.[43]

---

[42]Kaplan, p. 33.

[43]Kenneth Keniston, "Students, Drugs, and Protest: Drugs on Campus," Current, 103:9, 10 (Feb. 1969).

Whether one classifies oneself as a seeker or a head or somewhere in between, there is no question that most American students today—even some
of the most conservative—feel alienated from American society. Whatever
the cause of their alienation may be, marijuana is seemingly a symbol of it.
The conflict is not simply between the old and the young; it is between those
who support war and those who oppose it, the squares and the critics,
people concerned with running things and making money and people concerned with the quality of life. If one can generalize, it is between those who
fear change and those who feel change is imperative.

Only in terms like these can we understand the feelings of the many
people who, with Commissioner Giordano, see the attempt to legalize marijuana as "just another effort to break down our whole American system."[44]
As Erich Goode points out in "Marijuana and the Politics of Reality," this
reaction is more political than scientific: marijuana has become a symbol for
a complex of positions, beliefs, and activities in which those who use the
drug must also be politically radical, sexually promiscuous, and unpatriotic.[45]

Kaplan in his brilliant chapter "Marijuana as a Symbol" makes the
same point:

In a large portion of our population, then, marijuana is associated with a
life-style focusing on immediate experience, present rather than delayed
gratification, noncompetitiveness and lessened interest in the acquisition of
wealth. And even if one is not prepared to use stronger terms, such as irresponsibility, laziness, and a lack of patriotism, there is no doubt that the life-
style, like the use of the drug itself, involves a disregard for many of the conventions that the older society regards as dear. It is hardly surprising, then,
that many people will wish strongly that the criminalization of marijuana be
retained if only as a reminder to marijuana users—and indeed to many who
do not use marijuana but who are like users in other ways—that this life-style
and these values are less worthy.[46]

[44]Hearings . . . Before a Subcommittee of the House Committee on Ap-
propriations, 90th Congress (Feb. 8, 1967), p. 405, quoted in Kaplan, p. 9.

[45]Goode in Smith, p. 183.

[46]Kaplan, p. 5.

The drug laws, as William McGlothlin and Louis West point out, have "always been an attempt to legislate morality, although they have been justified in terms of preventing antisocial acts."[47] The Christian and achievement-oriented value system that fostered the drug laws and supports them so passionately today is bound to be threatened by a new culture that scorns those values. To supporters of the old system, marijuana is as surely the enemy's flag today as the swastika was thirty years ago.

Will pointing out the nonscientific basis of the feeling against marijuana help to get saner and fairer marijuana laws? Probably not for at least another ten years, says Kaplan. Too many people have an emotional investment, to say nothing of a political investment, in keeping the laws the way they are or making them tougher; and this emotional investment is probably the stronger and more dangerous for being largely irrational and subconscious. The most telling observation here comes from Erich Goode:

> A man is not opposed to the use or the legalization of marijuana <u>because</u> (he thinks) it "leads to" the use of more dangerous drugs, because it "causes" crime, because it "produces" insanity and brain damage, because it "makes" a person unsafe behind the wheel, because it "creates" an unwillingness to work. <u>He believes these things because he thinks the drug is evil</u>. . . . But everyone, Pareto says, seeks to cloak his prejudices in the garb of reason, especially in an empirical age, so that evidence to support them is dragged in <u>post hoc</u> to provide rational and concrete proof.[48]

This is a kind of thinking that most young people in my experience associate with their elders and try their best to avoid; in this sense marijuana is a generation-gap issue. But generations do not in the end seem to me all that different. Prohibition, after all, was repealed in 1933 by a generation my parents considered old fogies, and the abortion laws are in the course of being liberalized out of existence by my parents' generation. Marijuana's day will come, and perhaps sooner than Kaplan thinks.

---

[47]McGlothlin and West, p. 377.
[48]Goode in Smith, p. 176.

BIBLIOGRAPHY

Allen, James R., and West, Louis Jolyon, "Flight from Violence: Hippies and the Green Rebellion," American Journal of Psychiatry, 125:364–370 (Sept. 1968).

Buckley, William F., Jr., "Drugs: A Very Disturbing Study Comes from Canada," Los Angeles Times, Feb. 25, 1970, p. 14.

Etzioni, Amitai, "America's Social Frontiers: Why Not Smoke Pot?," Current, 95:38–41 (May 1968).

Glatt, M. M., "Is It All Right to Smoke Pot?," British Journal of Addiction, 64:109–114 (May 1969).

Kaplan, John. Marijuana—The New Prohibition. New York: World Publishing Co., 1970.

Kaufman, Joshua, et al., "Runaways, Hippies, and Marihuana," American Journal of Psychiatry, 126:718–720 (Nov. 1969).

Keniston, Kenneth, "Students, Drugs, and Protest: Drugs on Campus," Current, 103:5–19 (Feb. 1969).

Leonard, B. E., "Cannabis: A Short Review of Its Effects and the Possible Dangers of Its Use," British Journal of Addiction, 64:121–130 (May 1969).

"Marijuana or Alcohol—Which Harms Most?," U.S. News & World Report, 64:15 (Feb. 5, 1968).

McGlothlin, William H., and West, Louis Jolyon, "The Marihuana Problem: An Overview," American Journal of Psychiatry, 125:270–278 (Sept. 1968).

"The Nixon Drug Law," Life, 67:32 (Sept. 5, 1969).

Nowlis, Helen H. Drugs on the College Campus, with an Introduction by Kenneth Keniston. New York: Doubleday & Co., 1969.

Oursler, Will. Marijuana: The Facts, the Truth. New York: Paul S. Eriksson, Inc., 1968.

"Pot: Safer than Alcohol?," Time, 91:52–53 (Apr. 19, 1968).

"Potted Dreams," British Medical Journal, 1:133–134 (Jan. 18, 1969).

Samuels, Gertrude, "Pot, Hard Drugs, and the Law," New York Times Magazine, Feb. 15, 1970, p. 4.

Simmons, J. L., ed. Marihuana: Myths and Realities. North Hollywood, Calif.: Brandon House, 1967.

Oteri, Joseph S., and Silverglate, Harvey A., "In the Marketplace of Free Ideas: A Look at the Passage of the Marihuana Tax Act," pp. 136-163.

Smith, David E., ed. The New Social Drug: Cultural, Medical, and Legal Perspectives on Marijuana. Englewood Cliffs, N.J.: Prentice-Hall, Inc., 1970.

Goode, Erich, "Marijuana and the Politics of Reality," pp. 168-186.

Messer, Mark, "Running Out of Era: Some Nonpharmacological Notes on the Psychedelic Revolution," pp. 157-167.

Smith, Roger C., "U.S. Marijuana Legislation and the Creation of a Social Problem," pp. 105-117.

Solomon, David, ed. The Marihuana Papers. New York: New American Library, 1968.

Allentuck, Samuel, and Bowman, Karl, "Psychiatric Aspects of Marihuana Intoxication," pp. 411-416.

Ginsberg, Allen, "First Manifesto to End the Bringdown," pp. 230-248.

Leary, Timothy, "The Politics, Ethics, and Meaning of Marijuana," pp. 121-140.

Lindesmith, Alfred R., "The Marihuana Problem: Myth or Reality?," pp. 48-64.

"The Marihuana Problem in the City of New York," with a Foreword by Mayor F. H. LaGuardia, pp. 277-410.

McGlothlin, William H., "Cannabis: A Reference," pp. 455-472.

Solomon, David, "The Marihuana Myths," pp. xiii-xxiii.

Taylor, Norman, "The Pleasant Assassin: The Story of Marihuana," pp. 31-47.

Steinbeck, John. In Touch. New York: Alfred A. Knopf, 1969.

Tylden, Elizabeth, et al., "A Case for Cannabis?," British Medical Journal, 3:556 (Aug. 26, 1967).

Weil, Andrew T.; Zinberg, Norman E.; and Nelson, Judith M., "Clinical and Psychological Effects of Marihuana in Man," Science, 162:1234-1242 (Dec. 13, 1968).

The paper just presented has several characteristics worth noting. First, it illustrates most of the common problems encountered in handling quoted matter and footnotes. Second, its bibliography includes several publications that are not actually quoted or referred to but that the writer found helpful in shaping his thoughts; though teachers rightly discourage students from padding out their bibliographies with ill-digested or unread material, publications that have influenced the paper may properly be listed even if they have not been cited. Finally, the conclusion of the paper does not merely repeat or recapitulate what the writer has said already but goes on to suggest what the paper means, what message he thinks we should carry away from it. Anyone can summarize facts; what a reader wants is the writer's statement of what they seem to add up to.

FOOTNOTES

Common Abbreviations

In the footnotes and the bibliography of our marijuana paper, we used the conventional abbreviations "ed.," "et al.," and "*ibid.*" The first stands for "editor," or more rarely for "edited by," as in "*The Complete Works of Shakespeare,* ed. George Lyman Kittredge"; in its meaning of "editor" it takes the plural "eds." Its most common use is to indicate a man who prepares for publication either an edition of another man's works (as Kittredge did Shakespeare's) or a work by many hands (like the Solomon book on marijuana). As the preceding pages indicate, "ed." should be lowercased and should not be enclosed in parentheses. The same abbreviation also stands for "edition," as in "3d ed." or "rev. ed."

"Et al." is an abbreviation of the Latin *et alii,* "and others"; it may be either roman or italic. The use of "and others" instead of "et al." is also perfectly acceptable. "*Ibid.*" is another abbreviation from the Latin; the full form is *ibidem,* "in the same place." (Purists object to "in *ibid.*" because this would translate "*in in* the same place," but most professional editors accept the expression anyway.) "*Ibid.*" is used to stand for as much of the immediately preceding citation as applies to the present one:

thus if note 1 reads *"Paradise Lost*, Bk. 9, lines 115–121," note 2 might read simply *"Ibid."* (meaning that the identical passage is being cited again), or *"Ibid.*, lines 122–123," or *"Ibid.*, Bk. 10, line 8."

Short Forms

In citing a book or article for the second time when the first citation does not immediately precede, some authorities recommend *"op. cit.,"* an abbreviation of the Latin *opere citato*, "in the work cited": thus "Smith, *op. cit.*, p. 89." Increasingly, however, writers and editors are abandoning *op. cit.* for a short-title system. Suppose Smith's book is the only work you cite by anyone named Smith; then your second citation (and any subsequent citation) need only read "Smith, p. 89." This is the style we recommend.

If you cite more than one work by Smith, say a book titled *The Situation in Southeast Asia* and a magazine article titled "The Hong Kong Refugees," you need give just enough of the title in your next citation to make it clear which of the two works you are citing: "Smith, *Situation,* p. 89," "Smith, 'Refugees,' p. 191." Finally, if you cite works by more than one Smith, you should distinguish between Smiths by adding first names or initials: "H. E. Smith, p. 89," "Margaret Chase Smith, pp. 10–12."

Checklist of Footnote Forms

Here is a brief checklist of the most common footnote forms:

Books

First reference to a book:

> [1] C. G. Jung, *The Archetypes and the Collective Unconscious,* trans. R. F. C. Hull (New York, 1959), p. 185.
> [2] Wilhelm Windelband, *A History of Philosophy* (New York, 1958), II, 447.

Immediately following reference to the same page of the Windelband book:

> [3] *Ibid.*

To a different page of the same volume:

> ⁴ *Ibid.*, p. 449.

To a different volume of the same work:

> ⁵ *Ibid.*, I, 25–26.

Later references to the Windelband book if it is the only work by this author cited:

> ⁶ Windelband, II, 450.

If other works by this author are cited, distinguish between them by using a short form of the title:

> ⁷ Windelband, *History,* II, 450.

If a work by another author named Windelband, say George Windelband, is also cited, distinguish between them by using an initial:

> ⁸ W. Windelband, II, 450.

First reference to a book with two or three editors:

> ⁹ Cleanth Brooks, John Thibaut Purser, and Robert Penn Warren, eds., *An Approach to Literature,* 3d ed. (New York, 1952), p. 34.

Notice that "3d ed." is not included in the parenthesis; this is not parenthetical information, but an essential indication of which edition you are quoting from, since page 34 of the first or second edition might be very different from page 34 of the third. If there are four or more authors or editors, it becomes cumbersome to list all the names; it is conventional in this case to use the form "Cleanth Brooks and others," or "Cleanth Brooks et al."

Later references to the same book:

> ¹⁰ Brooks, Purser, and Warren, p. 80.

First reference to a chapter in a multiauthor volume:

[11] Joseph Frank, "Spatial Form in Modern Literature," in Robert Wooster Stallman, ed., *Critiques and Essays in Criticism, 1920–1948* (New York, 1949), p. 317.

Later reference to the same chapter:

[12] Frank, in Stallman, ed., pp. 323–325.

Alternatively, as in our marijuana paper, simply "Frank in Stallman, pp. 323–325." If there are many references to the Frank chapter in close succession, the citation can be abbreviated still further to "Frank, pp. 323–325."

Reference to another chapter in the same book:

[13] Edmund Wilson, "Historical Criticism," in Stallman, ed., p. 457.

Reference to an edition of the works of a single author prepared by an editor:

[14] *The Works of Schopenhauer,* ed. Will Durant (New York, 1955), p. 456.

Even though your concern may be exclusively with what Schopenhauer says and Durant's name may mean nothing to you, it is customary to cite the editor's name so that knowledgeable readers will immediately understand that you are using the Durant edition of Schopenhauer rather than any of the other English-language editions.

Reference to an encyclopedia article:

[15] "Etruscan Pottery," *Encyclopedia of Arts and Crafts* (New York, 1970), IV, 239.

Reference to a quotation available to you only in a secondary source:

[16] Axel Munthe, *The Story of San Michele,* p. 245, quoted in Karl Menninger, *Man Against Himself* (New York, 1938), p. 66.

Articles

First reference to an article in a periodical:

> [17] Thomas S. Szasz, "Moral Conflict and Psychiatry," *Yale Review*, 69:564 (Summer 1960)

Alternatively, "LXIX (Summer 1960), 564" or "69 (Summer 1960), 564." Whichever of these forms you use, stick to it for all articles cited in your paper.

Later references to the same article:

> [18] Szasz, p. 566.

This assumes that no other works by Szasz are cited in your paper. Otherwise use a short form: "Szasz, 'Moral Conflict,' p. 566."

Reference to a book review:

> [19] Joseph Frank, review of *Symbols and Civilization* by Ralph Ross, in *Sewanee Review*, 72:478 (Summer 1964).

Reference to an unsigned article in a newspaper:

> [20] "Black Power vs. 'White Guilt,'" *San Francisco Chronicle*, Oct. 15, 1971, p. 6.

Note that a periodical's dates are in parentheses when they follow a volume number. That is because the volume number is enough to enable the reader to locate the periodical in a library; the date is accordingly extra information, given parenthetically for whatever interest it may be to the reader. Where no volume number is given, the date becomes essential to finding the reference; it accordingly appears between commas, like a volume number, e.g. "*New York Times,* May 11, 1972, p. 12."

What to Footnote

If you have trouble with footnoting and need a single central idea to get hold of, it should be the concept of *retrievability*. In the last analysis, the use of parentheses or commas, italics or quotation marks, is a matter of form, a convention to be learned for your own convenience and your reader's, but not the heart of the matter. The basic purpose of footnotes is to tell your reader where you got your information so that he can decide for himself how much faith to put in it. Did you get it from the *New York Times,* May 11, 1972, page 12? Well and good. Your reader can either accept the information as true, dismiss it as biased (if he feels, for example, that the *Times* is generally biased), or look it up for himself to see whether your source really says what you say it says and to find out what else it says at the same time. Had you not footnoted your information, your reader would not have had these options. He would have had to take you on faith or to dismiss you as talking through your hat. Given these alternatives, skeptical readers will usually take the second.

In deciding what to footnote, it may help to imagine just such a skeptical reader, one disposed to question everything you say. He may ask, How do you know the Russian Navy is the world's second-largest? Your footnote is your answer: " 'Red Sails in the Sunset,' editorial in the *Topeka News,* Dec. 10, 1971, p. 28." How do you know that President Nixon was unpopular in Spain? "Letter from my brother, Lt. Eugene Hart, in Madrid, Sept. 20, 1970." Where did you learn that Mao Tse-tung was a lifelong champion of equal rights for women? "See Stuart Schram, *Mao Tse-tung* (Penguin Books, 1966), p. 43." Some sources are more trustworthy than others; your readers have the right to judge this matter for themselves.

Finally, make sure you include enough information in your footnote to take your reader straight to the right place if he wants to follow in your footsteps. "*Topeka News,* Dec. 10, 1971" is not enough; the reader may have to search through 50 pages of small type to find the passage you cite. "According to Stuart Schram" is not enough; Schram has written several books, each with several hundred pages, and dozens of articles. Even the citation of your brother's letter—not a recommended thing to do, by the way, but permissible where you have reliable information not readily accessible from more public sources—gains authority from the details. Your brother was a lieutenant, which means that he was not a child and probably not a mere tourist; and he was in Spain during President Nixon's administration, which means that his information is firsthand. "Letter from my brother" alone would tell us none of this.

To repeat, the content of footnotes is more important than their form. Get your information down first. You can learn the conventions of punctuation, italicization, and so on later.

PLAGIARISM

Plagiarism is literary burglary. At its worst it involves an outright intent to deceive, to pass off another's work as one's own. More often, it is the result of carelessness or ignorance. But whether intentional or unintentional (the distinction is often hard to draw), plagiarism is always an error, and a serious one.

Whenever you borrow another writer's words or ideas, you must acknowledge the borrowing. The only exceptions are information in the public domain (Columbus landed in America in 1492; oxygen was originally called phlogiston; oranges grow on trees) and opinions within anyone's range (*Hamlet* is a great play; time flies). Many undergraduates have trouble with this problem. Some react with an overnice conscience and footnote even dictionary definitions. Others change two or three words in a quotation and feel that they have somehow made it their own. The first practice is irritating, the second unethical. The right course is a generous and intelligent consideration of both the reader you are addressing (he will take 1492 on faith) and the writers you are using. When you use their words, their ideas, even their organization or sequence of ideas, say so—in a footnote or in the text. Claim as your own only what properly is your own.

The following examples may help to clarify the difference between legitimate and illegitimate borrowing. Here is part of the paragraph on Thoreau from Vernon Louis Parrington's *Main Currents in American Thought*:

At Walden Pond and on the Merrimac River Thoreau's mind was serene as the open spaces; but this Greek serenity was rudely disturbed when he returned to Concord village and found his neighbors drilling for the Mexican War, and when authority in the person of the constable came to him with the demand that he pay a due share to the public funds. The war to him was a hateful thing, stupid and unjust, waged for the extension of the obscene system of Negro slavery; and Thoreau was brought sharply to consider his relations to the political state that presumed to demand his allegiance, willing or unwilling, to its acts. Under the stress of such an emergency the transcendentalist was driven to examine the whole theory of the relation of the individual to the state.

The following examples will demonstrate some representative ways in which this passage, or parts of it, might be misused.[1]

Inadequate Acknowledgment: Outright Theft

When Thoreau was at Walden Pond or on the Merrimac River he knew considerable peace of mind, but when he returned to Concord this peace of mind was rudely disturbed. He came back to find his neighbors drilling for the Mexican War, a war he thought wrong, and when the constable came to him and demanded that he pay taxes to support that war, he balked. The war to him was a hateful thing, stupid and unjust, waged for the extension of the obscene system of Negro slavery; and Thoreau was brought sharply to consider his relations to the political state that presumed to demand his allegiance. In such an emergency, just how did the individual relate to the state?

In this example the writer has rephrased Parrington's first and last sentences, using some of his own words and some of Parrington's. He has made enough other minor modifications so that no full sentence of the original remains intact. But these trivial exceptions apart, he has copied the original word for word. His

[1] For simplicity we omit footnotes from the following discussion. A truly adequate acknowledgment to Parrington would of course include a footnote giving his name in full, the title of his book, the city and date of publication, and the numbers of the pages from which the writer's information is drawn.

intent to deceive is clear, the more so from his inept camouflaging of the first and last sentences. Had the writer put the directly quoted portion in quotation marks (or made it a single-spaced insert quotation) and footnoted it, he would not be guilty of plagiarism. He would have made it clear that he was contributing nothing of his own to the discussion, but was simply inviting us to listen to Parrington. As it is, however, he is passing off Parrington's words as his own, pretending to a knowledge (and style) he doesn't have. This is an inexcusable moral error.

Inadequate Acknowledgment: Paraphrase

> At Walden Pond and on the Merrimac River Thoreau's mind was calm as the open spaces; but this serenity was rudely disrupted when he returned to Concord and discovered his neighbors drilling for the Mexican War, and when the constable, representing authority, came to him and demanded that he pay his share of taxes for the war. He regarded the war as hateful, stupid, and unjust, and waged to extend the slave system, which he opposed. This experience caused Thoreau to reconsider sharply the whole question of the relation between the individual and the state.

This example represents only a negligible improvement on the last. The writer has made more changes in wording than the outright plagiarist, but has contributed no more of his own thinking or wording. Every idea in his paragraph and most of the words and phrases are taken directly from Parrington without acknowledgment. Though the writer has avoided copying whole clauses word for word, he is plainly guilty of plagiarism.

But what is a writer to do in such a case? Clearly it is impossible to enclose a paraphrase in quotation marks, for quotation marks may be used only where an author's words are reproduced exactly and completely. How then can plagiarism be avoided here? The best way is by running acknowledgments in the text, as in the following example.

Adequate Acknowledgment: Paraphrase

> According to Vernon L. Parrington, the "Greek serenity" of Thoreau's mind at Walden Pond and on the Merrimac

River was rudely disturbed when he returned to Concord and found his neighbors drilling for the Mexican War, and when the town constable, representing authority, came to him asking that he pay his share of taxes for the war. Thoreau regarded the war as stupid, unjust, and designed to extend the slave system, which he opposed. Now his direct experience of its effects, says Parrington, caused Thoreau to reconsider the whole question of the relation between the individual and the state.

In the two sentences in which Parrington's name appears, it is clear that the ideas are his. But what about the other sentence? Has the writer slipped in something of Parrington's as his own? An argument can be made either way; but since in general the writer is being straightforward about his debt, there can be little difficulty about giving him the benefit of the doubt.

Decisions like this are not always easy, since too many phrases like "Parrington says" or "Parrington goes on to point out" make writing graceless. If the claims of honesty and grace conflict, be honest first, but try also to be as graceful as you can. Every last comma need not be acknowledged. In the passage above, for example, only one phrase was placed in quotation marks even though other words—among them *stupid* and *unjust*—were used by Parrington. Since it was inconvenient to quote *stupid* and *unjust* in the exact phrasing used by Parrington, and since it would have seemed fussy to put *stupid* in one set of quotation marks and *unjust* in another, the writer decided that honesty was adequately served by his two general acknowledgments to Parrington. We think he was right.

Inadequate Acknowledgment: Forgetfulness

When Thoreau returned to Concord, he was shocked to find his neighbors drilling for the Mexican War. It was still worse when the government asked him to pay taxes for a war he didn't believe in, a war he considered hateful, stupid, and obscene. At Walden and on the Merrimac his thoughts had taken on an almost Greek serenity; now he was confronted with the dilemmas of real life. He did not hesitate. Putting aside his transcendental notions, he plunged into an examination of what the individual may legitimately be said to owe the state.

This writer has clearly mastered his material and knows what he wants to say. He has abandoned Parrington's sequence of ideas; he has added his own emphases; and his phrasing is largely his own. But in questions of acknowledgment, "largely" is not enough. Three bits of undigested Parrington remain: "his neighbors drilling for the Mexican War," "hateful, stupid, and obscene," and "Greek serenity." The first of these phrases is neutral enough to make its borrowing forgivable. The other two, and especially "Greek serenity," are not.

Given the writer's general performance, it seems likely that he has unconsciously drawn on his memory for the words in question, or perhaps that he has worked from slovenly note cards. He is nonetheless guilty of dishonest borrowing. At the very least, he should have put "Greek serenity" in quotation marks and acknowledged a general indebtedness to Parrington.

Adequate Acknowledgment: Mature Borrowing

There was a time when writers paid no attention to plagiarism. Chaucer and Shakespeare, for example, borrowed incessantly from other writers without acknowledgment, and never gave the matter a thought. But in the last century or so Western writers have taken an increasingly proprietary attitude toward their own work, and it is now considered common decency to give a writer credit for the use of his ideas, his words, or even the sequence in which his ideas are presented.

Many people who do not write much themselves feel that there is something natural or inevitable in a writer's sequence of ideas —they might feel that Parrington, for example, starting with Walden Pond and ending with the state, was simply recording the sequence established by history. But of course he was doing no such thing. History is written by historians; the shape of past events is the shape of the minds that set down these events. And so it is with the Parrington passage: what makes it useful is not so much its individual ideas and phrases as Parrington's general authority and intelligence.

If, therefore, you begin with Walden Pond and end with the individual and the state—no matter what words you use in between—you must make a bow to Parrington somewhere along the line and thank him for his help.   This is not only elementary honesty, but elementary courtesy.   Here is such a passage:

> Vernon Parrington pictures Thoreau at Walden as knowing a kind of "Greek serenity" that was rudely shaken when he returned to Concord and found his neighbors drilling for the Mexican War.   Yet the more one studies Thoreau, the more one wonders whether this contrast between the serene recluse and the embattled citizen is a valid one.   We are increasingly knowledgeable these days about the hostility implicit in an act, any act, of withdrawal.   Parrington implies that Thoreau was driven by events to take a political position, and in a sense he is right.   But was there no political content in his move to Walden?

Here the writer has used Parrington, but not exploited him; Parrington has helped him, and he admits as much in the very act of taking issue with one of Parrington's ideas.   Such a writer doesn't want to steal and doesn't have to.   The words of others are not some sort of mask or false identity that he puts on to deceive the world; they are elements in his search for truth. Why not honor those who have gone before and done good work? We need all the help we can get.   In the search for truth we have too few ideas, not too many; if we are honest men, we should let the world know what lights we are following and who lit them.

INDEX TO CURRENT USAGE

The following alphabetical sequence mixes words (e.g. *overall*) and categories (e.g. ANTECEDENT PROBLEMS), following the precedent of the first and greatest dictionary of current usage, Henry Watson Fowler's *Modern English Usage* (1926). We have followed Fowler also in including, as a sort of bonus to browsers, discussions under headings that no one with a problem would ever think to look up, e.g. CLASHING VALUES, *TIMEstyle*. Owing to space limitations, the present sequence is necessarily superficial. It should be supplemented as necessary by reference to Fowler, preferably in the second edition (1965), which was thoroughly revised and updated by Sir Ernest Gowers; or to Wilson Follett's *Modern American Usage* (1966), the best of several efforts to compile an American Fowler.

This section is intended essentially as a supplement to Parts 2 and 3 of the text. It does not relate to the text in any systematic fashion: indeed, some usage questions are discussed only in the text, some only in this section, and some in both places. Since cross-references have been kept to a minimum, users of this section may find it helpful to consult the main Index as well. The abbreviations W7 and AHD stand for *Webster's Seventh Collegiate Dictionary* and *The American Heritage Dictionary of the English Language*.

a, an. (1) A should be omitted after *kind* and *sort*: not *What kind of a fool do you take me for?* but *What kind of fool*; not *We thought it must be some sort of a trick*, but *some sort of trick.*

(2) *A half a* is illiterate: either *a half dollar* or *half a dollar*, not *a half a dollar.*

(3) *Historic, historical,* and *historian* are properly preceded by *a*, not *an*; the same goes for *heroic* and *humble.* The use of *an* before these words is an affectation.

(4) Distinctions of number often depend on the proper use of *a*. For example, *a secretary and treasurer* is one per-

son who handles both jobs; *a secretary and a treasurer* are two people. Such locutions as *a man and woman* and *a hat, coat, and tie,* by leaving out articles after the first, make a false, unpleasing, and sometimes puzzling amalgam out of elements inherently separate.

above. As an adjective (*the above figures*), *above* is acceptable, though good writers prefer *the figures above* or *the figures cited above.* As a noun (*The above is just one example of what I mean*), *above* is businessmen's jargon.

ACCENTS, on such words as take them, are as essential to correct spelling as the right letters. To spell a word like *émigré* or *résumé* with one accent or none, or with the wrong kind, is to misspell it. Newspapers are a source of confusion on this point; since their type fonts usually contain no accented letters, they accustom people to seeing words like *communiqué* and names like *Mendès-France* shorn of their accents. The best authority here is a dictionary. Where dictionaries disagree, take your choice.

actually. The use of *actually* as a mere intensifier in sentences like *I was actually afraid to speak* and *She actually begged him to stop* is rarely effective in making a description more vivid, and may lead to confusion with the proper use of *actually,* which is to contrast the facts with some incorrect prediction or version of them.

ADVERB CONFLICT. When a sentence begins with an adverbial phrase, every verb in the predicate of the sentence proper (independent clause) is modified by that phrase. Thus in *When I am sick, I get moody and snap at people* the opening phrase properly modifies both *get* and *snap.* A problem arises when the second verb is incompatible with the opening phrase. This often happens when a conflicting adverb is introduced, e.g. *In 1966 he taught at Harvard and returned to Yale a year later.* Clearly the man cannot have returned to Yale simultaneously in 1966 and 1967. The solution here, and to adverb-conflict puzzles in general, is either to introduce a second subject ("In 1966 he taught at Harvard; *he* returned to Yale a year later") or to subordinate the opening phrase clearly to the verb it belongs with ("He taught at Harvard *in 1966* and returned to Yale a year later"). In *By and large Lewis's opinions are reasonable and are invariably thought-provoking,* change to *reasonable, and they are.*

affect, effect. The verb *affect* means to influence or concern; the verb *effect* means to bring about or cause. A decision may *affect* your future, or *effect* a change in your way of life; taking some pills may *affect* your blood pressure, or *effect* your recovery. The noun *affect* (pronounced *AFFect*), a technical term in psychology, is rarely encountered; for all noun meanings but this one, the word is *effect.*

all that, in expressions like *I don't consider her all that beautiful,* is non-Standard. Use *that* alone if there is a suitable antecedent, otherwise *especially* or *particularly.*

allude. An allusion is an indirect reference or hint; for example, you may allude to a raucous Christmas party by asking a participant if he is still full of Christmas cheer, or you may allude to love by invoking Venus or Cupid. *Allude* is misused when the reference is direct, as in *I allude to your speech of February 24* or *I do not understand your allusion to "No. 4 tacks."* Change to *refer* and *reference.*

along with. A singular noun followed by a phrase beginning *along with* takes a singular verb: *Mark, along with his two brothers, has been seeing Dr. Bennett regularly.*

alternate, alternative. The adjective *alternate* means alternating with something else (*on alternate Tuesdays / alternately dozed and watched the movie*). The adjective *alternative* means involving a choice (*an alternative recommendation / by mail or alternatively by phone*). Partly by confusion with *alternative,* partly from the influence of the noun *alternate* in the sense of a second-level delegate to a convention, the adjective *alternate* is now widely used in the sense of substitute (*an alternate plan in case of bad weather*). Good writers continue to reserve this meaning for *alternative.*

ambivalent and *ambiguous* are not synonyms. *Ambivalent* refers to a feeling of simultaneous attraction and repulsion; thus a radical might feel ambivalent about his father's wealth. *Ambiguous* means capable of being understood in two or more possible senses, thus uncertain or obscure; the examples under MORE (p. 288) are ambiguous.

ANACHRONISMS.   One mark of a good writer is sensitivity to time and history in the choice of words. To say *Louis XIV was a teen-ager when he assumed full power* is technically correct but impossibly jarring: *teen-ager* is a twentieth-century word for a twentieth-century phenomenon. In *Here Donne uses a technique that is one of his trademarks* a great poet is diminished by the clatter of modern merchandising. Difficulties of this sort come down to a matter of connotation and denotation, on which see pp. 98–100.

and.   (1) It is perfectly permissible to begin a sentence with *And.*

(2) The precision of *and/or* may make it useful for legal documents, but its bizarre appearance and legalistic connotations make it unsuitable for any writing that aspires to please. Use *and* or *or*; if neither works, write *X or Y, or both.*

(3) When a series of two or more elements is referred to by a plural noun, the proper conjunction is *and,* not *or.   Or* should be *and* in the following rare lapse by Follett: "Others may be influenced by newspaper shortenings, which produce such unidiomatic phrases as *long-drawn recital, stave attack,* or *put in jail on charge he threatened president.*"

ANTECEDENT PROBLEMS.   (1) An antecedent should be an explicit noun, noun phrase, or noun clause, with the exception listed below for *which, this,* and *that.* An antecedent cannot be a verb: *The court tried to subpoena him but he would not accept it* should read *accept the subpoena.* An antecedent cannot be an adjective: the feature story headlined FEMININE IDEAS ON WHERE THEY WANT TO LIVE should have read WOMEN'S IDEAS. This error is particularly common with adjectives of nationality: *a Japanese view of their attack on Pearl Harbor* should read *Japan's attack.* Finally, an antecedent cannot be negative: *Although nothing important happened, it impressed me deeply* should read *I was deeply impressed.*

(2) *Which, this,* or *that* may refer to a preceding idea that is not grammatically a noun or a noun clause, provided the idea is completely clear. In *She is beautiful, which is more than you can say for Ada,* the idea is clear and the construction is accordingly admissible. In *We needed a flagpole, which was a problem,* it is not clear what the problem was and the sentence should be rewritten. In *His mother was happy; that was all he cared about,* the idea is clear and *that* is correct. In *Eileen was often angry, and this irritated her friends,* it is not clear whether *this* stands for her anger or its frequency.

(3) *Such* and *this* are not synonyms. *Such a man* means "a man of this sort"; *this man* means "the man just mentioned." *Such* should be *these* in *He would eat ice cream or sherbet, but even such desserts he did not really enjoy.*

(4) A pronoun should not precede its antecedent unless its meaning is immediately clear and any other construction would be demonstrably awkward. In *When his first play was performed, Shakespeare was 28,* either reverse the sequence of clauses or change *his* to *Shakespeare's* and *Shakespeare* to *he.*

See also NEGATIVE PROBLEMS (2).

anyplace is non-Standard. Use *anywhere.*

as. (1) *As to* should be restricted so far as possible to emphatic constructions like *As to my so-called duplicity, I deny it.* (In this use *as to* is interchangeable with *as for.*) *As to* should be used sparingly, if at all, as a straight preposition. *A clue as to* is an error for *a clue to; the question as to whether* should be the *question whether; doubts as to* might better be *doubts about.* Use *as to* only when you are convinced that no other preposition will serve your purpose as well.

(2) *As well as* takes the singular: *The doctor, as well as his nurse and his receptionist, is involved. As well as* cannot follow *both*: in *I invited both Henry as well as Ann and Bill,* delete *both.*

(3) Prepositional constructions in *as* must be properly related to the rest of the sentence. *As a man of experience, we would welcome your opinion* violates this rule by relating the *as* clause to *we*, an impossibility.

(4) Sentences requiring two *as*'s cannot get by with one. Technically speaking, an *as* has been swallowed at the indicated place in each of the following sentences: *"Old Foxy," as he referred to himself / , had won again. The cheese was as good / or better than Boursault. I thought of Mary not so much as my aunt / as my friend.* Since adding *as* at any of the slashes would be awkward, rewrite: *as he called himself, as good as Boursault or better, not as my aunt but as my friend.*

(5) Good writers do not use *as* to mean *because*. In *As Jane was ill, we did not go*, change *as* to *since* or *because*.

(6) *As* is not idiomatic with *consider, appoint, name, elect,* and *brand.* In *The senators considered the administration's behavior as an outrage,* delete *as* or change *considered* to *regarded*; in *He was appointed as district attorney in 1961* and *McCarthy branded him as a traitor,* delete *as.*

(7) *As* for the Latin *qua,* meaning in the capacity or character of, is overused by literary critics in such expressions as *Milton as polemicist* and even *speaking as polemicist, Milton.* Since the shade of difference between *as* and *as a* in these phrases can rarely be discerned, the popularity of the newer and more jarring *as* construction is hard to understand.

On *like* and *as,* see pp. 176–178.

bad, badly. See WELL, GOOD.

because. *Because* can lead to puzzles when carelessly used with *not.* *She did not go because she was ill* could mean either that she was too ill to go, or that she went (e.g. to the hospital) not because she was ill but for some other reason. The first meaning can be brought out unmistakably by adding a comma before *because*; the second meaning requires rewording, e.g. *It was not because she was ill that she went.* See also REASON (1).

between. (1) *Between* properly takes as its object two elements, or any number of elements thought of as relating or interacting closely, e.g. *The Constitution regulates relations between the states.* **Among** properly takes as its object more than two elements not thought of as interacting closely, e.g. *The book is about his life among the savages.* This distinction is not always easily made; when in doubt, use *between.*

(2) *Between* must be followed either by a plural noun or by a plural construction in *and.* In *Nonwhite family earnings grew between 1968–1972,* change to *between 1968 and 1972.* In *Between thirty to fifty persons are killed annually in hunting accidents,* change to *Between thirty and fifty* or *From thirty to fifty.* In *The choice was between going to jail or incriminating Larry,* change *or* to *and.* In *He soaked his foot in ice water between each act,* change to *between acts* or *after each act.* In *differences between the hospital in Akron and Canton,* the *and* is in the subordinate *in* phrase and does not make a true plural out of *hospital;* change to *and the one in Canton.*

biweekly, semiweekly. *Biweekly* means every two weeks, *semiweekly* twice a week. *Biweekly* is often misused for *semiweekly,* and some dictionaries, indifferent to the confusion they are authorizing, accord both meanings full status. The same is true of *bimonthly* and *semimonthly.* For years there are three words: *biennially* means every two years; *biannually* and *semiannually* both mean twice a year, with *semiannually* having the stronger suggestion of every six months. Our advice is to spare your reader confusion by spelling out what you mean: *twice a week, every two weeks,* or whatever.

black. See NEGRO.

blond, blonde. Use *blonde* for a woman, *blond* for a man, whether as noun or adjective.

brackets [ ], not parentheses ( ), should enclose words that you insert in a direct quotation from somebody else: *According to Delacorte, "Napoleon [III] was Bismarck's superior in all save persistence."* Newspapers use parentheses—*"That guy (Marichal) has never pitched better"*—because their simplified type fonts have no brackets, not because parentheses are right. If your typewriter lacks brackets, leave space and add them later in ink.

BRITISH SPELLINGS. See VARIANT SPELLINGS (2).

bureaucrat is not a neutral word like *official*. It is a disparaging word with strong connotations of stuffiness and narrow-mindedness.

case is often superfluous. *In Mary's case, there were two problems to be solved* might better read *Mary had two problems to solve,* and *In the case of the senior class gift, we tried hard to raise money* might better read simply *We tried hard to raise money for the senior class gift.* Use *case* when you must; avoid it when you can.

CLASHING VALUES. Avoid marrying words with no tolerance for each other's company. Three classes of such pairs may be distinguished: absolutes subjected to comparison or appraisal (*almost unique, more perfect, rather exhaustive*); absolutes with redundant modifiers (*sufficiently adequate, general consensus, dead corpse*); and words of great force qualified by tepid words (*slightly overwhelming, somewhat dreadful, a bit vile*). In the last class one sometimes finds the opposite phenomenon; thus a Japanese travel brochure describes Nikko as *unspeakably pleasant.* Combinations of opposites may occasionally be used deliberately to achieve a striking effect, as in the poetic device of oxymoron with its *sweet bitterness* and *harmonious discord*; but a little of this sort of thing goes a long way. See also ADVERB CONFLICT, ANACHRONISMS.

classic, classical. *Classical* has connotations of "established," *classic* connotations of "outstanding." Use *classical* for ancient Greek and Roman culture, literary forms of language (*Classical Arabic*), music of the educated European tradition, a curriculum centered on the humanities, or a standard body of knowledge seen as a necessary point of departure (*classical physics, classical military strategy*). Use *classic* where connotations of rank or importance are paramount: *a classic battle, a classic blunder, a classic case of mumps.*

cohort, in the sense of companion, associate, or crony, is non-Standard.

compare. (1) To compare X *with* Y is to appraise or measure X in relation to Y: *I compared my notes with hers.* To compare X *to* Y is to assert a similarity between the two: *You are wrong to compare Mao to Lenin.* The distinction is not always clear; when in doubt, use *with.*

(2) The quantities linked by *compare* should be comparable. In *My allowance was high compared with Sally,* they are not; change to *Sally's.*

compose, comprise. Compose means to make up; *comprise* means to be made up of, to consist of. The parts compose the whole; the whole comprises the parts. Since *comprise* is the rarer word and the harder to use correctly, and since its exact meaning is conveyed by the passive use of *compose*—i.e. *comprises = is composed of*—why not use *compose* in both senses and forget about *comprise?*

consensus. Thus spelled (not *-census*). A *consensus* is by definition general, and by definition has to do with matters of opinion or belief. Hence *general consensus* and *consensus of opinion* are redundant expressions.

contact as a verb meaning to get in touch with is non-Standard. As a noun meaning a person one is in touch with, *contact* is appropriate chiefly to spies, detectives, and others whose operations involve secrecy.

contemporary means "at the same time," but at the same time as what? Does *the contemporary view of Hamlet* refer to Shakespeare's contemporaries or the writer's? Unless your context makes your meaning unmistakable, replace *contemporary* with something unambiguous: *the prevailing view of Hamlet in Shakespeare's time* or *the current view of Hamlet.*

continuous, continual, constant. Continuous means uninterrupted: a string is continuous; the sound of an ambulance siren is continuous; a movie theater properly advertises "continuous performance." *Continual* means repeated at frequent short intervals: a bad cough may be continual; an executive may be continually interrupted by phone calls. *Constant* is a higher-voltage equivalent of *continual*.

convince. You do not convince a person *to* do something; you convince him *that* he should do it, or you convince him *of* its desirability. If *to* is irresistible, use *persuade* or *prevail on.*

council, counsel; council(l)or, counsel(l)or. A *council* is a group of persons with administrative or other functions. A *counsel* is a lawyer, and *counsel* are lawyers collectively or anonymously (*on advice of counsel*); *counsel* also means advice in general, and *to counsel* means to advise. A *councilor* is a member of a council; a *counselor* is one who gives advice. The teen-ager at a children's summer camp, though he may be a member of a council, is a *counselor*. The *-llor* forms are permissible but old-fashioned.

criteria is plural; the singular is *criterion.*

crucial has a connotation of finality or decisiveness. It is an absolute word, not to be used either with such comparatives as *more, less,* and *rather* or of relatively trivial matters. Above all, *crucial* should not be overused, as it persistently is by sports writers and other journalists.

data is plural; the singular is *datum*. *This data is* is fairly common and gaining ground, but most good writers still write *these data are.*

definite, definitive. *Definite* means specific or unmistakable; *definitive* has the further connotation of unalterably final or defined once and for all. Only when this connotation is present is *definitive* allowable as a dramatic intensifier of *definite*.

delusion, illusion. *Delusion* is a negative word; a person with delusions is typically disposed to act on them in such a way as to harm himself or others. *Illusion* is a neutral word; a person with illusions is merely mistaken or given to wishful thinking.

depends without *on* in such expressions as *It depends what you mean by power* is good spoken English but non-Standard in writing.

deprecate, depreciate. A century ago *deprecate* meant to protest against or disapprove of, *depreciate* to belittle, make light of, or lessen in value. Today *depreciate's* connotations are exclusively financial; *deprecate* has taken over its other meanings. It is found especially in the compounds *self-deprecation* and *self-deprecatory.*

dichotomy is a vogue word. In logic, from which it was needlessly borrowed, it means a division of a whole for analytical purposes into two mutually exclusive parts, as opposed to two overlapping parts, three or more parts, a continuum, or what have you. It has been extended by its borrowers to mean any division into two parts, whether analytically precise or not (*The Catholic-Protestant dichotomy is the only meaningful basis of discussion*), and thence to other meanings of *division,* notably rift or discord: *The French Revolution, however, deepened the dichotomy between radical and conservative.*

different than. Fastidious writers go to great lengths to follow *different* with *from,* and Follett, among others, supports them. It is not clear why. *Different than,* by analogy with *other than,* has been a staple of American spoken English for at least a century, and sometimes offers a brevity that *different from* cannot match. In *He used the word in quite a different sense than he did yesterday,* to require *from* would mean to replace *than he did* with no fewer than eight words: *from the one in which he used it.* Use *different from* where you can; but where it does not work and *different than* does, take the plunge.

discreet, discrete. Discreet means prudent; *discrete* means separate, or consisting of unconnected elements. The two words have nothing in common but their pronunciation.

disinterested means impartial, free of emotional interest in the issue at hand. A disinterested judge is not one who finds the case boring, but one who is well qualified to judge it fairly because he has no personal stake in the outcome. As Follett and others have remarked, the present tendency to equate *disinterested* with *uninterested* is not only depriving the world of an expressive word, but rendering less accessible a noble idea.

DUE TO must still be regarded as adjectival, and must accordingly attach itself to a noun or a pronoun rather than to a verb. In *He could not attend due to illness*, where *due to* improperly modifies *attend*, change to *owing to* or *because of*.

each, every. *Each* as a noun takes a singular verb and a singular noun or pronoun: *Each of the boys has his own car*, not *have*, not *their own car*, not *their own cars*. *Each* and *every* as adjectives take the singular when they precede what they modify: *Every man is his own worst enemy*, not *their own worst enemy*. When *each* follows what it modifies, it takes the plural: *They each are wearing the hats they wore yesterday*. Usage is wearing down these distinctions, however, particularly in the first and second persons. *We each have our own cars* is nominally correct, but *car* is almost universal; *Each of you should write his congressman* is nominally correct, but *your* is far more common. The rule is by now so far eroded that these departures may be considered correct.

Each and every, being simply an emphatic way of saying *each*, takes the singular despite the *and*: *Each and every one of them was found guilty*. So do compounds of the form *Each (every) X and (each/every) Y*: *Every man and woman here has a college education*. The compounds *everybody, everyone, anybody*, and *anyone* take the singular: *Everybody thinks of himself first / Does anyone want his money refunded?*

e.g. stands for *exempli gratia*, "for example": *Shakespeare's comedies, e.g. "As You Like It."* It is never used parenthetically: in *A fence or a railing, e.g., would give the necessary protection*, change to *for example*. It may be followed by a comma or not, at the writer's option. Being slightly pedantic in appearance and connotation, *e.g.* is better suited to footnotes and technical exposition than to the text of an essay. It should not be confused with *i.e.*, which stands for *id est*, "that is": in *the three triumvirs, e.g. Octavius, Antony, and Lepidus,* change to *i.e.*

either. (1) In constructions of the form *either . . . or,* what follows *either* should be parallel and grammatically equivalent to what follows *or*; see the text, pp. 161–163.

(2) *Either . . . or* may be used of three or more alternatives: *Either Heise, Shaw, or Butzaikis had to be traded.* As an adjective, however (*Take either road*), and as a pronoun (*Either is all right with me*), *either* is properly confined to two alternatives.

employment, like *utilization,* is often simply a ponderous word for *use.* In *The engineers recommended the employment of heavy earth-moving equipment,* change to *the use of* or *using.*

enable is incomplete without a following infinitive, whether active (*His fortune enables him to live as he likes*) or passive (*The new law enabled major improvements to be made*), preferably active. In *The committee's proposal would enable several changes in the clubhouse rules,* the infinitive is lacking; either add it or change *enable* to *make possible.*

enhance is not an exact synonym of *increase,* despite Governor Wallace's trip to Vietnam to "enhance my knowledge of the war." *Enhance* means specifically to increase in desirability, value, or attractiveness, and is properly said of something already to some extent desirable, valuable, or attractive. The word takes an abstract object: not *The simple tiara enhanced her,* but *The simple tiara enhanced her beauty.*

enormity means not great size but outrageousness or an outrage. The word for great size is *enormousness.*

enthuse is a verb of recent coinage from *enthusiasm.* Like *emote* and other formations of this sort, it has long outlasted the chuckles of its inventor without becoming Standard.

equally as. *Equally* cannot tolerate *as*: in *Her behavior was equally as foolish,* either delete *as* or change *equally* to *just.* In a complete *as . . . as* comparison there is no place for *equally*: delete it in *Her behavior was equally as foolish as his.* Constructions in between *equally X* and *as X as* should be resolved one way or the other: in *German wine is equally good, in its way, as French,* change *equally* to *as* or *just as.*

equate takes either *with* (*How can you equate Meyerbeer with Mozart?*) or *and* (*The new salary scale equates men and women*), or a plural resolvable into the equated components (*I equate the two sentiments*). Like BETWEEN, *equate* cannot take a singular: in *He appears to equate "democracy" in its American and Soviet senses,* either change to *equate the American and Soviet senses of "democracy"* or rewrite.

etc. is permissible in formal English to avoid a tedious and easily inferrable elaboration. Good writers, however, disliking its inelegant appearance and lazy-careless connotations, tend to use it chiefly where elegance is no issue, as in footnotes, lists, and tables. Getting rid of *etc.* elsewhere is usually no great trick; many phrases of the form *Castroism, Maoism, etc.* can be simply changed to *such as Castroism and Maoism,* and in the rest *etc.* can almost always be replaced by *and so on* or *and the like.* *Etc.* after *such as* or *e.g.* is redundant; see SUCH AS . . . AND OTHERS.

every, everybody. See EACH, EVERY.

everyplace is non-Standard. Use *everywhere.*

fabulous is the adjective form of *fable* and means legendary or fictitious. By extension it has come to mean amazing or marvelous, in which sense it has been so badly overused, especially by the young, as to have no force or credit left.

fact. Novice writers overuse *the fact that.* They write, for example, *I accepted the fact that I could not learn French* and *His lameness was due to the fact that he had had an accident* where they might better have written *I accepted my inability to learn French* and *His lameness was the result of an accident.* Use *the fact that* as sparingly as you can, and preferably where some fact as such is in question: *What I dispute is not the fact that he lied, but his motive in lying.*

farther, further. *Farther* tends to be used of physical distance: *Chicago is farther from New York than from Washington.* *Further* tends to be used of abstract distance: *We will go into this further at some later date.* When in doubt, use *further.*

female, feminine. *Female* means simply of the female sex as opposed to the male: thus *female doctor, female children, female rabbit, female hormone.* *Feminine* means having the characteristics commonly attributed to women as opposed to men: thus *feminine wiles, feminine pursuits, feminine features, feminine sensitivity.* To write *feminine* for *female* can be confusing. What is a *feminine doctor,* for example? One who uses a lot of makeup?

fewer, less. *Fewer* is used of countable units: *fewer cows, fewer days, fewer cups of coffee.* *Less* is used of abstract or inseparable quantities: *less air, less salt, less pain.* The same distinction is made between *less than* and *fewer than,* except that *less than* is used with countable units considered as single quantities (*less than five dollars, less than three weeks*) and with countable units in large numbers, where the mass dominates the individual: *less than 10,000 armed guerrillas, less than a hundred hotel rooms.*

firstly, secondly, etc. are old-fashioned; good writers and editors prefer *first, second,* etc.

flaunt, flout. To *flaunt* something is to parade it or show it off (*She flaunted her new mink wrap / The speaker flaunted his patriotism*); to *flout* something is to ignore or reject it publicly (*Khrushchev flouted the fundamental principles of diplomacy*). The two words have a common connotation of ostentation, but are otherwise opposite in meaning.

former, latter. *Former* and *latter* may be used, together or singly, only when immediately preceded by exactly two antecedent nouns, pronouns, or noun phrases of more or less equal weight, and then only when it would be awkward to repeat the nouns themselves. The following sentences violate the successive conditions of this rule. *Of the grants made to Oklahoma, Texas, and Louisiana, the largest went to the latter.* (More than two antecedents.) *A notice was sent to the dead man's next of kin, and the latter supplied the information.* (Only one antecedent.) *When they would not recognize Lyman's immunity, the latter was forced to resign.* (Antecedents not of equal weight.) *The judge and the court clerk had the same name; the former was apparently the latter's father.* (Better to repeat *judge* and *clerk*.) In general, avoid *former* and *latter;* good writers get along very well without them.

fortunate, fortuitous. Fortunate means lucky; *fortuitous* means accidental or unexpected. W7 to the contrary, *fortuitous* should not be used as a fancy way of saying *fortunate.*

fulsome does not mean full or complete, or even somewhat overblown and tending to excess; it means disgusting. Fulsome praise is praise so insincere or excessive as to be downright offensive to a person of taste.

gap. In 1958 a reporter coined the term *missile gap* to characterize an alleged American inferiority to the U.S.S.R. in the number of intercontinental missiles completed and under construction. Although this expression did some violence to the classic idea of a gap as a hiatus or break in continuity, it was apt enough to be given wide circulation. Inevitably there followed a large number of less apt imitations like *communications gap, credibility gap,* and *generation gap,* in some of which the idea of a gap could barely be discerned. *Gap* in this sense is today a vogue word; it could use a rest.

GERUNDS. A gerund is the *-ing* form of a verb used as a noun: *Swimming is fun / I am tired of fooling around / How about frying some eggs?*

    (1) Gerunds, like participles, should be attached as closely

as possible to their subject (if it appears in the sentence); in *By yelling at the top of their lungs, we finally heard them*, change to *they finally made us hear them*.

(2) An infinitive is sometimes erroneously used where only a gerund is idiomatic. Instead of *The Navy was committed to support the program*, idiom requires *to supporting*; instead of *I confessed to have found the question pointless*, idiom requires *to having found*. Only someone with an excellent sense of idiom will have no difficulty on this point. When in doubt, use the gerund.

For the distinction between gerunds, participles, and fused participles, see pp. 175–176.

good. See WELL, GOOD.

got, gotten. *Got* is the past of *get*; the past participle is sometimes *got*, sometimes *gotten*. *Gotten* is now the usual choice when a sense of progression is involved: *You have gotten much more cautious lately / Grandma has gotten worse again / I have gotten to know her better*. In other senses *got* and *gotten* are interchangeable: *I have got to bed late every night this week / We had got our feet wet*. As an intensive of *have* (*I've got the tickets / George has got to help us*), *got* is the only choice. Purists and Englishmen still reject *got* in this sense and disallow *gotten* altogether.

graduate. Forty years ago, *I was graduated from high school* was the only wording teachers considered proper. Today, *was graduated*, though still acceptable, sounds stuffy; the natural wording is *I graduated from high school*. The newer wording *I graduated high school* is non-Standard.

hardly. See SCARCELY.

help. When *help* is used in the sense of *avoid* or *refrain from*, the correct form is *I cannot help liking her*, not *I cannot help but like her*. The incorrect form, though widely used in speech, is not acceptable in writing. Further, the subject of *help* in this sense should be animate: in *The book could not help becoming a best seller*, change *help* to *miss*.

historic, historical. (1) *Historic* means historically important or famous (*a historic battle, Webster's historic speech*); *historical* is a neutral word meaning of, related to, or based on history (*places of historical interest, a historical novel*).

(2) *History* and words derived from it take *a*, not *an*.

home, house. A *house* is a building; a *home* is an abstraction. *Home* means the locus of family life (whether a building, a cave, or what have you), or the family itself, as in *a broken home*. Since *house* has neutral connotations and *home* favorable ones, advertisers have taken to advertising *homes, home furnishings, homewares*, and the like, and addressing themselves to *homeowners* and *homemakers*. The dictionaries have accepted—which is to say, recorded—these new locutions, but in good writing *home* remains inseparable from the idea of people. Any good writer will tell you that if *Dad sold our home in 1970*, Dad is a heel.

hopefully means in a hopeful manner: *She asked hopefully if there was a part for her.* Many writers, including 56 percent of the AHD's Usage Panel, oppose its extension to mean *it is to be hoped that*, as in *Hopefully the strike will be over by then.* Yet unattached adverbs of this form—e.g. *undoubtedly* for *it is not to be doubted that*—offer such notable gains in conciseness over the phrases they replace that we can scarcely understand, let alone join, the opposition to *hopefully*.

however. (1) When *however* comes at the beginning of a sentence or clause, it can be either a conjunction meaning *but* (*However, the children may feel cheated*) or an adverb meaning in whatever way or to whatever degree (*However the children may feel, we must proceed*). So that the reader may distinguish immediately between these two very different constructions, good writers always use a comma in the first.

(2) *However* should be placed early in the sentence if it is not to lose its force. In *The Secretary of Health, Education, and Welfare and two of his undersecretaries, however, opposed the change*, move *however* to the beginning.

(3) When *however* does not come at the beginning of a

sentence or clause, it has the effect of emphasizing the word it follows, and this emphasis must accord with the meaning. In *There was no official reply from the White House; the President, however, unofficially praised the plan,* the emphasis given by *however* seems to contrast the President and the White House, not the official and unofficial reactions. Change to *speaking unofficially, however,* or to *however, the President.*

I, me. (1) Although *I* is nominative and *me* objective, such technically correct expressions as *It is I* and *That was I* strike the American ear as prissy, with the result that *me* has all but replaced *I* in the predicate nominative: *It's me / Could it have been me that she saw? / The two people they forgot were you and me.* There is no opposing this development, and no reason to oppose it.

(2) People who would never dream of writing *They asked I to help* or *everybody except I* sometimes write *and I* for *and me* in the same constructions: *They asked my sister and I to help / everybody except Bob and I.* The cure for such illiteracies is a moment's thought.

i.e. stands for *id est,* "that is," and may be used as a substitute for *that is* or *namely* in footnotes and wherever else elegance is not an issue. *I.e.* should be distinguished from *e.g.,* which has the very different meaning "for example." In *The most populous states, i.e. Illinois, are the richest,* change to *e.g.*

implement as a verb is a vogue word of some 25 years' standing. It is especially beloved of big businessmen and government officials, perhaps because the scale and complexity of their operations make simple expressions like *carry out* and *put into effect* inappropriate, perhaps because *implement* suggests the sort of impersonal, deliberate, and orderly change-over that will disrupt things least, perhaps out of sheer pomposity. "With *implement,*" as Follett says, "the layman can sound technical." Good writers use *implement* rarely, if at all.

imply, infer. *Imply* means to suggest or hint, *infer* to deduce or surmise. A politician who is unwilling to announce his candidacy might *imply* his willingness to run by winking at an interviewer, from which the interviewer might *infer* that the politician would announce his candidacy later.

include, including. *Include* supposes the listing of some members, but not all, of the whole, as in *The jurors included two women.* In *Some of those arrested included schoolteachers,* either delete *some of* or change *included* to *were.* In *The guest list included Curtis, Watkins, and others,* change to *Curtis and Watkins.* In *The four countries to be considered include Syria, Lebanon, Jordan, and Iraq,* change *include* to *are.* What goes for *include* goes also for *including:* in *Twenty-one poems were read, including poems by Ginsberg, Patchen, and others,* change to *Ginsberg and Patchen.*

individual as a noun has only two legitimate uses of any interest: to designate the single organism as distinguished from the species, and to designate the single human being as contrasted with a group, an institution, or the state. The use of *individual* as an exact synonym for *person,* as in *Harry is a well-meaning individual,* is a "colloquial vulgarism" (OED) and, in a memorable phrase quoted by Fowler, "one of the modern editor's shibboleths for detecting the unfit."

infer. See IMPLY, INFER.

irregardless is non-Standard, a bastard mixture of *irrespective* and *regardless.* Use one or the other of these two Standard words.

it's, its. The first stands for *it is* or *it has;* the second is the possessive. *It's its size that bothers me.*

JARGON is the name commonly given to writing that is ugly and hard to understand. Originally, *jargon* meant the lingo of a particular science or occupation (especially as viewed from outside), and this meaning is still current. Among the jargons of American academic writing today, for example, as seen by its detractors, are that of the social scientists, with their *societal needs, functional capability, variables associated with organizational effectiveness,* and the like; and that of the literary critics, which numbers among its current delights *ambience, dualism,* and *Yeatsian.* More often, however, *jargon* today refers to the general blend of pompous diction and imprecise reference that has become America's style for ceremonial speech and writing. The mark of jargon in this sense is long words, pat phrases, and lifeless verbs; its function is not to communicate, but to impress or reassure.

JOURNALESE. Newspaper writing at its best has the great virtues of clarity and brevity. It also has certain defects that arise from the circumstances of its writing and printing. The newspaper writer has limited space, little time to reflect, and precious little a priori claim on the attention of his readers, who may be justly thought of as reading their newspapers hastily over breakfast or in the bus on the way to work. Neither subtlety nor complexity is possible in such circumstances, and the grays of truth give way to the facile blacks and whites of melodrama. The result of this process is journalese.

One mark of journalese is its heavy use of intensives: every difficulty is a *crisis,* every important decision *crucial,* every retrenchment *drastic,* every scientist *brilliant,* every death *tragic,* everything impressive *great.* Another mark is gimmicky noun-verbs like *pinpoint, highlight,* and *trigger,* which give the most prosaic proceedings a factitious liveliness. Headlines, with their premium on short, vivid words, have the same effect: critics do not criticize, they *rap;* a political opponent is a *foe;* a disagreement, however mild, is a *clash.* Activity, conflict, crisis are everywhere. The routine investigation of a Soviet complaint about an American aircraft is rendered seemingly ominous by the headline *Red Charge Spurs Probe.* This "tone of contrived excitement" (Follett) is the essence of journalese. Its characteristic exaggerations and oversimplifications have no place in serious writing.

See also TIMESTYLE.

latter. See FORMER, LATTER.

less. See FEWER, LESS.

let. (1) Either *let* or *leave* may be used with *alone* in the sense of not disturbing or interfering: either *We left him alone* or *We let him alone*. *Leave* is unacceptable, however, in analogous phrases carrying the sense of allow or permit (*Let sleeping dogs lie / Let him go*) and in the *let us* construction (*Let us face the facts / Let's ask Billy*).

(2) *Let* takes the objective case; in *I begged him to let George and I come along*, change to *George and me*.

lie, lay. *Lie* means to recline, *lay* to place or put in place. The following sentences exhibit the correct use of *lie* and *lay* and their various forms:

	Lie	Lay
Present	I *lie* down.	I *lay* the carpet.
Past	I *lay* down.	I *laid* the carpet.
Perfect	I *have lain* down.	I *have laid* the carpet.
Progressive	I *am lying* down.	I *am laying* the carpet.
Future	I *will lie* down.	I *will lay* the carpet.

like and *as*. See pp. 176–178.

literally is not a mere intensive. *Bill literally broke his heart over Mary* implies that his heart is now, or was at some time, in two or more pieces. Since this is impossible, *literally* should be omitted. *Figuratively* is no improvement; indeed, since all metaphors are figurative, *figuratively broke his heart* is as senselessly redundant as *literally ate his dinner*.

loan, lend. Use *loan* as the noun, *lend* as the verb.

-ly. (1) Avoid piling up adverbs in *-ly*: in *He acted completely honorably*, change *completely* to *altogether* to get rid of the singsong effect.

(2) Avoid forming adverbs in *-lily* from adjectives in *-ly* for the same reason: instead of *He answered surlily*, write *He answered sullenly* or *His answer was surly*.

(3) Avoid coining adverbs in *-edly* from participles in *-ed*. Some adverbs so formed have become unobjectionable by reason of manifest convenience and long use: *allegedly, repeatedly, undoubtedly*. But many assail the brain with a Germanic excess of syllables and components: *undisguisedly,*

animatedly, disappointedly. Worst of all, and intolerable to good writers, are *-edly* words in which the *-ed* syllable cannot be given full weight: *satisfiedly, puzzledly, discouragedly*. If an *-edly* word cannot be confidently pronounced, it should not be written.

(4) Do not hyphenate compounds formed by adverbs in *-ly* and participles or adjectives: *the newly married pair*, not *newly-married*; *the brightly lit room*, not *brightly-lit*.

mad for *angry* is non-Standard.

majority. *The majority* is often an unnecessarily long way of saying *most*, as in *The majority of my friends go to college*.

materialize means to take material or effective form, as in *Our plans for a Free University never materialized*. It is not properly used as a fancy synonym for *happen* or *occur*. In *Nothing important materialized at the San Francisco conference*, change to *happened* or *was decided*.

mean for is non-Standard in such sentences as *I never meant for him to do all that work* and *She meant for the plan to be taken seriously*. The difficulty can often be repaired by simply dropping *for*; alternatively rewrite with *meant that* or *intended that*.

media is invariably plural. In *The press is generally a more reliable media than television*, change to *medium* or rewrite.

militate, mitigate. *Militate* means to count or have weight, and is used exclusively with *against*: *Three things militated against our accepting the offer*. *Mitigate* means to lessen in severity: *Her pleasure mitigated his grief*. The combination *mitigate against* does not exist.

more can be ambiguous. What is meant, for example, by *The proposal called for more fully integrated restaurants*? More restaurants that were fully integrated, or restaurants that were more fully integrated? What is meant by *We need more unbiased reporting on Vietnam*? Only a more carefully chosen wording can tell us.

most. (1) *Most* for *almost*, as in *Most everybody was there* or

You can come most any time, is a colloquialism that should never find its way into formal writing.

(2) *Most* for *very,* where the idea of comparison is at best implicit, is opposed only by a rear guard of retreating purists: *We had a most enjoyable evening in Paris / They saw the most remarkable horse.*

nauseous, despite its similarity to *bilious,* means sickening or repulsive, not sick or beset by nausea. It is a synonym of *nauseating,* not of *nauseated,* the word for which it is frequently misused.

NEGATIVE PROBLEMS. (1) Few sentences can easily tolerate more than one or two negative words. In *Cohen did not consider the chance of failure negligible,* readers will have to pause and sort out the three negatives (*not, failure, negligible*) before they can be sure what Cohen thought. Better to do the sorting for them: *Cohen saw a clear chance of failure.*

(2) A negative noun compound or pronoun is not an acceptable antecedent for a positive pronoun. In *No member was allowed to smoke in public, and they were not to wear short skirts,* change *No member was* to *Members were not.* In *Since no one was home, we left them a note,* omit *them.* In *The police expected no trouble but were prepared for it if it came,* change to *did not expect trouble.*

(3) A negative noun compound or pronoun (e.g. *nobody*) cannot serve as the subject of a verb requiring a positive subject: in *Neither the Yankees nor the Mets gave up, but kept on playing to win,* change the comma to a semicolon and *but* to *both.* See also NEITHER; NOR.

Negro should be capitalized, whether as a noun or as an adjective. *Black,* which articulate Negroes now seem to prefer to *Negro,* is seen both ways (capitalized and lowercase) in both uses (noun and adjective), but lowercase will probably prevail by analogy with *white.*

neither. (1) Make sure that with *neither* you use *nor,* not *or.*

(2) *Neither . . . nor* may be used of three or more elements, as in *Neither illness, bad weather, nor financial re-*

verses ever dimmed his good spirits. As an adjective, however (*Neither one is any good*), and as a pronoun (*Neither
will do*), *neither* is properly confined to two elements.

(3) Whatever part of speech follows *neither* should also
follow *nor*; see pp. 161–163.

none may take either a singular or a plural verb; see p. 149.

nor. Poetic diction apart, *nor* has only two legitimate uses: as
the second (or subsequent) element in the correlative pair
neither . . . nor, and as a conjunction introducing a clause
(*Nor do I agree with Senator Kennedy / There was nothing
to say, nor was there anything Jean could do*). The correct
word after *not* or *no* is not *nor* but *or*. In *The word does
not occur at all in Dickens, nor to my knowledge in Thackeray,*
change *nor* to *or*; in *She had received no word from the city
desk, nor any other messages,* change *nor any* to *and no*.

not only . . . but also. (1) *Also* is optional in this formula: it is
commonly used when the second element is simply added to
the first (*We will be seeing not only Dr. Shapley but also
the surgeon*) and omitted when the second element is an in-
tensification of the first (*She is not only the fattest girl I
know, but the fattest girl I have ever seen / We drove not
only to Southampton, but all the way to Plymouth*). When
also is used, it need not immediately follow *but*.

(2) The same part of speech that follows *not only* should
also follow *but also*; see pp. 161–163.

(3) *Not only* may be used without *but* to get intensive
effects, as in *He not only smelled, he reeked.* The comma
splice here is intentional.

not un- is a construction that persists despite Orwell's celebrated
suggestion that writers cure themselves of it by memorizing
the sentence *A not unblack dog was chasing a not unsmall
rabbit across a not ungreen field.* This construction may be
used sparingly, but only where the positive wording has been
considered and found wanting. In *I have not infrequently
been bored to tears by his stories,* change to *I have frequently.*

off.   Good writers never use *off of.*   In *somewhere off of the coast of Venezuela* and *jumping off of the garage roof,* change *off of* to *off.*

O.K. and *okay* are unacceptable in formal writing.   For the distinctions made by the AHD's Usage Panel between *O.K.* as a noun, an adjective, a verb, and an adverb, see the Usage Note reproduced on p. 107.

one.   (1) The pronoun *one* has two uses, the numeral (*One of them must be Michael*) and the impersonal (*One cannot please everybody*).   In the numeral use, *one* is followed by *he, his, him,* etc.: *One had his dog with him; another had a parrot.*   In the impersonal use, *one* is followed by *one, one's, oneself*: *One cannot take one's dog into a restaurant.* The common error is to follow the impersonal *one* with *he, his,* etc.; in *One has a hard time keeping his temper in such circumstances,* change *his* to *one's* or *One* to *A man.*

(2) Even sophisticated writers sometimes come to grief with the construction *one of those men who,* as in this sentence from a recent novel: *Richard is one of those men who is always bragging about his accomplishments.*   The intent of this construction is always to assign an individual to a class; the class here is *men who are always bragging about their accomplishments,* and the novelist's wording should be changed accordingly.

(3) *One or more* conventionally takes the plural: *One or more of them were kept overnight / One or more waitresses have been hired since June.*   Oddly enough, the more unambiguously plural *more than one* conventionally takes the singular: *More than one example comes to mind / More than one has been found wanting.*

(4) *One another* and *each other* are interchangeable.

only.   A vocal class of purists maintains that the placement of *only* is a matter of high importance: thus *Only Martin heard the crash* means no one else heard it; *Martin only heard the crash* means he did not see it as well; *Martin heard only the crash* means he heard none of the other noises in question.

Strong though this argument seems in principle, going against it rarely produces ambiguity in practice and is sometimes downright preferable on rhetorical grounds. Our advice is to put *only* wherever you think it best serves your purposes.

or. On number and gender problems in sentences having subjects linked by *or,* see pp. 147–148. See also AND (2), (3); EITHER; NOR.

overall is a vogue word for *whole, total, comprehensive, general,* etc.; good writers rarely use it. *In overall terms the new gymnasium made sense* presumably means either *broadly speaking* or *in long-run terms*; if one of these phrases had been used, we would know which meaning was intended. In *The overall cost came to $650,* change *overall* to *total.* Sometimes *overall* is simply redundant, as in *Harvey's overall speed for the 100-yard dash was 10.0 seconds.*

overly, once a perfectly acceptable word, has been displaced by the prefix *over-* (as in *overenthusiastic*) and now sounds bumpkinish to a fastidious ear. It is also superfluous, given the availability not only of the *over-* compounds but of *too* and *excessively.*

pair is usually singular: *The other pair of scissors was broken.* It can be plural (*The more experienced pair tend to share the driving equally*), but never after a number higher than one: *He bought two pairs of pants,* not *pair.*

past, passed. The adjective *past* should not be confused with the verb form *passed.* Either *The time for caution was past* or *The time for caution had passed,* but not *was passed* or *had past.*

per should be avoided except in heavily technical contexts. For *30 miles per hour,* say *30 miles an hour*; for *two new trainees per annum,* say *two new trainees every year*; for *1,800 calories per person,* say *1,800 calories each.* Such expressions as *information per central office memorandum of May 12* and *as per your request* are commercial jargon and have no place in formal writing.

percent, percentage, proportion. *Percent* and *percentage* refer to degree or amount reckoned on a scale of 100: *What percentage of applicants are accepted?* *Between 70 and 80 percent.* *Proportion,* as currently used, is a synonym for *percentage* except for the scale of 100: *What proportion of applicants are accepted?* *Perhaps seven or eight out of ten.* Do not use *proportion* to mean nothing more than *part;* in *A large proportion of the beef was spoiled,* change *a large proportion* to *much* or *most.*

personal formerly meant simply the opposite of *impersonal;* something personal involved a person, as contrasted, for example, with a machine or a block of wood. In recent years, *personal* has increasingly been used to mean *individual* and even *private*: schools now offer *personal counseling,* not individual counseling, and where a man once spoke of his private life and his private secretary, he now speaks of his *personal life* and his *personal secretary.* A still further extension has made *personal* a mere intensive, in which sense it is unnecessary and virtually meaningless. More often than not, it should simply be eliminated from such expressions as *my personal opinion* and *my personal friend,* as should *personally* from such expressions as *I personally liked the play very much.* As for *personalized,* which rarely means more than imprinted or monogrammed and often means nothing whatever (*personalized cosmetic care*), leave it to Madison Avenue.

phenomena is plural; the singular is *phenomenon.*

PLURAL CONFUSIONS. The plurals of Latin words ending in *-ex, -ix, -um, -us,* and *-a,* and of Greek words ending in *-on,* sometimes take the English endings *-s* and *-es,* sometimes the original Latin or Greek endings (usually *-ices* for *-ex* or *-ix, -a* for *-um* and *-on, -i* for *-us,* and *-ae* for *-a*), and sometimes both. Two questions arise. First, how is one to know which form to use, *indexes* or *indices, appendixes* or *appendices, spectrums* or *spectra, cactuses* or *cacti, formulas* or *formulae, criterions* or *criteria?* Second, how is one to know whether Latin or Greek words ending in *-a* like *agenda, criteria, data,* *memoranda,* and *phenomena* are singular or plural? The answer to both questions is the same: consult a dictionary. The complexities are many: *genus,* for example, does not take *genuses* or *geni* but *genera, stigma* not *stigmas* or *stigmae* but *stigmata.* Patterns are unpredictable and inconsistent: *agenda* and *opera,* for example, once strictly the plurals of *agendum* and *opus,* not only have become strictly singular but have engendered the new plurals *agendas* and *operas,* whereas other words of the same form remain strictly plural and still others (e.g. *insignia*) are both plural and singular. Finally, to compound the confusion, usage is rapidly changing: thus *data,* once strictly the plural of *datum* and still used only as plural by careful writers into the 1960's, is accepted as singular by 50 percent of the AHD's Usage Panel. Clearly, only a good and reasonably up-to-date dictionary can steer you through these troubled waters.

Other plural problems are discussed in the text (see Index) and under specific words in this section.

possess should not be used as a fancy synonym for *have.* In *Bismarck possessed a keen intellect,* and in *That was all the money I possessed,* change to *had.*

POSSESSIVE PROBLEMS. (1) On the formation of complicated possessives, see pp. 152–154.

(2) When a name must be added in brackets to a quotation, avoid the intolerable forms "*George's* [*Cook*] *bat*" and "*George* [*Cook*]'*s bat*"; whatever the newspapers may say or do, the only acceptable solution to this problem is "*George's* [*George Cook's*] *bat.*"

(3) *Time* magazine, as part of its effort to minimize wordage, uses such possessive constructions as *at week's end* for *at the end of the week* and *London's Institute for Strategic Studies* for *the Institute for Strategic Studies in London.* Despite the efficiency of this construction, good writers eschew it, as they do *TIMEstyle* in general.

practically means in practical terms or for practical purposes; good writers do not use it to mean *almost* where the idea of practical application is absent. In *I practically never get to sleep before midnight,* change *to almost*; in *She practically broke down and cried,* change to *virtually.*

precipitate, precipitous. The first as an adjective means with headlong speed, hence hasty or rash; the second means steep. An action is *precipitate,* a cliff *precipitous.*

prefer takes *to* or *rather than,* not *than.*

PREPOSITIONS. (1) It is no easy matter to choose a preposition in such sentences as *We succeeded (by) (through) sheer good luck* and *Many men go to pieces (in) (under) such conditions*; and it is too complex a matter to tackle here. The leading treatise on the subject is Frederick T. Wood's *English Prepositional Idioms* (New York: St. Martin's, 1967). A useful list of 67 preposition choices that give many writers trouble appears in Follett, pp. 257–259.

(2) It is nonsense to say that a sentence cannot properly end with a preposition. Winston Churchill, finding a change made on this ground by a printer's proofreader in the proofs of one of his books, allegedly wrote, "This is the sort of impertinence up with which I will not put." Yet the error persists, leading at times to such painfully unidiomatic sentences as this one, from a 1971 United Press story: *Baker told a reporter Wednesday he expects the Lehi VI to cost around $250,000 and that he doesn't know from where the money is coming.*

presently is widely used as a synonym of *now* or *at present,* but many writers, with 51 percent support from the AHD's Usage Panel, restrict it to the sense of *soon,* as in *He said he would be along presently.*

principal, principle. The first is an adjective meaning leading or foremost, a noun designating the top official of a school or an important person in various legal contexts, and a noun designating the money on which interest is calculated. The second is a noun only and means a fundamental truth, law, or assumption. Derivation apart, the two words have in common only their sound; in *My principle worry was Margie,* change to *principal.*

proportion. See PERCENT.

protagonist means the leading character in a drama or other literary work, and by extension the most conspicuous personage in any affair. It is neither etymologically nor in current correct usage the opposite of *antagonist*; being an absolute word, it cannot properly be qualified by *chief* or *leading*; connoting as it does uniqueness in a given context, it cannot take the plural in respect to that context, i.e. we cannot speak of the *protagonists* of a drama; and it is not a synonym of *advocate* or *champion*. Since the temptation to misuse *protagonist* in all four of these ways is seemingly overwhelming, our advice is not to use it at all.

provided, providing. If you cannot make do with *if,* the word you want is *provided,* not *providing.* In *They agreed to support Muskie providing he honored his pledge,* change to *provided,* or better still to *if.* The full form *provided that* should be used only where omitting *that* would cause confusion.

quote for *quotation* is non-Standard.

rack, wrack. *Rack* is right, *wrack* wrong or at best no improvement on *rack,* in all the common expressions in which both are sometimes used, notably *rack and ruin, on the rack, racked by pain, nerve-racking, storm-racked,* and *rack up points.* *Wrack* has no important meanings all to itself.

rather is a halfhearted word and should never be used with all-out words like *spectacular* or *magnificent.*

re-. To *reform* does not mean to form again; to convey this last meaning without confusion we must write *re-form.* Similarly, we *re-solve* a recurring problem, *re-cover* our furniture, witness a *re-creation* of a historical event. Though correct, these hyphenated forms are irritatingly self-conscious; use an *again* construction if you can.

really is used by young writers either to persuade the reader of the intensity of their response (*I really loved that dog*) or to solicit his agreement to an argument for which no evidence is offered (*We really made a mistake at Yalta*). Invariably the strategy misfires and *really* comes through as a bankrupt effort to win the reader's respect or attention on the cheap. Good writers do not make this mistake. It takes more than an adverb to convey intensity of feeling or persuade the unpersuaded.

reason. (1) Generations of grammarians have deplored the *reason is because* construction: in *The reason I phoned was because she asked me to,* they say, *because* must be changed to *that.* The grammatical argument for *that* is impeccable, yet *because* persists and may someday become accepted usage, as it has in the reverse syntax: *Just because Diana likes parties is no reason why Tom should.* Until that putative someday, use *that.*

(2) *Reason why,* though deplored by purists, is universal in speech and Standard in writing, even when *why* is not followed by a clause: *It won't work, and there are two reasons why.*

regards. Of the constructions *in regards to, with regards to, in some regards,* and *as regards,* only the last is Standard. The first two require *regard,* the third *respects.*

respectively is used to relate the individual components of one sequence to their proper counterparts in another sequence: *Jane, Lois, and Greta married a soldier, a sailor, and a Marine, respectively.* The word is obtrusive and should be used only where it is absolutely necessary. In *With people like my father and mother, poker parties and bridge clubs are a way of life,* it would be gratuitous to add *respectively*; the reader can sort things out for himself.

restive, restless. The two words are interchangeable according to modern dictionaries, but many writers prefer to restrict *restive* to its more distinctive meaning of balky or unwilling to cooperate.

ring takes the past form *rang*: *He rang the bell,* not *rung.*

scarcely, hardly, and *barely* take *when* or *before,* not *than*; in *Scarcely had I got my coat off than the telephone rang,* change to *when*.   Double negatives like *without hardly a word of protest* and *couldn't barely find enough money for groceries* are illiterate; use *with* and *could*.

-self, -selves.   (1) *Ourself*, not *ourselves*, is the reflexive pronoun for the imperial or editorial *we*: *We found ourself last week at a party for Mae West.*

(2) The forms *themself*, *theirself*, and *theirselves* do not exist.

(3) Never use the reflexive pronoun where the simple pronoun will serve as well.   In *My sister and myself arrived early,* change *myself* to *I*.

SENTENCE FRAGMENT.   A sentence fragment is any word or combination of words that is preceded and followed by a full stop (period, question mark, exclamation point) and that does not contain an independent subject and predicate: for example, the second, third, and fourth elements in *What did Scott need?   A guide who knew the country.   What else?   Money.*   Sentence fragments are perfectly legitimate in expository writing if used with proper respect for three caveats. First, do not use many; the repeated use of sentence fragments, as in some humorous newspaper columns, marks the writer as committed to striving for cheap effects.   Second, do not use them in highly formal or abstract writing, where their informality would be out of place, or in passages of routine exposition, to which their abrupt, emphatic quality would be unsuited.   Third, do not separate them unnaturally from a preceding or following sentence of which they logically form part; in *He must have meant Truman.   Because Roosevelt would never have said that,* change to *Truman, because.*

service as a verb is best confined to repair or maintenance work on specified equipment or machinery; thus one services a television set or a car.   Any extension to people (*We serviced over a hundred customers*) or even to abstractions (*The office was serviced twice a day by a man from Vend-o-Mat*) risks drawing a titter because of the word's strong sexual connotations (*This bull services four cows*).

shall, will. In American usage *shall* is now for the most part restricted to the first person interrogative, and then only when a decision or recommendation is requested: *Shall we go?* / *Shall I tell him or will you?* In all other uses *will* is idiomatic: *I will be 21 in March* / *We will be lucky to escape alive* / *Will you want a picnic lunch?* / *Will I be the only girl there?* Though *shall* remains permissible in the classical uses—simple future in the first person, determination in the second and third—*will* is now equally idiomatic in these uses and far more widely used. In general, you will not go wrong by writing whatever you would say.

-ship. (1) One of the best-known entries in Fowler bears the title "Love of the Long Word." It is hard to imagine any other motive for the present-day practice of saying *leadership* for *leaders, membership* for *members,* and *readership* for *readers.* The *X-ship* form is properly used to indicate the quality or state of being an X (*courses in leadership, an application for membership*), or the body of X's considered as a quantity (*a larger membership, a readership of over 20,000*); it is improperly extended to mean some or all X's as people. In *The party's leadership was discredited,* change to *leaders were*; in *Many of the membership disapproved,* change to *members.*

   (2) *Gamesmanship* and *one-upmanship* were coined by the British humorist Stephen Potter; they should be used only in a jocular or ironic context.

should, would. In American usage *should* means *ought to.* In the conditional, *would* is proper with the first person as well as the second and third: *I would be glad to call on her* / *Would we be welcome there?*

similar is not an adverb. In *She dresses similar to Lucy,* change to *like* or *rather like.*

sink takes the past form *sank,* not *sunk*: *The ship sank* / *German planes sank two ships.*

situation has the combination of vagueness and polysyllabic weight that insecure writers love because they think it makes them sound impressive. Sometimes the word can be simply dropped: in *It is an awkward situation when no one understands English,* change to *It is awkward when.* Almost always some less pretentious equivalent can be found: in *The situation called for prompt action,* for example, we could change to *They had to act promptly,* and in *if I were in John's situation* to *if I were John.*

so. (1) Some writers, chiefly women, mistakenly use *so* and *such* as synonyms for *very* in sentences like *Ireland is such a lovely country* and *We were so glad to get home.* Whatever its virtues in conversation—"Lydia is *so* beautiful tonight, don't you think, Mr. Palmer?"—this feminine intensive has no place in writing.

(2) *So* for *so that* is non-Standard; in *They saved money all year so they could have an expensive vacation,* change *so* to *so that.* *So* in the sense of *and therefore,* though still frowned on by purists, is now accepted by 83 percent of the AHD's Usage Panel: *They had saved money all year, so they could afford an expensive vacation.* Since these two uses of *so* are not easy to distinguish, it may be helpful to note that where a comma seems natural before *so* the construction is probably the acceptable one.

some is non-Standard for *somewhat* or *occasionally.* In *Things improved some,* change to *somewhat;* in *He played football some,* change to *played football occasionally* or *played a little football.* The expression *some better* for *somewhat better* is now confined to elderly rustics.

someplace and *someway* are non-Standard; use *somewhere* and *somehow.*

SPELLING. See SUFFIX CONFUSIONS; VARIANT SPELLINGS.

strata is strictly plural; not *every strata of society* but *every stratum* or *all strata.*

structure as a verb, meaning to organize or arrange, is social science jargon, and should be restricted to social science uses: e.g., one might contrast a structured psychiatric counseling session with one carried out by the technique of free association. Beyond this domain, *structure* tends to be vague. What is meant, for example, by *Miss Jones works best in a highly structured situation?* That she needs supervision? That she likes clear rules? That she feels more comfortable in a highly stratified or bureaucratic office than in a more informal work setting?

substitute as a verb means to put in place of, and *substitution* means putting in place of; they are not synonyms for *replace* and *replacement*. *Substitute* takes *for* (*They had substituted a Chevrolet for my Ford*); *replace* takes *by* or *with* (*I replaced my old Ford by/with a new Chevrolet*). In *The wartime board was substituted by a new nine-member board,* either change *substituted* to *replaced* or turn the sentence around: *A new nine-member board was substituted for the wartime board.* In *The substitution of Ed's plan by Harry's seems unwise,* change to *The substitution of Harry's plan for Ed's.*

such. See ANTECEDENT PROBLEMS (3); SO; SUCH AS . . . AND OTHERS.

such as . . . and others, like *including . . . and others,* is a redundant construction. *Such as* selects one or more items from a class; *and others* asserts that the items selected do not constitute the whole class. Since *and others* tells us nothing that *such as* has not told us already, it is pointless to use both expressions; we should choose one or the other. Change *Confederate generals such as Lee, Jackson, and others* either to *Confederate generals such as Lee and Jackson* or to *Lee, Jackson, and other Confederate generals.*

SUFFIX CONFUSIONS. Three main kinds of confusion arise with suffixes: (1) choosing the correct word from two or more words with the same root but different suffixes; (2) choosing the correct spelling for a word having a suffix that is spelled different ways for different words; (3) determining whether to double a consonant before a suffix. The solution to all three problems is to consult a dictionary. The rest of this entry will simply document the existence and suggest the extent of these problems.

(1) *Definite* and *definitive, precipitate* and *precipitous, principal* and *principle,* are discussed elsewhere in this section. Other often confused adjective pairs are *unexceptional* (routine) and *unexceptionable* (acceptable without change);

seasonal (according to season) and *seasonable* (appropriate to the season); *sensuous* (pertaining to gratification of the senses in general) and *sensual* (pertaining to physical, especially sexual, gratification). Still other confusions arise between different parts of speech: *predominate* (verb) for *predominant* (adj.); *populous* (adj.) for *populace* (noun); *callous* and *phosphorous* (adj.) for *callus* and *phosphorus* (nouns). These distinctions are made clearly in your dictionary, where you have only to look them up.

(2) Some variant spellings of same-sounding suffixes are as follows:

First spelling	*Second spelling*	*Third spelling or spelling optional*
indispens*able*	indefens*ible*	—
gene*alogy*, miner*alogy*	archae*ology*, soci*ology*	—
resist*ance*, venge*ance*	insist*ence*, indig*ence*	intransig*ence* (-*eance*)
defend*ant*, attend*ant*	superintend*ent*, resplend*ent*	depend*ent* (-*ant*), pend*ant* (-*ent*)
men*tion*, preven*tion*	ten*sion*, preten*sion*	—
interpret*er*, advertis*er*	operat*or*, inspect*or*	advis*er* (-*or*), invent*or* (-*er*)
boist*erous*	disast*rous*	dext*rous* (-*erous*)
station*ery*, monast*ery*	statu*ary*, secret*ary*	—
critic*ize*, organ*ize*	advert*ise*, exerc*ise*	anal*yze*, paral*yze*
publ*icly*	diplomat*ically*	frant*ically* (-*icly*)
question*naire*	million*aire*	—
her*oes*, embarg*oes*	Ner*os*, larg*os*	zer*os* (-*oes*), carg*oes* (-*os*)

Many, many other examples could be given of suffix confusions of this sort, not to mention confusions extending beyond suffixes, e.g. *questionnaire / millionaire / debonair, proceed / precede / supersede.* No one can find his way through this swamp without a dictionary.

(3) In American usage, the *New Yorker* to the contrary, suffix forms of verbs ending in *-l* and *-r* double the consonant when the last syllable of the verb is accented (*occurred, transferring, rebellious, abhorrent*) but not otherwise (*rivaling, offered, traveler, marvelous*). The *New Yorker* follows British usage in doubling *-l* even where the syllable is unaccented.

teen-ager and *teen-age* are relatively new words, dating only from about 1942; for better or for worse, they have strong connotations of the social concerns and commercial preferences of young middle-class Americans of the present era. Their use should accordingly be restricted to where these connotations are more or less appropriate: e.g., it would not be appropriate to refer to Keats's early poems as the work of a teen-ager.

terrific for splendid, as in *a terrific dinner*, is best left to the very young.

than. (1) A few sentences of the form *I like Mary better than Bob* need an extra verb to be clear: is it *than Bob does* or *than I like Bob?* Most such sentences, however, are clear enough in context to get by without elaboration: *The state chairmen liked Taft better than Eisenhower / The Senate committee was more courteous to Budenz than the House committee.* Don't add the clarifying verb unless you have to. If you have to, add it after its subject, not before: *than Bob does,* not *than does Bob,* which has the artificial ring of something never heard in speech.

(2) Pronouns take the objective case in the expression *than whom* and after *other than: Anyone other than her would have turned him down.* Otherwise pronouns following *than* take whatever case they would take if the clause introduced by *than* were spelled out: *I like Mary better than he* [does] / *I like Mary better than* [I like] *him.*

See also DIFFERENT THAN; PREFER; SCARCELY.

the. (1) When a possessive precedes a book title (or the equivalent) beginning with *The,* it is permissible to omit *The*: thus "Hardy's *Mayor of Casterbridge,*" "Jonson's *Alchemist* and Shakespeare's *Tempest.*"

(2) In writing the names of magazines and newspapers beginning with *The,* it is permissible to omit *The* for convenience: "his *New Yorker* articles," "a *New York Times* reporter." When *the* is retained, it should be lowercased and roman rather than capitalized and italic: "as the *San Francisco Chronicle* says," "the *New Republic's* coverage." The lowercased, roman form is of course inevitable when *the* attaches not to the title but to a following noun, as in "the *Times* editorial."

The unidiomatic omission of *the* before abstract nouns followed by *of* is discussed on pp. 112–113.

thereof, therein, thereto, etc. are sometimes substituted for the rhetorically weak *of it, in it, to it,* etc., especially at the end of a sentence: *The book was tedious, and he longed to get to the end thereof / Morgan knew of the plot but not of Nye's part therein.* However serious the *of it* disease may seem, the pompous and archaic *thereof* cure is fifty times worse. If no other cure for *of it, in it,* etc. can be found, live with the disease.

TIMEstyle is a word made up by an exasperated rival editor to denote the unique style of writing created and purveyed by the magazine *Time.* The word is a good one: with its ironic bow to the magazine's ritual capitalization of TIME, its echo of such lunatic *Time* amalgams as *cinemactor,* and its hollow, tinny ring, it comes as close as any single word can to capturing *Time's* distinctive spirit, which may be described as self-important, verbally daring, but ultimately without substance. TIMEstyle is one of the great influences on present-day American English. A student reads words like *kooky* and *pad* in *Time* and presumes that they are suitable for an essay on Charles Lamb; another student confidently uses TIMEstyle possessives like *at week's end* and *California's Senator John Tunney*; a third achieves a bogus briskness by dropping *and's*; a fourth piles up human-interest adjectives before his nouns (*genial, balding, 48-year-old Colonel*

Possiel); a fifth becomes addicted to sentence fragments, a sixth to facetious asides, a seventh to impudent global pronouncements (*Every so often an art needs to go a little crazy*). To be sure, such devices make for lively writing, writing that will tell people something interesting in only four minutes about Vietnam or the stock market or the newest Italian movie—writing, in short, that will sell magazines. But that is all one can say for TIMEstyle. What it cannot do is examine serious questions seriously or subtle questions subtly; chained as its writers are to the proven commercial negotiability of the short and snappy, they are as likely to produce an eloquent statement on Christianity or civil rights or war as Hollywood is to produce a genuine Abraham Lincoln. If *Time's* inventiveness and editorial discipline are to be admired—and they surely are—it must be for their contribution to journalism, not to the higher uses of English.

together with. A singular noun followed by a phrase beginning *together with* takes a singular verb: *The emperor, together with his ministers and his household, was exiled.*

too. *Not too* for *not very* in such sentences as *I was not feeling too good that morning* and *Fuentes was not too pleased with the verdict* is non-Standard. A number of alternatives are available, among them omitting *too,* changing *too* to *very,* and switching to the Standard idiom *none too.*

tortuous means winding, twisting, circuitous, or devious. It is not related to *torture* except by remote derivation, and has no connotation of physical pain.

total. *A total of X* takes the singular or the plural according to whether X would take the singular or the plural. Thus *Five hundred signatures was their goal / A total of 500 signatures was their goal*; but *Five hundred signatures were obtained / A total of 500 signatures were obtained.*

towards is an old-fashioned spelling; use *toward.*

trigger in the sense of touch off, as in *The announcement triggered a three-day strike,* is a vogue word popularized by journalists. We agree with Follett, who called it "one of the most overworked words of the century."

try and, as in *We felt we should try and get Senator Cranston to support us,* though acceptable to the British authorities Fowler and Gowers, is unacceptable to 79 percent of the AHD's Usage Panel. Use *try to.*

type. (1) *Type* is overused for *kind* or *sort.* Properly used, *type* implies a strong and clearly marked relationship to a well-defined class. Where the relationship is less clear or the class less well-defined, as in *He is the type of person who kicks cats,* change to *kind* or *sort.*

   (2) *Type* without *of,* as in *the type person* or *this type record player,* is illiterate.

   The suffix *-type* is discussed on p. 105.

underway is an adjective only, and occurs exclusively in the attributive position in such seldom-used technical compounds as *underway refueling;* the adverb is two words, *under way.* In *We had a hard time getting the project underway,* change to *under way.*

unique should not be compared or qualified. Something unique is the only one of its kind. A thing is accordingly either unique or not; it cannot be *rather unique, very unique, more unique* or *less unique* than something else, the *most unique* thing of its kind, or (a choice specimen from a London editor) *unique even by Middle Eastern standards.*

upcoming is a journalist's vogue word; use *approaching.*

use as an auxiliary verb is inflected: *I used to go,* not *use to.*

utilize and *utilization* are ugly and unnecessary synonyms for the verb and noun forms of *use.* In *The committee praised our utilization of Russian and Spanish materials,* change *utilization* to *use.*

VARIANT SPELLINGS. (1) W7 and most other dictionaries distinguish two kinds of variant spellings: the OR spelling (*orangutan* OR *orangoutan* / *optimum* n, pl *optima* OR *optimums*) and the ALSO spelling (*fogy* ALSO *fogey* / *learn* vb *learned* ALSO *learnt*). When OR is used, the two spellings are alleged to be of equal status and currency but rarely are in practice, as one can infer from the nonalphabetical order of entries like *orangutan* OR *orangoutan*.   When ALSO is used, the second spelling is alleged to have less status or currency than the first.   Dictionaries differ in these matters: thus W7 lists *marihuana* and *cookie* first, the AHD prefers *marijuana* and *cooky,* and the *Penguin Dictionary* gives only *marijuana* and *cookie.*   Barring an occasional screwy preference like *cooky,* our advice is to use the first spelling given in your dictionary.

(2) British spellings like *theatre* and *centre, neighbour* and *honour, criticise* and *analyse,* are no more appropriate to American writing than British terms like *lift* for elevator and *lorry* for truck.   The only exception is proper names of British offices and institutions: *Minister of Defence,* not *Defense*; *Labour Party,* not *Labor.*   Some American spellings, e.g. *glamour, advertise,* do not follow the customary pattern; when in doubt, consult your dictionary.

See also SUFFIX CONFUSIONS.

very is overused by young writers.   Often it can be simply eliminated without changing the meaning of a sentence or weakening its force, e.g. in *She lived in a very big house in Winnetka* and *I was very sorry to hear of Abe's illness.*

wait on for *wait for* is non-Standard; in *If we had waited on Harry, we would still be waiting,* change *on* to *for.*

ways for *way,* as in *quite a ways from home* or *a long ways to go,* is non-Standard.

we, EDITORIAL.   The editorial *we,* as used, for example, in the "Talk of the Town" section of the *New Yorker,* has a persistent fascination for young writers, who see it as the very hallmark of the light touch.   As it happens, however, few constructions are more difficult to master, and not one in a thousand college writers can achieve and sustain the sought-after tone of modest, twinkling urbanity; the usual effects range from arch to cloying to intolerably self-conscious.   Our advice is to experiment with the editorial *we,* if experiment you must, in your extracurricular writing; use *I* in your themes.

well, good. *Well* as an adjective, apart from the cast-iron idiom *all's well* and the obsolescent *it is well* (*It is well not to anger him*), implies good health. Thus *she was good* means that she behaved or performed well, *she was well* that her health was good; the same general distinction can be made between *she felt good* (happy) and *she felt well* (healthy), and between *she looked good* (attractive) and *she looked well* (healthy).

The distinction between *bad* and *badly* is less clear-cut. Even good writers occasionally use *bad* as an adverb (*want something bad enough to fight for it*) and *badly* as an adjective (*feel badly about losing*). Our advice, however, is to use *bad* only as an adjective and *badly* only as an adverb: *The victim was not so badly off / Sundberg was hurt so badly that he had to leave the game / She has been feeling bad ever since.*

what as a pronoun can be either singular (*what bothers me most*) or plural (*what seem to be clouds*), but not both at once. In *What takes longest are the field events,* change *takes* to *take* or *are* to *is.*

where. (1) *At* with *where,* as in *Tom could not remember where the car was at,* is a colloquialism of the South and Southwest; it is not acceptable in writing.

(2) *Where* for *that,* as in *I could see where somebody might think so,* is non-Standard.

whose may be freely used as the possessive of *which;* whether the antecedent is animate or inanimate makes no difference, so long as it is clear. *Caves for the treasures of which men have given their lives* is clumsy; change to *caves for whose treasures.*

worst. *Webster's Third Unabridged* prescribes "if *worse* comes to worst," the AHD "if *worst* comes to worst." Though the Webster version is the more rational, we prefer the AHD version, for which the *Oxford English Dictionary* cites examples as far back as 1594.

wrack. See RACK.

INDEX

Catalog

If you are interested in a list of fine Paperback
books, covering a wide range of subjects
and interests, send your name and address,
requesting your free catalog, to:

McGraw-Hill Paperbacks
330 West 42nd Street
New York, New York 10036